JULES FERRY

And the Renaissance of
French Imperialism

JULES FERRY
And the Renaissance of French Imperialism

By THOMAS F. POWER, Jr.

OCTAGON BOOKS

A DIVISION OF FARRAR, STRAUS AND GIROUX

New York   1977

Copyright 1944 by Thomas F. Power, Jr.

Reprinted 1966
by special arrangement with Thomas F. Power, Jr.
Second Octagon printing 1977

OCTAGON BOOKS
A DIVISION OF FARRAR, STRAUS & GIROUX, INC.
19 Union Square West
New York, N.Y. 10003

LIBRARY OF CONGRESS CATALOG CARD NUMBER: 66-18042
ISBN 0-374-96555-2

Manufactured by Braun-Brumfield, Inc.
Ann Arbor, Michigan
Printed in the United States of America

To
MY PARENTS

CONTENTS

PREFACE

This volume is concerned with the driving forces of the great French expansionist movement in the early years of the Third Republic, and addresses itself especially to the problem of the motives of Jules Ferry, the Premier under whom the greatest expansion occurred in 1881–1885. It attempts a reexamination of some of the commonly ascribed motives, particularly that of economic determinism. It undertakes to show the relatively small role that markets and financial penetration actually did play in French colonization. It tries for the first time, to correlate the colonial undertakings of the greatest French imperialist with the rest of his political activity and fortunes, as well as to draw together in one volume the story of almost simultaneous French action in Tunisia, West Africa, the Congo, Oceania, Madagascar, Egypt and Indo-China.

The secondary problem examined is the attitude of the French Parliament toward colonial expansion. Previously it has been generally assumed that Parliament was strongly and purposefully anti-colonial in feeling during these years. This work attempts to demonstrate that, in fact, Parliament was little perturbed about such questions, and gave Jules Ferry the same amount of support on his colonial ventures as on domestic questions.

The war and the fall of France forestalled my hope of study in Paris. However, there is little documentary evidence remaining abroad that could materially affect the findings incorporated here. In large part, the book is, therefore, a revaluation of material already available in printed form; for the most part it is based on the voluminous published collections of diplomatic documents, parliamentary debates, newspapers, memoirs and secondary works. The exception has been some useful material found in the National Archives among the State Department Archives.

The best biographer of Jules Ferry, M. Jean Dietz, very kindly advised me on several problems and has informed me that there is little unpublished data among the papers of Jules Ferry that bears on foreign or colonial matters. The *Fondation Jules Ferry* of Paris was good enough to supply me, in 1939, with considerable information on the documents in their possession regarding Jules Ferry. My sincere thanks are also due and gratefully rendered to the librarians of Columbia University, the Library of Congress, Harvard University, the National Archives and the University of Chicago.

The subject under consideration was suggested to me by **Professor Shepard B.** Clough in 1938, and an examination of parliamentary reaction to imperialism was developed into a Master's essay under his direction. The scope of the study was broadened in the seminar of Professor Carlton J. H. Hayes, under whose direction the dissertation was completed at Columbia University. To Professor Hayes I am deeply indebted for his stimulating guidance, his searching criticism. His breadth of knowledge and wisdom has been indispensable in the preparation of this book. To Professor Clough I owe a profound debt of gratitude. His careful attention to the form, detail and content of his students' work is a constant source of encouragement. Although burdened by his own research while on leave from Columbia, he very kindly gave a hand in reviewing the manuscript when Professor Hayes was suddenly called to his ambassadorial post. I am also most appreciative of the careful reading and helpful criticism offered by Professors Lindsay Rogers, Jacques Barzun, Charles W. Cole, Robert T. Schuyler, Ross Hoffman and Walter C. Langsam. To Amherst College I wish also to express my thanks for two successive appointments as Amherst Memorial Fellow in History and to Columbia University for an appointment as University Fellow in History.

Many friends have contributed substantially of their time to assist me in the preparation of the manuscript under trying wartime conditions. Among them are especially Ensign Joseph A. Doyle, Dr. Eugene Fubini-Ghiron, Ensign Edgar F. Taber and my parents. Above all, I am grateful to my wife whose patient and cheerful attention to the manuscript and proofs was unflagging despite the heavy pressure of her own professional work.

T.F.P., J<small>R</small>.

Washington, D. C.
August, 1943

Chapter One

THE PROBLEM AND THE MAN

The Third French Republic inherited an overseas empire of a million square miles and, during the first ten years of its existence, paid almost no attention to it. The administration of the colonies cost the central government thirty million francs a year, accounted for only a small part of French trade, and held little attraction for emigrants or for the general public. On no side was there much interest in cultivating or enlarging the empire, and it languished except for the sporadic labors of a few colonial administrators.

Then between 1880 and 1885 the French Empire mushroomed to an area of over three million square miles. It became the second largest European overseas empire, possessing great natural resources and a large population. New lands, many only recently explored by Europeans, were placed under the French flag, and areas formerly held by only shadowy claims were securely bound to the mother country. Tunisia, Annam, Tonkin, Madagascar, much of the Congo basin, Upper Senegal, the French Sudan, numerous points along the West Coast of Africa, part of Somaliland, and many islands in the South Pacific including the Society Islands and several lesser archipelagoes—all were added to it as protectorates or as annexations.

The most important French statesman in this colonial expansion was Jules Ferry. Most of the new French territories were acquired during his two terms as Premier, 1880–1881 and 1883–1885. Heir to several half-finished projects, he was, more than any other one man, responsible for the renaissance of the French Empire. Movements earlier prepared by agents in the field needed the vigorous support of the government. Aided by a fortunate diplomatic balance in Europe and a secure political position at home, Ferry, through his determination, skill in diplomacy and political adroitness, won this series of colonies for France. By a show of military force he extended protection to weak Moslem rulers like the Bey of Tunis; he subsidized exploration in West and Equatorial Africa and, by judicious mixture of military conquest and diplomatic bargaining, secured the new-found lands for France; he waged war on the Queen of Madagascar, the King of Annam, and the Emperor of China; his agents bribed into submission various petty sovereigns from Polynesia to the West Coast of Africa. All this he accomplished with little support from the French Parliament and in the face of bitter criticism from his enemies among the French Radical Republicans and Conservative Clericals. Aided by professional military men, career diplomats, colonial officials, explorers and a few merchants, and supported at home by the moderate Republicans, he presented France with an empire and for his efforts received public humiliation and hatred.

The motivation of the great upsurge of imperialism experienced in the last quarter of the nineteenth century by all the major European countries except Austria-Hungary has been long and hotly debated. Marxist historians, and economic determinists in general, have explained the phenomenon as the effort of a glutted European capitalist economy to find outlets for its surplus capital and manufactures, and cheap sources of labor and raw materials. By nationalistic historians and speakers it has been portrayed as a great patriotic movement intended to carry overseas the blessings granted by possession of a certain flag, be it French, English, German or other.

The motive forces of imperialism, like those of so many other great phenomena, were undoubtedly most complex with labyrinthine intertwinings of political, economic, military, diplomatic, and nationalistic considerations. The extension of European control over vast areas in Africa, Asia, and the distant seas was undertaken not for any single reason but for many reasons. It was undertaken by many men who at different periods had various purposes; and sometimes it was undertaken more by accident than by design.

Much light may be thrown on the origins of French colonial expansion after 1870 by an examination of the career and the colonial policy of the greatest French imperialist, the man who by action acquired the empire and by speech gave a justification and rationalization for it. Such an examination is attempted in the following pages. It endeavors to determine what factors in the character, background, and connections of Ferry may have disposed him to embark on an imperialist policy; to investigate in detail each of his colonial undertakings and the relationship between French imperialism and French domestic politics.

In the early career of Jules Ferry [1] there was nothing to mark him as the future arch-champion of the French colonial renaissance. This man, who was also the father of the French elementary school system and consolidator of the Republican institutions of the Third French Republic, sprang from a long line of solid bourgeois Lorrainers. [2] From

[1] 1832–1893.

[2] Originally farmers at Saint Dié in the Vosges Mountains, the family turned to clock-making with apparent success in the eighteenth century. During the Directory, Consulate, and Empire, the grandfather of Jules was mayor of Saint Dié, where he owned a tannery.

his earliest years the future Premier lived among partisans of the bourgeois French Revolution.[3]

Jules' father was a lawyer, his mother the daughter of a judge. The family resources were such that the father, never physically strong, needed to devote only part of his time to his legal practice. Ferry, *père*, read the Parisian Republican newspapers *Siècle* and *National* and, like a good liberal, was a severe critic of Guizot's authoritarian regime during the July Monarchy. He served on the *conseil général* of the department for some years. During the Revolution of 1848 he was profoundly disturbed by the rumors that reached Lorraine of a Socialist revolution in Paris. A bourgeois skeptic, he allowed his wife and children to go to church, although he never took his own religious duties seriously.

The biographers of Jules Ferry have professed to see him as "a typical *Vosgien*" [4] from his childhood days. However typical he may have been, he was a timid, selfish, rather awkward child in frail health who preferred reading or drawing to taking part in more active youthful pursuits. At the *Collège de Saint Dié*, he showed himself to be, if not a brilliant student, at least a good, hard-working, intelligent one who managed to win some academic prizes.[5]

Jules' mother died in 1834 at the birth of his younger brother Charles. The Ferrys moved to Strasbourg in 1846, his father having left the bar due to failing health, so that Jules and Charles might pursue their education. Jules did well at the *Collège Royal* at Strasbourg, particularly in rhetoric and philosophy. In 1848 he began the study of law. The family moved to Paris in 1850, again in order to facilitate the education of the children. Jules pursued his legal studies and began to practice law at the early age of nineteen on December 20, 1851—the day of the plebiscite electing Louis Napoleon President for ten years. For some time Ferry was secretary to one of the ablest lawyers in Paris, a M. Thureau.[6]

Ferry's financial position during this period was such that he could

---

[3] His great-uncle was a member of the Convention and voted for the death of the King. His uncle was a lieutenant in Napoleon's army who had refused to serve under the restored Bourbons, and turned to paper manufacturing. As a boy, Jules heard the Revolution extolled by his grandfather (†1847), the glories of the Napoleonic campaigns told by his uncle.

[4] Jean Dietz, "Les débuts de Jules Ferry," *Revue de France*, année 12, V (1932), 503. The series of biographical articles by this author comprise the best biography of Ferry except for matters of foreign policy which the author never covered. Except for that lacuna, these articles constitute one of the best studies of the French Republican groups from 1865 to 1885.

[5] A prize won in religion class strikes an ironic note in the career of the author of the French Republic's laic laws.

[6] Alfred Rambaud, *Jules Ferry* (Paris, 1903), p. 3. The author of this biography served as Ferry's *chef de cabinet* 1880–1881 and, besides being a competent historian of Eastern Europe, was an active colonial propagandist.

devote most of his time to study, painting, and travel. He consistently pursued his studies and research in law, economics, and history—interests later developed further. But his main avocation now was painting. Indeed, he thought seriously of a career as an artist, going so far as to travel to Venice to paint and study. Few lawsuits came to the artist and it appears that at this time he did not plead even those well.[7] He had not yet developed the forcefulness and clarity of speech he later demonstrated.

That he was considered one of the promising young lawyers of Paris, however, is shown by his appointment as a secretary of the *Conférence des avocats*. His colleagues were the rising, rabid young Republicans of the day. In this training ground the leaders of the future Third Republic, such men as Gambetta, were developed. A paper on the *Influence des idées philosophiques sur le barreau du dix-huitième siècle,* delivered here in 1855, classed Ferry among the open critics of the Emperor Napoleon III and revealed that he was strongly under the influence of eighteenth-century rationalism.

After the death of their father in 1855, the Ferry brothers lived on in Paris. Their home became a gathering place for a coterie of young Republicans, mostly lawyers. One of the most important intellectual influences on these young men and especially on Jules Ferry was that of Positivism.[8] He came into contact with the liberal positivist school of Emile Littré,[9] and a study of Ferry's works shows a striking identity of view and even of phrase between Littré and Ferry. The former frequently came to Ferry's salon and when, in 1867, the old scholar founded *La philosophie positive,* a review devoted to the propagation of positivist ideas, Ferry worked under him. Two years later he gave further testimony of his identification with the school of Littré.[10]

What particularly appealed to Ferry was the positivist method that placed emphasis on fact-finding, and its corollary of ascertainable and absolute laws, in accordance with which society could be controlled and

---

[7] Dietz, *loc. cit.,* p. 506.

[8] A. Dupront, "Jules Ferry s'opposant à l'empire," *Revue historique,* CLXXVII (1936), 356.

[9] Littré was a great scholar and philologist, the author of the still-standard French dictionary, translator and commentator on Hippocrates, and the popularizer of the doctrines of Auguste Comte. He had been Comte's star pupil and heir-designate, but they had become estranged, and Littré led the liberal wing of the Positivists, especially after the death of Comte in 1857. He rejected the Religion of Humanity that Comte had erected as the capstone of his system of Positivism and was more friendly to liberal and democratic institutions than had been his master.

[10] *La philosophie positive,* I (October, 1867), 297. Speaking of his collaboration on *La philosophie positive,* he said: "That is the mark of my philosophic position and I believe that I shall not change." Letter quoted in *Intermédiaire,* XLVIII (1903), col. 327–328.

shaped. Positivism's professedly empirical, factual approach, its anti-clericalism, its opposition to Napoleon III, its praise of representative government, its admiration for England, and its belief in the importance of an enlightened public opinion for self-government all appealed to him. Positivism, in brief, bolstered his middle-of-the-road bourgeois views; it gave new and stronger support to his eighteenth-century rationalism and his belief in natural law and continual progress. It furnished an explanation, a proof of the inevitability and correctness of the opinions he held. Positivism's optimism, enthusiasm, and complete self-assurance made it extremely agreeable to a man of Ferry's background. He was quite typical of his colleagues in his adoption of liberal Positivism, which was a lifelong influence.

It was with such inspiration that Ferry undertook studies in economic history. Some results of his research were embodied in two long articles which he unsuccessfully tried to have published in the *Revue des deux mondes*.[11] They were in essence attacks on the government-sponsored monopolies and credit institutions of the Empire and therefore dangerous for the magazine to print.[12]

These articles [13] traced the struggle, which Ferry believed to be the essence of economic history from the Middle Ages to his time, between small-scale individualistic production and production and control by monopolies supported and encouraged by the government. After describing the growth of Mercantilism from the fifteenth to the eighteenth centuries, with especial praise for Colbert, whom he believed to be the champion of the bourgeoisie, he hailed the period after the French Revolution as the happiest for France because she then enjoyed a system of competitive, small-scale production. But he was alarmed by the recrudescence of monopoly under imperial control. He believed Napoleon's new banks and credit monopolies to be dangerous, for they enabled a government, absolute in the political sphere, to achieve absolute control in the economic sphere, too.

As a disciple of John Stuart Mill, Ferry believed that a free state with

[11] A. Robiquet, *Discours et opinions de Jules Ferry* (Paris, 1898), VII, 449. This collection will hereafter be cited simply as *Discours*.

[12] The editor would accept them only if they were reduced by two-thirds. This is understandable for, although the research was accurate and the argument reasonably clear, the organization of the material was poor.

[13] Entitled "On the Origins of the Modern Industrial System in France" and "Industrial Concentration," *Discours*, VII, 451–535. The first was written in 1859, the second in 1863, both were revised in 1865 but refused by the *Revue des deux mondes* in 1863 and again in 1865. Dupront, *loc. cit.*, p. 359. As a good Positivist, he used a great deal of source material, including: the *Fonds 500 de Colbert*, reports of Venetian Ambassadors, Depping's collection of decrees, decrees of the Valois kings, and decrees and laws of the Revolution. He read Bodin, Malestroit, Laffemas, Savary, Boisguilbert, Vauban, Dupont de Nemours, Adam Smith, and many lesser writers.

free institutions could control its industrial giants and avoid the dangers of industrial feudalism.[14] Ferry was a free trader and an economic liberal, favoring enterprise as completely free as was compatible with the interests of the petty bourgeoisie which should control its government through an enlightened public opinion.

Ferry played a minor role in Republican politics beginning with the elections of 1863, when he collaborated in drawing up a *Manuel électoral* for the *Union Libérale* of Orleanists and Republicans. This called for an end of the regime of personal government and the restoration of civil liberties. After the campaign, in which the Republicans made some small gains, he drew up an indictment of the official corruption in the elections, containing the complaints of the opposition candidates and pleading for free and honest elections under universal suffrage.[15] Probably as a result of these brochures, he was arrested, along with twelve others, on the charge of forming an unauthorized association. All were convicted and fined five hundred francs.[16]

Shortly afterwards Ferry became convinced that it was impossible to secure a reform of the imperial institutions to which he objected and that the only hope for France lay in overthrowing the Empire. Despite the many concessions to liberal demands made by Napoleon III, real power still lay in the hands of the Emperor and the bureaucracy who paid scant regard to institutional limitations. Ferry would not lead men to violent revolt, but henceforth he steadily called for the end of the Empire in his writings.

Wide travels throughout Europe had led him to a journalistic career. On his frequent trips to Germany, Italy and Switzerland he had combined purposeful study with his interest in painting and government. He visited political exiles in Switzerland, was angered by Turkish despotism he observed in Constantinople and by the vain court displays he saw in Spain. At first Ferry's articles for the Paris papers were merely descriptive and anecdotal but they grew increasingly political in their content.

He became a regular political writer on the staff of the recently founded *Temps*, the champion of the moderate Republican viewpoint. Although not the most important political commentator on the staff, he wrote hundreds of articles, sometimes more than one a day. The high point in his career as a journalist was between 1868 and 1870. Then he poured out articles exposing imperial illegalities and kept up a running fire of caustic comment on the arbitrary use of power by the government and on the restrictions of civil liberties.

[14] *Discours*, VII, 534.   [15] Jules Ferry, *La lutte électorale en 1863* (Paris, 1863).
[16] Rambaud, *op. cit.*, p. 10.

A new, more tolerant press law in 1868 gave him greater opportunities with the plethora of new publications. He wrote for the Radical Republican *Tribune* and especially for the *Electeur* whose outspoken Republicanism he preferred.[17] He was several times fined heavily for savage attacks on the Empire. He was even more clearly stamped as a chief opponent of the Empire by publication of a volume bitterly criticizing Haussmann, the Prefect of the Seine, responsible for the execution of the Napoleonic rebuilding of Paris.[18] He accused Haussmann of undertaking unnecessarily expensive public works, floating huge unauthorized loans and wasting much of the money expended. This attack brought the author great notoriety throughout France and materially aided his legal practice which now became quite substantial.[19]

Ferry entered the lists in the election of 1869 as one of the Radical Republicans. Six years before he had demanded the "necessary liberties;" now he called for the "necessary destructions." His platform was typical of the radical wing of the Republican group. He demanded freedom of the press, speech, association, teaching, assembly; truly free elections; an end of the personal power of Napoleon; administrative decentralization; absolute separation of church and state; the reform of judicial institutions by a broad development of the jury system; and a transformation of permanent armies.[20]

The last demand, which he had changed from "suppression" to "transformation" upon Gambetta's advice,[21] was a cardinal tenet in the platform of the Liberals who saw the army as the instrument of power of the Empire and the Empire's means of carrying on a capricious foreign policy. The immediate object of attack was Napoleon's very unpopular new army law of 1868 which was intended to make military service universal and create a reserve force with men who had finished their military training.[22] The Liberals proposed to rely on a small professional army and a *levée en masse* for defense.

With the backing of the leading Republicans, including Gambetta, Ferry was elected from his Paris constituency on the second ballot over his liberal Catholic opponent. However, his parliamentary career under the Empire was neither long nor fruitful. As a member of the intransigent opposition, the new deputy hurled at the Government criticism so vitriolic that it destroyed its possible effectiveness. He nearly broke up a session of the *Corps législatif* in July, 1869, by informing the majority that it was illegally in office because of the official pressure brought

---

[17] Letter of Ferry in *Intermédiaire*, XLVIII (1903), col. 327–328.

[18] J. Ferry, *Comptes fantastiques d'Haussmann* (Paris, 1868), 95 pp.

[19] Dietz, *loc. cit.*, p. 617. [20] *Discours*, I, 190–192. [21] Dietz, *loc. cit.*, p. 615.

[22] Gordon Wright, "Public Opinion and Conscription in France, 1866–70," *Journal of Modern History*, XIV (March, 1942), 44.

to bear on its behalf.[23] In the session of 1869–1870 Ferry devoted himself to bitter attacks on the Empire and its chief minister Emile Ollivier, a former friend. With Gambetta and Arago, Ferry submitted an electoral reform bill that was never seriously considered, for it would have suppressed the system of official candidacies and altered the method of voting.

Ferry and Imperialism under the Empire

Ferry's views on colonial and foreign policy during the Empire present a striking contrast with his championship of French overseas expansion during his own terms as Premier. An attempt to discover a philosophy of imperialism in the Ferry of the 1860's is fruitless. The plain fact is that foreign and colonial affairs were not so important to him during the period of the Empire as were questions of domestic policy. He was absorbed in fighting against official corruption and official pressure in elections, for a real universal male suffrage, a parliamentary government, and for a decentralized administration. Overseas expansion, moreover, brought the kind of state intervention which he detested. It implied colonial restrictions, and these he abhorred. His lack of interest is patent in the very small number of his speeches and articles devoted to foreign and colonial policy during these years.[24]

It is significant for a study of Ferry's imperialism that in 1865 his articles on Mercantilism expressed neither praise nor blame for Colbert's attempts to found an overseas empire. The fact that colonial and trading companies were tried and failed, or met with indifferent success, was recorded; but there was no editorial comment on it, no regret for the loss of a golden opportunity.

It was not for lack of opportunity that Ferry made few comments on foreign policy. Napoleon III sent military expeditions to Mexico, Syria, Cochin-China, China, Oceania, and North Africa. His war in the Crimea, his war with Sardinia against Austria, his proposals for a conference every time that European diplomatic circles stirred—all these presented Ferry with ample opportunity for criticism.

Mexico was referred to three times in articles in the *Electeur* in 1868-1869.[25] But none of these references was of more than a passing nature. The Mexican expedition was just one of the many crimes of the Napoleonic government: not only did it violate the rights of small nations, but it also left France unprepared on the eve of Sadowa. In the *Temps*

---

[23] *Discours*, I, 199.

[24] Only three or four of his nineteen speeches, and five of some 300 articles in the *Temps* before 1870 touch at all on these matters. *Discours*, I.

[25] *Discours*, I, 175, 181.

Ferry took the Government to task for sending troops to Mexico to defend the interests of Jecker, a Swiss. He stated that if the intervention had been for French interests he would not object. It was secrecy and poor management, rather than imperialism as such, that drew his fire.[26]

About Napoleon's activities in the Far East and Oceania, Ferry said nothing. Nor was Syria ever mentioned. North Africa figured only when Ferry complained in June, 1870, that the "provisional" government, now forty years old, had been maintained too long.[27] His objection was to the military rule under which the colony lived.

Once he agreed with the opinion that "the French race has only a mediocre aptitude for the colonial life" and appeared to be satisfied that this should be so. All he asked for French colonists in the remaining colonies was the same justice and political liberty that should exist in France.[28] He expressed no opinion on the value of the North African holdings or other colonies. Certainly there is no evidence here that Ferry had any imperialistic leanings before 1870.

Napoleon's European activities drew more fire from Ferry. The Italian policy received one barbed shaft in an article in the *Temps* when he sarcastically referred to the "government which has taken up the inheritance of Charlemagne in Roman affairs." [29] The relations between France and Germany drew more of his attention than did any other question of foreign affairs. As a liberal and a Frenchman, Ferry hated Bismarck, referring to him in 1866, when the Duchies question was pressing, as "the arrogant and faithless minister who is at the present time the most insolent enemy of the parliamentary regime." [30] The year before, when he was visiting Bavaria, of which he was very fond, he wrote in high glee to his brother to describe what he held to be a stubborn, firm resistance on the part of the Bavarians against this "madman of the North." [31]

When the Austro-Prussian war broke out in 1866, Ferry took sharp issue with those imperialists who sympathized with Prussia. With keen foresight he maintained that a victory for Prussia, far from being a victory for progress, would bring an "enslaved Germany with the constitutional regime wiped out from the Elbe to the Danube; militarism and absolutism winning, by the hand of M. Bismarck, the most brilliant, the most perfidious of its victories." [32] If Bismarck won, he told his readers that "the establishment of a great Germany, or rather of a great absolutist and military Prussia, can bring our country only dangers yet un-

---

[26] *Le Temps*, July 28, 1868.　　[27] *Discours*, I, 327-334.
[28] *Le Temps*, January 23, 1869.　　[29] *Discours*, I, 563.　　[30] *Ibid.*, p. 346.
[31] J. Ferry, *Lettres de Jules Ferry*, ed. Eugénie Ferry (Paris, 1908), p. 39. Hereafter this will be cited as *Lettres*.
[32] Rambaud, *op. cit.*, p. 13.

known in its history." This line of attack was the same as that taken in the *Corps législatif* by Thiers, who wrote Ferry to compliment him on his stand.

On the eve of the Franco-Prussian war of 1870, he once more assailed the Government's foreign policy that had allowed Prussia to gain sway over all Germany. The occasion was the proposed construction, with German backing, of the St. Gothard railroad line in Switzerland.[33] Seeing this as a link between Germany and Italy and a danger to Switzerland's neutrality, Ferry criticized the Government for not having made strong representations to Switzerland to get a new guarantee of her neutrality. He told the Government that "You will never heal the wound of Sadowa. That is an irreparable misfortune—but by a wise policy you will at least be able to attenuate it." This should be done chiefly by:

> . . . the cultivation of those alliances that you have lost. . . . You so cleverly maneuvered that you delivered Germany to the giant of North Germany, while you were losing the friendship of Italy: and it is because of that that Italy has gone to North Germany. . . . This state of affairs is what your mistakes have created. The alliance of Germany and Italy has been made against you; don't forget it.[34]

Among Ferry's speeches and writings previous to 1870 there are found only a few other discussions of French foreign policy. In 1860 he wrote in favor of friendship with England when relations were strained over France's acquisition of Nice and Savoy from Piedmont.[35] But about the actual acquisition of the latter provinces he wrote nothing. In 1864 a letter to Pelletan expressed his deep sympathy for the Poles who had recently rebelled and were being subjected to a ruthless suppression by Russia with the backing of Bismarck.[36] In 1869, at a conference at Lausanne, he told the utopians assembled there that a United States of Europe was impossible then, for the great nations of Europe had "too much military ambition."[37] When there were rumors of French preparations to move into Belgium and the Rhineland, Ferry came out unequivocally against aggression. He took issue with those who saw France as greatest "when she is most feared and when she enlarges about herself the circles of her bellicose and triumphant nationality." He denied the contention of those who said that France should hold Belgium and the Rhine provinces because she once held them or because they are part of the "hereditary patrimony of the Gallic race" or because "Providence has predestined the French nation to extend to

[33] *Discours*, I, 338–341.　　[34] *Ibid.*, p. 344.　　[35] *Ibid.*, p. 29.
[36] *Lettres*, p. 28.　　[37] Dietz, *loc. cit.*, p. 620.

the Rhine." Only the "Yankees" believed themselves so predestined and he deplored their "chauvinism." [38]

When the nature of Jules Ferry's background and aspirations before 1870 is considered, it is not surprising to discover that he was not then an imperialist. The acquisition of colonies was not part of the liberal creed.

From the time of Adam Smith, the economists of the *laissez-faire* school were unsympathetic to or opposed to colonies. Smith himself opposed the old colonial system and was dubious about the value of colonies at all.[39] Jeremy Bentham had sent out an appeal to the French to free their colonies.[40] The Utilitarians felt that colonies were unproductive, costly, and undesirable because of the restrictions they imposed on native populations. The same argument was upheld by John Stuart Mill [41] who would allow colonization only if it were accompanied by free trade and were carried on for the economic benefit of the whole world. Colonies as exclusive national markets, sources of supply and investment would be unnecessary for national prosperity in a world run according to Mill's doctrines.

Liberal economics supplied no economic justification for colonies. Nor did it condone aggressive overseas imperialism. Liberalism was pacific and cosmopolitan. The only wars it excused were wars of national unification, the regaining of *irredenta*. This creed, which had such an influence on Ferry, would have led him away from colonial expansion if he had considered the matter. Similarly the tenets of the Positivism that influenced Ferry were cosmopolitan and peaceful. It opposed the military adventures of Napoleon. It hoped to see all the world live together in peace and prosperity. Imperialism had no place here before 1870.

Colonies were not a popular cause in the Europe of the 1860's. England was at the height of her "Little England" movement.[42] Her empire was neglected, even scorned. Prussia under Bismarck was notoriously uninterested in acquiring colonies. Like Italy, she was too busy at home to cast longing eyes overseas.

Jules Ferry was not a man of much originality. He was an uncommon

---

[38] *Discours*, I, 25–29.

[39] Adam Smith, *Wealth of Nations* (J. C. Bullock, ed., Harvard Classics, ed., 1909), Bk. 4, Chap. VII.

[40] In a pamphlet, *Emancipate Your Colonies*, written in 1793, Bentham, speaking of the belief that colonies enriched the mother country, said: "All the common ideas on this subject are founded on illusions." *Jeremy Bentham's Works* (J. Bowring, ed., Edinburgh, 1843), III, 32.

[41] John Stuart Mill, *Principles of Political Economy* (London, 1873), p. 584.

[42] R. L. Schuyler, "The Climax of Anti-Imperialism in England," *Political Science Quarterly*, XXXVI, 537–560.

man with common tastes. Perhaps that was why he was a successful politician. He did not lead the way himself although he was in the vanguard of a minority. His energies and interests were absorbed in domestic questions. As a pacific liberal, a liberal nationalist, a man of the *juste milieu,* he would not want to engage in overseas campaigns. Before 1870 there was no reason why he should want colonies. France had no wounded prestige to be salved, she had no pressing need for new markets, the Republicans did not seek military glory. It is really not surprising that Jules Ferry was not an imperialist under the Napoleonic Empire.

War and Revolution

When the war of 1870 broke out, Ferry parted company with many of his liberal Republican colleagues to vote appropriations for preparations and for war, although he opposed the press's saber-rattling that helped persuade Napoleon to embark on a trial of arms with Bismarck. As a patriot, he preferred even Napoleon III's rule to French defeat. During the course of the conflict he advocated a full war effort and, like a good heir of the Revolution, called for placing arms in the hands of all citizens to repel "the enemy race [that] throws itself on us." [43]

The crushing defeat and surrender of the Emperor at Sedan gave the Republicans the opportunity of creating a new government in Paris. Ferry was in the vanguard of the band of deputies which led the crowd to the Hotel de Ville on September 4 to proclaim the Government of National Defense with its curious hodge-podge of leaders. Through the siege of Paris in the winter of 1870–1871 Ferry was a member of the Government, serving as mayor of Paris. In this capacity he shared with Magnin, the Minister of Commerce, the difficult task of supplying the city. When the Government of National Defense took over the provisioning task, there were only thirteen days remaining before Paris was completely invested on September 19. There was no time, no organization to move people out or large quantities of food in.

In mid-November (when he knew it to be already insoluble),[44] Ferry was put in charge of the provisioning problem. When the mayors of the arrondissements refused to sanction rationing, it was necessary to reduce the bread to a twenty-five per cent wheat content. That winter there was real hunger in the city, which was not relieved by the expedients of killing elephants in the zoos and rats in the sewers. The wonder was that two million people were kept alive for four and a half months with such slim resources. Ferry seems to have done a fair job in a post for

---

[43] *Discours,* I, 375.   [44] Rambaud, *op. cit.,* p. 51.

which he had neither experience nor assistance. But much of Paris always held this "Faim Ferry" against him.

During the tumultuous days of the siege Ferry showed himself a cool, moderate official determined to run an orderly government. An uprising of October 31 held the members of the Government prisoner in their offices. At great personal risk Ferry led a detachment of soldiers in a surprise entrance that freed the Government and quelled the disturbance. He won the admiration of all his colleagues for that feat of bravery.[45]

He was not an advocate of a war to the last ounce of French strength and the last foot of French soil. He saw the utter hopelessness of long French resistance without supplies, troops, and leaders.[46] When Paris was finally starved into surrender he broke with Gambetta, who wanted to carry on the war in the provinces. The split between the two men over this issue led to a long estrangement, bridged eventually by only a partial reconciliation.

Following the surrender of the Government of National Defense on February 28, Ferry remained at his post trying to establish order in the war-torn city. His was a most difficult position, especially when the newly elected Monarchist National Assembly proceeded to antagonize the population of Paris by terminating the moratorium on commercial debts and rents. Thousands of civilians were threatened with bankruptcy or eviction in a city whose economy was paralyzed. As the temper of Paris became menacing it was deemed essential to remove the arms still in the control of the National Guard. Ferry suggested the removal of the cannon held by the National Guard on Montmartre,[47] cannon paid for by popular subscription, and very dear to the working class population. It was the Government's attempt to seize them that precipitated the uprising of the Commune.[48]

When the population rose against the National Assembly, Ferry wanted to keep in Paris the Government and the troops already there, bring in other troops to end the rebellion. Thiers, however, thought otherwise, and, over Ferry's strong objection,[49] ordered the army and the administration to evacuate Paris on March 18. Ferry was the last member of the Government to leave, hoping to the end to get troops to

[45] J. Dietz, "Jules Ferry au Gouvernement de la Défense Nationale et pendant la Commune," *Revue de France*, année 14, II (1934), 510; Emile Marcère, *Entretiens et souvenirs* (Paris, 1899), II, 8.

[46] Dietz, "Jules Ferry au Gouvernement . . . ," *loc. cit.*, p. 510.

[47] *Ibid.*

[48] D. W. Brogan, *France Under the Republic* (New York, 1940), pp. 57–58.

[49] Rambaud, *op. cit.*, p. 57.

defend the Hôtel de Ville. He was actually pursued by a mob intent on murder and had to flee through the streets alone.[50]

During the second siege of Paris and its bloody recapture in the Spring of 1871, Ferry, in Versailles, took no part in the government. He was exhausted and sick at heart at the spectacle of civil war in his beloved city. He hated "those Jacobins in Paris" hardly more than he detested the Monarchists who were working to block a liberal republic to prepare for a restoration.[51] When the Versailles troops broke into Paris, Ferry went with one of the advance units. He was revolted at the sight of the casualties inflicted on both sides. He hoped to retake possession of the Hôtel de Ville to save what he could, but he found only ruins. He did restrain the troops from wreaking vengeance along the Quai d'Orsay.[52] Appointed Prefect of the Seine, May 26, he undertook to restore some order to the bloody, burned city. Almost before he had begun his tasks he was forced to resign. No man associated with September 4 was acceptable to the royalist majority at Versailles.

The war and the Commune tremendously affected the outlook of men like Ferry. They were profoundly shocked. The crushing defeat of France in the war destroyed their hopes of a peaceful, liberal world; and the uprising of the Commune their confidence in the lower classes. Militarism was to be a keynote of their generation, and to blight their bright hopes. A later generation that has seen France overwhelmed again can appreciate the upheaval, the torment and soul-searching that the catastrophe brought.

Ferry himself wrote, "that year [1870–71] had divided into two parts the lives of all men who lived through it or witnessed its events."[53] He blamed the Empire for having so weakened and stifled France's moral fiber that she had no "reserves of energy and character" with which to fight the enemy. The nation had been badly led, dazzled with an optimism that led to defeat. His generation had not been prepared for the task that confronted it and therefore had fumbled for a long time before finding an adequate solution. The bloody struggle of the Commune disturbed Ferry most. He had loved the Paris populace from a distance, but this bourgeois lawyer never understood the desperation that brought the uprising.

The loss of Alsace and part of Lorraine in the Treaty of Frankfort was of course a severe blow to a Lorrainer. He grieved deeply over

---

50 Dietz, "Jules Ferry au Gouvernement . . . ," *loc. cit.*, p. 518.
51 Rambaud, *op. cit.*, p. 64. Citing a letter to his brother.
52 *Ibid.*, p. 66.
53 "Au lendemain du Second Empire," *Revue politique et parlementaire*, CLXVIII (1931), 136. This is a fragment of a letter found among Ferry's papers, written some time after 1875, reflecting on the events of 1870–1871.

France's loss and dishonor but he was never a violent *revanchard*.[54] As a good Frenchman, he hated Germany, but, unlike some of his contemporaries, he was never fanatical about it. His only direct connection with the Treaty was to urge Thiers to include a few small communes on the French side of the border when the head of the Government had intended to cede them to Germany without protest.[55] As he was from Lorraine, Ferry's attitude is notable, but it may be explained partly by his preoccupation with attempts to form a Republican bloc to support Thiers and secure a republican form of government for France. He had no time to spend in vain recrimination; he was too busy with the important problems of the day.

Elected to the National Assembly from his home in the Vosges country, his early position in that body was not a happy one. On the one hand, he was unpopular with the conservative groups of the Right whom he had fought during the days of the Empire. They thought him a dangerous radical, especially since he had been associated with the September 4 revolt. On the other hand, he was unpopular with Gambetta's following, the largest of the Republican groups. This unpopularity sprang from his split with Gambetta during the war and from his own harsh personality.[56]

An appointment as Minister to Greece was a fortunate outlet for him at that time. After having refused a post in Washington, he was sent by Thiers in June, 1872, to Athens, where he remained for a year.[57] His chief problem was the settlement of the controversy over the Laurium mines (which, though of slight importance, was now of eight years' standing). These mines had been expropriated by the Greeks without a settlement satisfactory to French and Italian claimants. After some delay, in the course of which Thiers refused to present the Greeks with the ultimatum Ferry wished, the latter succeeded in settling the affair to the satisfaction of all.[58]

There was little to absorb his energies in Greece and when, upon returning home for a visit, he found himself in the midst of the political crisis that defeated Thiers on May 24, 1873, Ferry decided to resign his post and return to the National Assembly.

Birth Pangs of the Republic

He now was a secondary Republican leader in an Assembly whose Monarchist majority was hopelessly deadlocked with three claimants to

[54] *Lettres*, p. 140.   [55] *Ibid.*, pp. 128–129.
[56] Juliette Adam, *Mes angoisses et nos luttes* (4th ed., Paris, 1907), p. 287.
[57] J. Dietz, "Jules Ferry et les débuts de la Troisième République," *La Grande Revue*, CXXXIX (1932), 551.
[58] *Ibid.*, p. 554.

the French throne. Since the Bourbons, Orleanists, and Bonapartists could not unite, the Republicans were able to increase their strength and bide their time. Ferry turned as eagerly to the task of attacking the "Moral Order," which the conservatives professed to uphold, as he once had attacked the Empire.

France backed into the Republic in 1875 as the Assembly, unable to delay longer than four years, finally adopted a constitution. Ferry appears to have been quite well satisfied with its provisions although it had many shortcomings. He was content to have a democratic instrument with universal suffrage and a parliament,[59] whereas Gambetta and his followers were greatly dissatisfied with it.

Late in 1875 Ferry joined the majority of his Republican colleagues by becoming a Freemason. At that time membership in French Freemasonry was almost essential for Republican leaders. There was a striking identity of view between them and the Masons. Ferry disliked the secrecy of the order but liked its program, with its free thought, stress on public education, belief in progress, and its outlook of philanthropic Jacobinism.[60]

In the same year he married Eugénie Risler, daughter of a wealthy Alsatian family with strong Republican leanings, history, and interests.[61] It proved a valuable political asset to be connected with this prominent family from the "lost" provinces.[62]

In the elections of 1876 Ferry's campaign platform called for a "resolutely conservative" policy, pursuing "appeasement, freedom, and liberty" for the new Republic.[63] There was no hint of the ambitious educational, anti-clerical, and colonial program he would undertake soon after his election by his Vosgian constituency. He defeated his opponent, Buffet, who was the incumbent Premier and Minister of the Interior, despite the active support the latter received from the government and the local clergy.[64]

There was a general Republican victory throughout France in this February election: 340 Republicans to 155 Conservatives were chosen.[65]

---

[59] *Lettres,* p. 204.

[60] Dietz, "Jules Ferry et les débuts . . . ," *loc. cit.,* p. 561.

[61] The Rislers were in chemical manufacturing at Thann. His wife's grandmother was a Kestner, a family long active in Republican politics. The uncles of Mme. Ferry were Victor Chauffong and Col. Charras, both Republicans in 1848; Auguste Scheurer-Kestner; and Charles Floquet. Dietz, "Jules Ferry et les débuts . . . ," *loc. cit.,* p. 565.

[62] *Ibid.*   [63] *Discours,* II, 202–204.

[64] He was defeated not only by Ferry, but in the other three districts where he stood for election. Ferry was elected 11,739–6,204.

[65] The Senate elections on the preceding January 30 had also been a victory for the Republicans when they obtained 92 of the 221 seats at stake, so that the Republicans could muster a slight majority by combining with the Center.

The Republican preponderance was not so great as the number of deputies would indicate, however, since they obtained only fifty-one per cent of the vote.[66] But the political power was not yet held by men of Ferry's point of view. The conservative wing of the Republicans was still dominant. Dufaure, the new Premier, backed by the rather conservative center bloc of Republicans, drew some support from the Left. Ferry stood behind Dufaure's cabinet, although Gambetta would not.[67]

The Republican party was then, as always, divided into groups. That known as the Republican Left was headed by Ferry. It maintained a position politically to the right of Gambetta but just left of Center. Despite repeated overtures Ferry refused to form a coalition with the Great Tribune's group, saying, like a good Republican, that union came through diversity. It was his belief that the Republicans should pursue what he termed a "policy of results," being satisfied with half measures until the time should be ripe to press on.[68] He expressed the same view in the Republican journals for which he continued to write.

In the famous *Seize Mai* crisis of 1877 Marshal MacMahon forced the Premier, Jules Simon, out of office, although the latter had a good majority in the Chamber. At this time Ferry campaigned energetically for the Republican bloc as well as for himself. He clearly defined the issue at stake in a speech to the Chamber when he stated that there was a choice for France of being ruled by "a government of caprice or a government of the majority . . . the sword of a marshal of France or under a regime of laws." [69] Like the other Republicans, he was fighting for the rule of a responsible ministry.

Throughout the campaign he denounced the Government's restrictions on civil liberties. The restrictions do not seem to have hampered him personally. He reiterated that the Republicans were by no means dangerous radicals but sensible men anxious to run a peaceful government and prevented from so doing by the vagaries of the Conservative party.[70] To his wife he wrote in great delight that he found his electors not at all worried about the pretended dangers from the Republican program. Jacques Bonhomme in the Vosges was quietly but firmly Republican.[71] Ferry's confidence was justified by his victory with a comfortable margin: 13,320 to 8,729 for his opponent.

[66] Charles Seignobos, *L'Evolution de la Troisième République 1875–1914*, Vol. VIII of *Histoire de la France contemporaine* (ed. Ernest Lavisse, 10 vols., Paris, 1921), pp. 7–8.

[67] Marcère, *op. cit.*, II, 15.

[68] J. Dietz, "Jules Ferry et les traditions républicaines," *Revue politique et parlementaire*, CLIX (1934), 524.

[69] *Journal Officiel de la République Française—Annales des Députés: Débats parlementaires, Chambre des Députés*, 6/17/77. Hereafter this series will be cited as *J. O. C.*, and the debates of the Senate as *J. O. S.*

[70] *Discours*, II, 414.   [71] *Lettres*, p. 227.

The Republicans won an unmistakable victory in the October voting with 52 per cent of the votes and 327 of the 363 Republican deputies returned despite the herculean efforts of the Conservatives.[72] This proved to be the end of the Conservative party as a formidable threat. It could fight a delaying action in the Senate for another year, but from now on the Republicans were free to quarrel among themselves until danger arose from a new quarter.

Educational Reform and the Laic Laws

Ferry first entered the Government as Minister of Education in the Waddington cabinet, formed shortly after the retirement of Marshal MacMahon and the election of President Grévy. For the next six years Ferry was almost continually in ministerial office.[73] Variously Minister of Education, President of the Council, and Minister of Foreign Affairs, he came to be the dominant figure in the Republican ranks on the basis of his record of accomplishment. At first he shared the leadership with Gambetta, but after the latter's death, he became unquestioned chief for several years.

In his new office Ferry had the opportunity to undertake a program of educational reform that had long been dear to his heart, and which was a major part of the Republican program. In a series of laws enacted between May, 1879 and March, 1882, France was given a public school system providing for free, compulsory, and lay elementary education. State schools and lay school teachers largely replaced a dual system of state and church schools, both formerly staffed in large part by members of religious orders.

Ferry's program of educational reform was part of a broader anticlerical campaign. The Republicans gained political control of France by 1878 and their Chamber undertook a war on the conservative parties and their clerical allies. Republican success marked the end of a society ruling France since the Restoration.[74] Henceforth the Republic was to be run by and for the bourgeoisie belonging to the professional and lower middle class with considerable attention paid to the interests of the peasantry, and very little to the welfare of the proletariat. This balance characterized France to the end of the nineteenth century. Jules Ferry was a chief engineer in the construction of the framework which

---

[72] Seignobos, *op. cit.,* p. 38.

[73] February 7, 1879–November 11, 1881; January 30, 1882–August 7, 1882; February 21, 1883–March 30, 1885. He was Premier: September 23, 1880–November 11, 1881, and February 21, 1883–March 30, 1885. The balance of the time he was Minister of Public Education.

[74] Daniel Halévy, *La décadence de la liberté* (Paris, 1931), p. 86.

necessitated securing Republican control of France's institutions, including the educational, administrative, and judicial systems and the army. In 1878 only Parliament was republicanized; by 1885 all but the army was to be brought under control. The Republicans then would have what they termed the "necessary liberties" of political democracy.

The Church was to be restricted, not annihilated. Clerical control or influence over education, marriage, funerals, cemeteries, the army, and holidays was to be sharply curtailed. This was another of the long and numerous anti-clerical struggles in France. Its ideology had long roots in eighteenth-century rationalism. The various materialistic philosophies of the nineteenth century, Positivism, the vogue of science, natural law, and evolution culminating in Darwinism all contributed to the intellectual heritage of the Republicans who had more immediate cause to dislike the Church in their own political battles.[75]

Ferry, as early as April, 1870, had publicly committed himself to the cause of educational reform.[76] As a Positivist and as a liberal, he believed in the power of education to enlighten and improve men. As an anticlerical he desired to curb the great influence of the Church on the youth, since the Church was free to establish and run its own schools, and had supervisory powers over the state schools. He added few ideas to the Republican program but he gave them vigorous execution.

The strongest arm of the Church at the time was the Jesuit Order. It had the best schools, the ablest teachers and preachers, the greatest resources. Therefore Ferry undertook first to curtail the powers of the Jesuits. This was a matter of good strategy. The allegation was fairly widely believed that the Jesuits were constant plotters. Moreover, they were actually closely tied by sympathy, work and money to the upper classes—those same classes which had opposed the Republic. The ultramontanism of the order offended many of the faithful still devoted to the Gallican liberties. Ferry could count on a disposition of a certain part of the clergy and laity to be not over-sorry to see the Jesuits brought low.[77]

The blow fell from an unexpected corner. Article Seven of a bill to re-establish the state monopoly of conferring degrees, provided that no one belonging to an unauthorized religious order could direct or teach in any school.[78]

The battle over Article Seven was the greatest and most difficult in Ferry's educational program. The measure soon became the rallying

[75] E. Acomb, *The French Laic Laws, 1879–1889* (New York, 1941), pp. 110 ff.
[76] *Discours*, I, 283–305.   [77] Brogan, *op. cit.*, p. 148.
[78] For many years the Jesuits and other orders had been tolerated, but eighteenth-century and revolutionary bans against them had never been repealed, and they were not authorized to operate in France.

point of the Republican majority.[79] The bill was introduced by Ferry himself. It appears that his colleagues approved it in a Cabinet meeting without realizing the significance of this provision.[80] But the Clerical party was not slow in realizing its portent. When the battle was once joined, violent anti-clericalism was rampant in France. The bill passed the Chamber after a bitter fight on July 9 by a 333–164 vote. The debate continued throughout the summer. Ferry spoke in defense of his bill at several conventions, making an extensive tour through the Midi speaking for his proposal.[81] But in the Senate the old-time liberals, who were now conservative Republicans, joined the Monarchists in opposition. Despite Ferry's vigorous defense and the plea of the new Premier, Charles Freycinet, the Senate defeated Article Seven.[82]

Backed by a vote of the Chamber of Deputies, the Government invoked the laws against unauthorized associations. Decrees published on March 28, 1880, gave the Jesuits three months to dissolve their order, except for their teaching houses which could finish the school year. A second decree gave the other congregations three months to ask authorization before the laws would be applied to them. They determined to stand together against the decrees. Upon the expiration of the time limit, the Jesuits were expelled from their houses by the police—after they had refused to depart by themselves—but their property was not confiscated. There were few protests except from some notables in Paris, for the fate of the Jesuits could elicit little sympathy from the bulk of the French population.[83]

Freycinet was most unhappy over the turn of events and endeavoured to negotiate a compromise with Rome. As his talks were about to bear fruit they were nullified by the premature publication of the news by a legitimist paper.[84] The Cabinet had known nothing of the actions of its chief and the Gambettists promptly resigned, killing both the Government and the negotiations.[85]

Ferry as Premier—Domestic Affairs

It was under these circumstances that Ferry became Premier on September 23, 1880. He continued the expulsions that were already under way. There was the same sort of passive resistance on the part of the congregations but with no popular outcry. However, he expelled none of

[79] Brogan, op. cit., p. 150.
[80] Charles Freycinet, Souvenirs, 1878–1893 (Paris, 1913), p. 74; Marcère, op. cit., II, 23.
[81] Lettres, pp. 290–295.   [82] Seignobos, op. cit., p. 64.
[83] Gabriel Hanotaux, Histoire de la France contemporaine (Paris, 1908), IV, 594.
[84] Seignobos, op. cit., p. 63.
[85] Dietz, "Jules Ferry et les traditions républicaines," loc. cit., pp. 508–510.

the women's orders, none of those in Algeria, nor the Carthusians nor Trappists. Altogether two hundred and sixty-one monasteries were closed and 5,643 men expelled.[86] Thereafter the decrees were not strictly enforced. Actually, many Jesuits were allowed to return provided they were not blatant about it.[87] Nevertheless, resentment against Ferry still ran high in Catholic, conservative circles.

With this preliminary battle won, Ferry proceeded during the next several years with other major parts of his program. Elementary education was made compulsory and free for all children. "Civic" instruction, designed to mold all school children into staunch Republican patriots, was substituted for religion in the curriculum. Secondary education was made available to girls. Requirements for teacher-training and ability were established with a system of state examinations for all teachers, religious and lay alike. A system of state normal schools was set up to train a lay personnel. By March, 1882 these measures had been enacted, and thereafter the problems were chiefly administrative ones, including the development of an adequate plant and personnel for the new school system.

Although Ferry, compared with some of his radical, violently anti-clerical Republican colleagues, was moderate in his anti-clericalism, both in the laws he proposed and in administering the new system, he earned the bitter hatred of the Right. He was especially hated for the formulation of Article Seven, the subsequent expulsions, and the creation of the schools termed "godless" by the conservatives. These anti-clerical measures served to alienate the conservatives from Ferry's subsequent imperialistic policy.

His first Cabinet did not differ materially from the two that had preceded it and in which he had already been the dominating figure.[88] Ferry held the Presidency of the Council and the portfolio of Public Education. To satisfy the Senate, the post of Minister of Foreign Affairs was given to Jules Barthélemy Saint-Hilaire. This elderly professor of Greek, former secretary of Thiers, proved to be a model of probity but rather dull, a minister who was no asset in the rough-and-tumble of debate in the Chamber. The other Cabinet members were good, solid Republicans, politically to the left of Center with the same general views as those of Ferry.[89]

---

[86] Seignobos, *op cit.*, p. 66.

[87] Dietz, "Jules Ferry et les traditions républicaines," *loc. cit.*, p. 513.

[88] Seignobos, *op. cit.*, p. 61.

[89] They were: Cazot, Justice; Constans, Interior and Cults; Magnin, Finance; General Farre, War; Vice-Admiral Cloué, Navy and Colonies; Sadi Carnot, Public Works; Tirard, Agriculture and Commerce; Cochery, Post and Telegraph. Of these, Cloué and Sadi Carnot were new, together with Barthélemy Saint-Hilaire. The under-secretaries

Nevertheless, the political position of the new President of the Council was not a strong one throughout his first term. He held the office and the title, but Gambetta held the real power in the Republican party although he retained his post as presiding officer in the Chamber of Deputies.[90] The maintenance of his position on the basis of mere toleration hung over Ferry like a threatening shadow during the first year and a quarter he had the Premiership. His majority was sustained only by the coalition of Gambetta's Republican Union with his own Republican Left group. Ferry realized the weakness of his situation and once tried to step down in favor of Gambetta but the latter would not take office.[91] Gambetta generally supported Ferry because he agreed with most of his aims,[92] but he made it clear to all that he was biding his time.[93] Gambetta was not called to the Premiership largely because of Grévy's dislike for him—a dislike that was both personal and political.[94]

There was a fundamental personality clash between the two most important leaders of the Republican groups who were old friends and comrades in arms. But Gambetta was as violent and impulsive in his political opinions and speeches as in his personal life; Ferry, the prudent bourgeois, was repelled by the mannerisms as well as by the ideas of the unstable Gambetta.[95] There never was a violent break between the two; each was too wise openly to challenge the other, but their relations remained cool.

The personality of Ferry was a handicap to leadership of his party. He was not capable of arousing great enthusiasm in his audiences. He was respected but not loved by his adherents. While Gambetta could move men deeply with his warm, impassioned oratory, Ferry imposed his opinion with vigor and cold logic.[96] He never became a subtle juggler of Parliament, but rather drove it on.[97] Ferry's own supporters found him rather stiff, dry, and silent. Indeed they found his silence somewhat baffling and his cold calculation embarrassing.[98]

Ferry, as a lover of sound, good order, wanted a substantial government that really governed, not one dependent on the latest whim of Parliament. His methods were those of a cold legist without a trace of

---

of State were: Turquet, Fine Arts; Horace de Choiseul, Foreign Affairs; Martin-Feuillée, Justice; Faillières, Interior; Wilson, Finance; Raynal, Public Works; Girerd, Agriculture and Commerce. Two future Presidents of the Republic served here: Carnot and Fallières.

[90] J. Dietz, "Jules Ferry: sa première présidence du conseil," *Revue politique et parlementaire,* CLXV (1935), 99.

[91] *Lettres,* p. 307.   [92] Seignobos, *op. cit.,* p. 61.

[93] P. Gheusi, *La vie et la mort singulières de Gambetta* (Paris, 1938), p. 216.

[94] Freycinet, *op. cit.,* p. 63.   [95] G. Hanotaux, *Mon Temps* (Paris, 1938), II, 179.

[96] Marcère, *op. cit.,* II, 33.   [97] Freycinet, *op. cit.,* p. 167.

[98] Hanotaux, *Mon Temps,* II, 391.

sparkle or glamor. He fought hard for his beliefs and pursued his ends tenaciously once he had decided on a course of action. He displayed little originality, but compensated for this with a prodigious fund of knowledge, a capacious memory, and indefatigable toil. His colleagues respected his wide knowledge of history, economics, law, government, and administration.[99] His best talents were displayed in his debates on the school laws and on foreign policy.

While devoting the major part of his energies to the task of educational reform in the early months of his first Premiership, Ferry found time to carry through a program to establish the political and civil liberties long sought by the Republicans but left hanging under previous conservative governments.

He broadened the provisions of a pending bill to establish freedom of assembly in France and carried it through both Chambers. Full freedom to hold public meetings unsupervised by the police was granted.[100] A law guaranteed practically unlimited freedom of the press both as to publication and sale. Few countries had such a liberal press code as that given France.[101] The restrictions on both liquor and newsstand licenses were lifted, as were restrictions on Sunday and holiday labor.[102] The laws on civil liberties represented an important and long-promised realization of democracy in France.

A series of anti-clerical measures, aside from those concerned with education, were also passed during this period. The number of chaplains in the army was reduced.[103] Cemeteries were taken from clerical control,[104] and the administration of charities and hospitals, in which the clergy had played a prominent role, was placed in the hands of the municipal authorities.[105] Ferry did not play an active part in these particular steps. He was not always pleased by them, but he usually acquiesced. He several times urged and argued the Chamber into a more conciliatory attitude toward the Church but it won him no friends on the Right as his sins were in any case too great for them to forgive.

The long-standing problem of electoral reform rose to plague Ferry in the Spring of 1881. An old demand of the Radical Republicans had been to change the method of voting to the *scrutin de liste*.[106] Gambetta

99 Freycinet, *op. cit.*, p. 77.
100 Dietz, "Jules Ferry: sa première présidence du conseil," *loc. cit.*, p. 97.
101 Seignobos, *op. cit.*, p. 73.　　　　102 *Ibid.*, p. 72.
103 Acomb, *op. cit.*, p. 187.　　　104 *Ibid.*, p. 204.　　　105 *Ibid.*, p. 209.
106 The problem of *scrutin de liste* and *scrutin d'arrondissement* was one long and often debated in French politics and is quite confusing to the foreign student. *Scrutin d'arrondissement* quite simply provided for voting and representation from single-member constituencies (as in the United States). This was the system from 1870 to 1885. The radicals contended that this political mirror gave France a "broken reflection" by emphasizing narrow local considerations. They held for *scrutin de liste*

now had a private bill introduced in the Chamber providing for that system. However, the Cabinet was divided over the question, Ferry and Saint-Hilaire being opposed, while Constans and others were as strongly in favor of it. The Cabinet could only hold together by refusing to take a stand on the problem in the Chambers.[107] But Gambetta succeeded in having the bill passed.[108]

It was a different matter in the Senate, however. Gambetta was still suspected by many conservative Republicans to be a dangerous radical. It was believed that this new voting procedure was intended to provide a method for building a party which he himself could closely control. When the *scrutin de liste* came before the Senate, the Cabinet still refused to declare itself. Without its support the bill was doomed. The adverse vote of June 9, 148–114, was intended to be, and was in truth, an affront to Gambetta.[109]

The Gambettists were furious at Ferry's failure to support a bill passed by the lower house. From this time on they attacked him vigorously in the Chamber and in the press: Gambetta's *République française* was especially bitter.[110] This change in the balance of power was important as it coincided with the attacks on Ferry arising over the expedition to Tunisia. Had there been anyone to replace Ferry, he would have been overthrown at this juncture; but Gambetta did not want to take the Premiership on the eve of the elections.[111]

New elections for the Chamber of Deputies normally would have taken place early in the Fall of 1881. Ferry, however, thought to gain an advantage by moving the date forward to late August. He was interpellated on the matter and secured a vote of confidence by a very narrow margin on July 25. His majority was only thirteen—the votes of the Cabinet itself were all that saved it.[112] It was already clear that Ferry was on the way out unless some striking change occurred.

The election campaign that Summer was not a very bitter one as such elections went.[113] The case against the Ministry was clear enough for the

---

which provided voting on the basis of several representatives to be elected from larger districts. Presumably this would elect men with a broader view on national problems and elect more Republicans. It was Gambetta's pet reform, suspect to many because of that. His insistence was later to cause his fall. Ironically, the Chamber elected on *scrutin de liste* in 1885 nearly killed the Republic, and the Republicans hastily reverted to the old system.

[107] Freycinet, *op. cit.*, p. 160.   [108] Hanotaux, *Histoire*, IV, 676.
[109] Seignobos, *op. cit.*, p. 79.
[110] Dietz, "Jules Ferry: sa première présidence du conseil," *loc. cit.*, p. 174.
[111] Freycinet, *op. cit.*, p. 174.   [112] *J. O. C.*, 7/26/81.
[113] There is some disagreement among authorities on this point. Dietz, "Jules Ferry: sa première présidence du conseil," *loc. cit.*, p. 101, considers the campaign "very violent," but a seasoned observer and historian like Seignobos thought it quite calm. Seignobos, *op. cit.*, p. 80; Hanotaux, *op. cit.*, p. 705.

Right. It hated the anti-clerical measures of the past year and a half and accused the Government of various degrees of radicalism and atheism. It also criticized the heavy expenditures made for roads, railroads, school buildings, and the cost of the Tunisian expedition.

The intransigence of the Right was to be expected. More significant was the division among the Republicans. In the platforms of the candidates the burning question was that of constitutional revision.[114] The next most important demand was for military reform, followed in frequency of occurrence by a demand for protection and extension of the new free, compulsory, lay education.

The Premier's personal platform was modest enough. He reminded his electors of his establishment of democratic press and assembly laws, touched briefly on his educational work and promised to carry it forward to completion. He made no point of his Tunisian policy. Indeed, foreign affairs were skimmed over with a generality about defending "the essential interests and legitimate prestige of France abroad." He promised in the future to continue with the same firmness and wisdom the course he had already set. Specifically, he pledged the completion of pending laws on the magistracy, on the Associations, and on aid to agriculture in its current distress. There was no hint that might alarm his constituents of plans for overseas expeditions.[115] His reiterated appeal was to the Republicans to unite to defeat the Monarchist candidates.

During the campaign Ferry changed his position on the important question of constitutional revision. On August 10 he rallied to a moderate proposal of Gambetta's. He declared he could approve of "temperate, partial and mitigated revision" and would serve as Gambetta's "first lieutenant" to achieve it. His capitulation removed a major point of difference within the chief Republican groups. Yet, Ferry remained firmly opposed to the *scrutin de liste,* still so dear to Gambetta.[116]

The balloting brought new victories to the Republicans. The Monarchists, by losing some fifty seats, were now reduced to ninety members. Ferry himself was re-elected 7,331 to 1,600.[117] However, the real victory belonged to Gambetta. The contest within Republican ranks was in reality centered on the latter, who was making his great bid for power. More than two hundred deputies with his blessing had been elected.[118]

It was apparent from the end of the Summer that Ferry's defeat in the Chamber was at hand. Gambetta so obviously held the controlling

[114] Seignobos, *op. cit.,* p. 80. [115] *Discours,* VI, 83–84.
[116] Seignobos, *op. cit.,* p. 80.
[117] Dietz, "Jules Ferry: sa première présidence du conseil," *loc. cit.,* p. 102.
[118] The new division of the house majority as nearly as the Republicans were classifiable was: Center Left: 39; Republican Left (Ferry's group): 168; Republican Union (Gambetta's group): 204; Extreme Left: 46. Seignobos, *op. cit.,* p. 82.

power that not even the reluctant Grévy could longer deny him the leadership if he chose to take it. Ferry spent some days with the President at the latter's country home late in September. They found themselves in agreement on the future course. It was decided that Ferry should retire and Gambetta be called, if he would agree to form a moderate cabinet. Despite Grévy's urging, Ferry refused to accept any portfolio in the new combination.[119] It was the President's hope that Gambetta would soon fall.

Apparently, Gambetta was not over-anxious to take the Premiership at this moment. He was well aware of Grévy's hostility as well as that of the moderate Republicans and the Extreme Left in the Chamber. However, a more propitious moment could not be foreseen and he decided to assume office.[120]

The Cabinet made it generally known that it would retire shortly after Parliament reconvened.[121] Nevertheless, Ferry was determined not to resign without first defending his action in Tunisia as a last defiant gesture.[122] After two days of debate he was defeated, November 10, 1881, on a vote of confidence on his Tunisian policy. To end a tumultuous session, Gambetta stepped in to secure the new colony for France.[123] This intervention marked his certain entrance to the ministry. On November 14 he formed the long-awaited "Grand Ministry," great only in the extent of its failure.

Second Premiership

The death of Léon Gambetta at the close of the year 1882 left Jules Ferry the undisputed leader of the Republican groups, and for two years thereafter, as Premier, he controlled the government of France. During this second Premiership he embarked on a thoroughgoing colonial policy much more definitely planned and directed than during his first term in office. From the very first days of his Ministry new expeditions were sent out and others were strengthened. New energy and direction were given to the already inaugurated French designs on West Africa, the Congo, Madagascar, Egypt, Annam, and Tonkin. In these two years France acquired a really firm hold on a greatly enlarged colonial empire.

Considerations of domestic politics and enmities based on French political battles prevented Ferry from doing as much in colonial matters

---

[119] *Lettres*, p. 314.
[120] J. J. Weiss, "La situation parlementaire," *Revue politique et litteraire*, 3 me sér., t. 17, (1881), p. 516.
[121] C. Hohenlohe-Schillingsfürst, *Denkwürdigkeiten* (Stuttgart, 1907), II, 320.
[122] *Ibid.*
[123] For details on this question and debate see the succeeding chapter.

as he would have liked to do. Even though Parliament was little consulted until his projects were well under way, Ferry was constantly hampered by a coalition of the Right and the Extreme Left which objected violently to everything he did. Finally the growing forces of opposition seized on the excuse of a defeat of French troops in Tonkin to oust him from office.

During his second term Ferry demonstrated a greater maturity and political acumen than before. He was conciliatory, better controlled than when he was first Premier. But he was still a leader who was not really loved, did not inspire great enthusiasm, but did command respect from the coalition of his own adherents and the former followers of Gambetta.

He consolidated the Republican position by mastering the Monarchist judiciary, amending the constitution, legalizing trade unions, completing a few laic laws, and nearly balancing the budget through the reduction of the state public works program. In the field of education he had only administrative tasks left, for the last of his major school reforms had been established during a term as Minister of Education in 1882.[124] The educational battles, which were his first interest, having been won, he could devote more of his energies to the conduct of foreign affairs.

The Cabinet he formed on February 23, 1883, included several of the important moderate Republican leaders and a group of promising young Republicans.[125] The strongest men in the Cabinet were Paul Challemel-Lacour and Pierre René Waldeck-Rousseau. Both, like Ferry, believed in the need for a firm and active Ministry in contrast to the procrastinating, insipid ones that had immediately preceded. However, Challemel-Lacour soon proved to be a disappointment, for this misanthropic, dyspeptic professor of philosophy was not only ill but no match for the Radicals and Bonapartists in the rough-and-tumble of parliamentary debate. Easily discouraged, he became a drag on Ferry who, from the beginning, not only determined foreign policy but had to direct much of it even when Lacour nominally held the post. Ferry was not fortunate in his choice of foreign ministers.

[124] January 30–August 9 in the Freycinet Cabinet.
[125] The Cabinet included: Challemel-Lacour, Foreign Affairs; Martin-Feuillée, Justice; Waldeck-Rousseau, Interior and Cults; Tirard, Finance; Thibaudin, War (succeeded by General Campenon, October 9, 1883–January 3, 1885 and General Lewal, January 3, 1885–April 6, 1885); Brun, Navy and Colonies (succeeded by Admiral Peyron, August 9, 1883); Raynal, Public Works; Hérisson, Commerce; Méline, Agriculture; Cochéry, Post and Telegraph; Ferry besides being President of the Council was Minister of Education and Fine Arts until November 20, 1883, when he was succeeded by Faillières. The under-secretaries were: Noirot, Justice; Margue, Interior; Labuze, Finance; Baihaut, Public Works; Faure, Navy and Colonies; Casimir-Périer, War. Ferry's *chef de cabinet* was the young historian, Gabriel Hanotaux. Among these men were eight future premiers and three future presidents of France.

The Cabinet crisis that preceded Ferry's accession as Premier the second time was occasioned by Prince Napoleon's posting of a Bonapartist manifesto. Ferry quickly put an end to the affair, which had led to street rioting in Paris, by retiring the Orleanist princes from the army. He bluntly told the Monarchists that the Republic had the right to defend itself.[126] Thereafter he turned to his program of moderate reform.

He secured passage for a bill temporarily suspending the rules of tenure for the magistracy in order to purge the bench of the Monarchist and Bonapartist appointees who had been harassing the Government in every crisis. The removal of 453 judges earned him more hatred from the Right but assured Ferry's moderate supporters that the laws of the Republic would hereafter be administered by good Republicans.[127]

In the Summer and Fall of 1883 Ferry had a falling out with the Extreme Left. He was initially annoyed by their demonstration against Alphonso XII of Spain when he visited Paris.[128] In October, in speeches at Rouen and Havre, he castigated the Left for the sterility of its political program and its irresponsible and intransigent sniping at every ministry.[129] This declaration of hostilities and his moderate policies combined to alienate the Radical Republicans.

The anti-clerical program was greatly curtailed during his second Premiership.[130] He postponed a bill on Associations, and buried a bill to cut Church appropriations and take back certain properties from the clergy. Many public schools were allowed to keep their religious emblems and many teachers to teach Catholicism during school hours. Numerous expelled congregations were allowed quietly to resume their work.[131]

Demands for tariff protection were being voiced loudly by the agricultural interests during the lean years France was then experiencing. Ferry was persuaded to abandon his former belief in free trade [132] by Méline, the great champion of tariff protectionism. Tariffs on cereals, beet sugar, cattle and alcohol were increased.[133] Although Ferry had

---

126 Henri Leyret, *Waldeck-Rousseau et la Troisième République* (Paris, 1908), p. 233; Rambaud, *op. cit.*, p. 203.

127 *Lettres*, p. 337.   128 Seignobos, *op. cit.*, p. 100.

129 J. Dietz, "Jules Ferry, sa seconde présidence du conseil," *Revue politique et parlementaire*, CLXV (1935), p. 308.

130 During this time laws were passed to legalize civic funerals and make divorce possible. Ferry did not approve of the latter, but Naquet, the perennial champion of such a measure had secured enough supporters to pass it, although the Ministry took no part in the debate. Ferry intervened only to eliminate provisions for divorce by mutual consent.

131 Dietz, "Jules Ferry, sa seconde présidence du conseil," *loc. cit.*, p. 304.

132 He had already supported small tariff increases in 1881.

133 Rambaud, *op. cit.*, p. 214.

some misgivings on the matter, a law was passed allowing the foundation of syndicates, or trade unions.[134] This measure was insisted upon by Waldeck-Rousseau who pushed it through Parliament.[135] To relieve the badly unbalanced French budget as the depression deepened, Ferry abandoned the railway construction under the Freycinet plan of public works. A series of conventions with the railroads handed all lines over to them, and further building by the State ceased. But the Extreme Left was greatly angered because the State did not retain the right to repurchase the railroads if it wished. Ferry was charged with having sold out to the railroad and banking interests.

The long discussions on constitutional reform and the form of municipal government for France were temporarily ended by the moderate solutions to these questions carried out by Ferry and his Ministry. The communes of France, except Paris, were given a uniform system of government by the law of April 5, 1884. Really effective power was left in the hands of the departmental prefect. This form of municipal government endured without substantial change throughout the life of the Third Republic. To effect a very limited and partial revision of the constitution, a National Assembly was convoked at Versailles in August, 1884. After a week of debate made noisy by the Monarchists and Radicals, the Ferry program triumphed. Four minor changes were made by the Republican majority.[136] These made no appreciable alteration in the constitutional structure but did serve to show the members of the extreme parties that thoroughgoing revision was out of the question.

Changes in the manner of election to the Senate were called for, following these revisions. The Republicans wanted to abolish the system which provided for seventy-five life senatorships and the appointment of one senatorial elector to each commune regardless of its size.[137] But, over the Ministry's objection, a coalition of the Right and Extreme Left passed a motion providing for direct election of Senators by universal suffrage, by a 267–250 vote.[138] Waldeck-Rousseau thereupon handed in his resignation and urged the whole Cabinet to follow him.[139] However, Ferry succeeded in arguing and cajoling the Ministry into remaining until he could place the issue squarely before the Chamber. On December 9 he demanded and secured from the deputies a vote of confidence and a reversal of the December 2 action. He then pushed through a compromise whereby, as vacancies occurred through death, the seventy-

---

[134] Actually syndicates, although outlawed under a 1791 law, had been tolerated under the Third Republic, but henceforth they were freed from government control. Seignobos, *op. cit.*, p. 104.

[135] Leyret, *op. cit.*, p. 397.   [136] Seignobos, *op. cit.*, p. 105.   [137] *Ibid.*, p. 106.

[138] Leyret, *op. cit.*, p. 404.   [139] *J. O. C.*, 12/3/84.

five life seats should be distributed among the departments roughly according to population.

The perennial *scrutin de liste* proposal came up again during the reform of the constitutional laws. Since Ferry and his friends did not have to fear that the bill might be a measure of Gambetta's to insure his personal power, the Cabinet acquiesced in, but did not support it. Under the guidance of the old Gambettist, Waldeck-Rousseau, it easily passed the Chamber with a show of hands on March 19, 1885.[140]

Ferry was faced with a coalition of the extremes, a frequent phenomenon in French politics. His middle-of-the-road, opportunistic policy had made him many enemies on both political flanks. It is remarkable that such an aggressive and energetic Premier should have been tolerated for over two years by a Parliament used to dethroning its leaders after short terms.

The Monarchists had scant hope of founding a kingdom of France now and devoted their energies to criticizing the Government from the conservative viewpoint. They objected to the conduct of the State finances and accused the Republicans of fraud and corruption; they were bitter over the reform of the magistracy which hit their ranks. Their greatest objection was to the laic program. They continued their vitriolic attacks on the neutrality of primary education and the dissolution of the congregations. From platform and altar their members preached against the "godless schools" that Ferry had established. Because Ferry was so intimately connected with the laic program and other Republican reforms, the conservative groups fought his colonial program on nearly all occasions. Their ostensible reason was the heavy expense of the colonial undertakings for an already unbalanced budget.

Ferry met with no less bitter opposition from the Republican Left. Unpopular since the siege of Paris and made more so by his insistence on moderation in constitutional reform and the religious questions, he was thoroughly detested by the Radicals. His personality, his thoroughly bourgeois attitude, his determination to govern firmly, served only to increase the split with the Left.

These two groups had to sacrifice no fundamental principles to agree more or less tacitly upon concentrating their attacks on Ferry's colonial program. Their coalition grew stronger on questions of domestic and foreign policy throughout 1884,[141] finding its real strength in December when it defeated and nearly killed the Cabinet. During the first quarter of 1885 Ferry's power was waning, his majorities were falling off steadily. One untoward incident could pull the Ministry down, and such an in-

---

140 It came before the Senate after Ferry's fall and was passed in May.
141 See Appendix.

cident was furnished by a military reverse in Indo-China. With that Cabinet fall, came to an end a long series of French colonial gains stretching from Tunisia, along the West coast of Africa through central and East Africa to the China Seas and the South Pacific.

Chapter Two

NATIONAL RIVALRIES AND THE ACQUISITION OF TUNISIA

The most striking French imperial expansion undertaken by Jules Ferry during his first Premiership was the acquisition of a protectorate over Tunisia in May, 1881. Together with the Tonkin affair, seizure of this North African Regency is the best known of Ferry's colonial exploits. It was the first of a series of notable additions to the French Empire that followed in swift succession. In Tunisia the Third Republic ran into one of its first conflicts with the imperial interests of other powers, principally Italy and England. There, too, in order to enforce its claims the young Republic had to send out its first military expedition of considerable size. The successful acquisition of Tunisia had extremely important effects on the Republic's development, for it encouraged further colonial expansion and contributed in large measure to the formation of the European diplomatic alignment of the 1880's.

Jules Ferry has often been presented as the chief instigator and author of the Tunisian affair. But the truth is that he had little to do with preparing the way for it. Sometime after he came into office, having no previous intention of pursuing an aggressive colonial policy, he was persuaded to take the last in a long series of steps which had been preparatory to French acquisition of this protectorate. To use a Bismarckian expression, Ferry plucked the Tunisian fruit which was already ripe. The heat to ripen that fruit had been turned on by Ferry's predecessors and by Italians with imperial ambitions. To Ferry belongs the credit for assuming responsibility for the final decision to thwart the Italians in Tunisia and take for France an area long conceded her by England and Germany, as well as the credit for carrying the affair through to a successful conclusion despite opposition at home and abroad.

The Tunisian affair has been studied often and intensively.[1] It has

[1] Among the best studies on the basis of post-1918 publication of diplomatic documents and a critical approach are: W. L. Langer, "The European Powers and the French Occupation of Tunis," *American Historical Review*, XXXI (1925–1926), 55–78, 251–265; Eugene Staley, *War and the Private Investor* (New York, 1935), Chapter XII; and F. L. Schuman, *War and Diplomacy in the French Republic* (New York, 1931),

been cited as one of the classic cases of economic imperialism; as a great example of power politics; and as an unconscionable trade in international diplomacy. It is all these things. It is also illuminating and crucial for a study of the reasons Jules Ferry embarked on an expansionist course.

Tunisia before Ferry

Tunisia in the nineteenth century was a virtually independent Regency. Once under the suzerainty of Turkey, this tie had been, to all intents and purposes, practically discarded. Under a succession of Beys more extravagant than able, Tunisia fell under French domination after Algeria was acquired. Contiguous with that French colony, Tunisia was considered by many Frenchmen to be their "natural" zone of interest. Until about 1860 French influence was paramount.[2] Napoleon III allowed it to wane while English and Italian interests grew apace.[3] In financial affairs France remained predominant, however, for the Beys floated a series of loans in Paris[4] that proved most unfortunate, as had similar borrowing for other Mohammedan princes. Poor revenue collections and excessive expenditures led to the institution of a Tunisian Debt Commission in 1869 which soon became an International Commission to insure payment on the debt of 160,000,000 francs.[5]

Italian ambitions became the chief stumbling block for the French in the Regency. There was among Italian nationalists a sentimental attachment to the site of Carthage and the dream of rebuilding the imperial glories of Rome. Tunisia, so close to Sicily, would have given Italy strategic control over the narrow waters of the Mediterranean. Moreover, there were far more Italian than French colonists in Tunisia.[6] Italy made her first attempt to seize Tunisia in 1871, when she demanded

---

Chapter IV. The two later works, in particular, explore the interplay of economic, nationalistic and diplomatic factors in the case of Tunisia. A now outdated, more strictly economic interpretation of French penetration into Tunisia may be found in L. Woolf, *Empire and Commerce in Africa* (London, 1919), pp. 79 ff.

[2] As was evidenced by such privileges as a monopoly of Tunisian telegraph lines granted the French in 1859. Langer, *op. cit.*, p. 56.

[3] The English consul, Sir Richard Wood, secured an important railway concession for the line from Tunis to the port of La Goletta in 1859.

[4] The first loan was floated in 1863, followed by another of thirty-five millions in 1865.

[5] It was originally a Franco-Tunisian Commission because French investors held virtually all the bonds, but the English and Italian consuls in Tunis forced the Bey, despite French protests, to set up an International Commission with representatives of their respective nations. Staley, *op. cit.*, p. 333.

[6] Stephen Roberts, *History of French Colonial Policy* (London, 1929), I, 286. There were about 11,200 Italians and 700 Frenchmen in Tunisia in 1881.

great privileges for the Italian colony there,[7] following friction between Italian citizens and natives. France was helpless to do more than protest, but England intervened to halt the Italians and force arbitration of the incident in March, 1871.[8]

Soon afterwards the Sultan tried to reassert his suzerainty over the Bey. France refused to recognize his claims in October, 1871, and successfully insisted upon the maintenance of the *status quo*.[9] The Sultan's claims to suzerainty remained of antiquarian interest.

After the Franco-Prussian War, France had no intention of immediately annexing Tunisia or any other place. She was more than busy rebuilding her governmental and economic structure, and paying the war indemnity imposed on her by Germany. There were no energies or soldiers for export. Upon several occasions she assured England that she had no intention of moving in on the Bey in whom England had a friendly interest.[10] The French consul in Tunis, who in 1872 suggested that France annex the Regency, was told that the Government meant to do no such thing and that he should put such thoughts from mind.[11] At the same time it was made clear to all that France was determined to keep other powers out of Tunisia and maintain her important position there.

When rumors circulated that France was going to act in Tunisia, the German ambassador, Count von Arnim, told the Duc Decazes in January 1874 that Germany would not tolerate French annexation.[12] Decazes asserted that such an idea had not entered the official mind of France. Bismarck first indicated a changed opinion on this matter during the war scare of 1875 when he began to encourage Decazes to move into North Africa.[13] After the crisis had passed, Bismarck clearly adopted a more conciliatory policy toward France which he demonstrated by urging her to undertake some overseas expansion.[14] From this time forward, Bismarck constantly supported France in Tunisia, very definitely intending that his policy should divert French attention from the lost provinces of Alsace and Lorraine.[15] However, France was in no position to act

[7] A. M. Broadley, *Tunis, Past and Present: The Last Punic War* (London, 1882), I, 149–150.

[8] *Commission de publication des documents relatifs aux origines de la guerre de 1914. Documents diplomatiques français, 1ère série* (Paris, 1929–1934), I, No. 65. Hereafter this series will be cited: *DDF.*

[9] *Ibid.*, No. 106, note.   [10] *Ibid,* Nos. 65, 252.   [11] *Ibid.*, No. 106.

[12] Lord Newton, *Lord Lyons* (London, 1913), II, 60; Hohenlohe, *op. cit.*, II, 199, puts this in December, 1873.

[13] *Grosse Politik der europäischen Kabinette 1871–1914* (Berlin, 1922), I, 303. This series will hereafter be cited: *GP.*

[14] Pearl Mitchell, *The Bismarckian Policy of Conciliation with France* (Philadelphia, 1935), p. 56.

[15] *GP.*, I, 303.

in the Regency; she was also still suspicious of gifts from Berlin.[16]

Tunisia stumbled her way to bankruptcy, and a series of quarrels began over commercial rights, concessions for public utilities and struggles for influence among the European consuls in the Regency. The French consul after 1874, Theodore Roustan, was passionately devoted to the cause of French Empire [17] and for years struggled mightily against English and Italian interests. Aided by the Governor of Algeria, he outmaneuvered the English consul to push a French firm into buying a strategic but economically worthless railroad between Tunisia and Algeria, with the aid of a subsidy granted by Parliament in 1877.[18] While the English and French consuls wrangled in Tunis, the fate of the Regency was really determined at the Congress of Berlin in 1878.

The Congress of Berlin

Although primarily interested in the problems of Southeastern Europe, the Congress of Berlin proved to be a decisive turning point in North African and French colonial history.[19] France went to this conference [20] surrounded by an international atmosphere more favorable to herself than she had enjoyed for some time. Bismarck pursued his conciliatory policy, working carefully to forestall a possible Franco-Russian alliance. French relations with England were amicable and carefully preserved by French statesmen as the cornerstone of their international policy.

Before the conference opened, England had arranged with Turkey that she should occupy the Turkish island of Cyprus in return for a promise to defend Turkey's Asia Minor possessions against Russian advances.[21] It was then thought that France should be given some compensation for this increase in English power. Despite all the published documents, it is still not perfectly clear who first suggested that France

[16] Robert Wienefeld, *Franco-German Relations, 1878–1885* (Baltimore, 1929), p. 80.

[17] Hanotaux, *Mon Temps*, II, 251.

[18] *DDF*, II, Nos. 49, 193; Staley, *op. cit.*, pp. 336, 377.

[19] This conference was called in 1878 to settle problems arising from the peace imposed on Turkey by Russia in March 1878, following the Russo-Turkish war. The major powers, especially Austria and England, were displeased with that peace, and a European conference, called by Bismarck in his famous "honest broker" role, set aside the provisions of the treaty and made a new settlement.

[20] The Republicans had at first been reluctant to attend a Congress in the erstwhile enemy's capital. The invitation to participate was accepted only when Gambetta was persuaded that it was essential for French prestige and interests to be represented. E. Pillias, *Léonie Léon, amie de Gambetta* (Paris, 1935), p. 106. The acceptance was conditional upon there being no discussion of French interests in Egypt and the Near East, including the Holy Places. Freycinet, *op. cit.*, p. 32.

[21] Dwight Lee, *Great Britain and the Cyprus Convention Policy of 1878* (Cambridge, 1934), p. 85.

be given a free hand in Tunisia. The latest evidence indicates that the idea came from London.[22] At any rate, it appears that Bismarck and Salisbury agreed on the Cyprus-Tunisia trade either just before the Congress opened or very soon thereafter.[23]

In a letter to Waddington on July 6, 1878 Salisbury revealed the arrangement with Turkey concerning the cession of Cyprus.[24] Waddington was greatly upset, having expected England to ask only for such a small point as Mytilene.[25] But Tunisia was offered to France in an interview between Waddington and Salisbury on the 7th. According to the French statesman's account, Salisbury said that England would be glad to see France in Tunisia, flatly stating, "Do what you like there," and later adding: "You cannot leave Carthage in the hands of the barbarians."[26] This offer was confirmed by Disraeli at the Congress and later by the Prince of Wales in Paris.[27] The French delegate was cautious about committing himself, at first being content to say that France was interested in a protectorate over Tunisia but not in outright annexation.

When Waddington reported the conversations to Bismarck, the Chancellor gave his full support to the arrangement. The French statesman mistakenly thought that this was Bismarck's first knowledge of the proposal.[28] Italian ambitions in Tunisia were disregarded by Bismarck and Salisbury.[29]

The news of England's occupation of Cyprus caused considerable unfriendly comment in the French press, especially in Gambetta's *République française*.[30] The bargain about Tunisia had to remain a state secret for the time being. But Waddington returned from Berlin delighted to have Tunisia in his pocket, as he put it, and nearly as delighted that

[22] *DDF*, II, No. 330. It is barely possible that it was Bismarck who suggested that France be compensated and that Tunisia be the payment. Langer believes that the Cyprus-Tunisia trade was probably arranged between England and Germany in May with Bismarck suggesting the Tunisian compensation for France. Langer, *op. cit.*, p. 66.

[23] Langer, *op. cit.*, p. 67.

[24] Ministère des Affaires Etrangères, *Documents diplomatiques, Conférence de Berlin, 1878* (Paris, 1878) pp. 304–306. Publications in this series are generally known as *Livres Jaunes* and will be so cited hereafter, abbreviated as *L. J.*

[25] *DDF*, III, *Annexe* I.   [26] *Ibid.*, II, No. 330.

[27] *Ibid.*   [28] *Ibid.;* Newton, *op. cit.*, II, 148; Lee, *op. cit.*, p. 100.

[29] Salisbury did venture the suggestion that Italy might move into Tripoli, but he was not really concerned over Italian interests. Bismarck was currently annoyed with the Italians and not interested in their ambitions. Apparently his Foreign Minister, Bülow, did once offer Tunisia to the Italians, although he may not have known about the offer of that state to France when he did so. At any rate, the suggestion was soon dropped. Count Corti, the Italian Foreign Minister, learned of the Cyprus convention from the newspapers. Corti, who was opposed to compensations in principle and whose colleagues wanted compensation in Trentino and Trieste, returned to Italy with what he termed "clean hands." His critics termed them "empty hands," and he narrowly escaped being stoned in the streets of Milan. Langer, *op. cit.*, pp. 67–71.

[30] Lee, *op. cit.*, p. 106; Newton, *op. cit.*, pp. 151–152.

France once more was at the council tables of Europe as a Great Power.[31] He soon showed that he fully accepted the idea of a protectorate over Tunisia, despite his initial hesitancy. With the approval of Marshall MacMahon, he was determined that France should act quickly to take advantage of this change in British policy.[32]

At once, after returning to Paris, he proceeded to secure England's formal, written consent to French occupation of Tunisia and her assurance in regard to Egypt and Syria in a form that could be published if necessary. The day after his return, he told Lord Lyons, the English ambassador, of his conversations with Salisbury.[33] The latter was disturbed by the "lurid touches" in Waddington's account. He protested that Tunisia was not his to give away as freely as the French Minister made it appear.[34] To the French ambassador he asserted that his suggestion was not a "provocation to seize Tunis," but an expectation that France could do so if Turkey should be further weakened.[35] Finally changes were made that satisfied Salisbury and on July 26 he conceded what was in essence a free hand for France in Tunisia.[36] A few days later he displayed belated concern over Italian and Turkish objections to the proceedings,[37] but Waddington had his promises and was already pushing on.

Four days after his return to Paris, Waddington asked Roustan whether the Bey would accept a protectorate if it were presented to him, and how much military resistance he could offer.[38] Roustan replied that either a generous money payment or the use of military force would be needed, that simple persuasion would be of no use.[39] The same day that he received his assurances from England, Waddington asked Roustan to draft a protectorate treaty.[40] Roustan returned to Paris and conferred with Waddington at length between August 11 and 27. No record of these talks exists, but apparently the two men drafted a treaty of protectorate that was never presented to the Bey.[41] Roustan returned to Tunis on a warship that remained stationed at La Goletta.[42] However, on September 1 Waddington cabled him to postpone all further action,[43] saying he was concerned about the reactions of Turkey and Italy to any move at the moment. He thought he must first find a suitable compen-

[31] *DDF,* II, No. 328. [32] *Ibid.,* No. 330.

[33] Newton, *op. cit.,* II, 154. The French ambassador to London, d'Harcourt, was instructed at the same time to get a categorical written reply from England giving France *carte blanche* in Tunisia. *DDF,* II, No. 330.

[34] Newton, *op. cit.,* II, 156; *DDF,* II, Nos. 334, 335.

[35] *DDF,* II, No. 330. [36] Ibid., III, *Annexe* II.

[37] A. Lebon, "Les Préliminaires du traité de Bardo," *Annales des Sciences Politiques,* VIII (1893), p. 402; Newton, *op. cit.,* I, 158.

[38] *DDF,* II, No. 328. [39] *Ibid.,* No. 329. [40] *Ibid.,* No. 337.

[41] *Ibid.,* note. [42] *Ibid.,* No. 364. [43] *Ibid.,* No. 339.

sation for the Italians.[44] The Foreign Minister had a domestic political situation to worry him, too, for Gambetta was now opposed to any move into Tunisia.[45] Waddington could undertake no major venture until he was sure of his home front as well as his international position.

Italian Designs

The Italians began a series of counter moves in the struggle for Tunisia in the Fall of 1879. Cairoli, the Prime Minister of Italy, feared that France had been given a free hand there. When he asked in London about the truth of this rumor, he received a noncommittal answer. When he inquired of Waddington concerning France's intentions, Waddington told him that he would not act without previously consulting Italy.[46] A bellicose new consul, Signor Licurgo Maccio, was now sent out to Tunis to uphold Italian interests. He was soon to engage in a battle of "affairs" with Roustan who was a good match for him. In Rome, Corti and the Ministers of War and Navy resigned rather than be associated with such a dangerous policy as that which Cairoli pursued after October.[47] Maccio arrived in Tunis with a great fanfare, including a band and a military escort, much to the disgust of Roustan. From the first moment a consular war was on.[48] Roustan found his new opponent much more difficult than the Englishman, Wood, ever had been.

The new turn of events did not escape Paris, and Italy was warned in mid-October through the French minister to Rome, the Duc de Noailles, that France would allow no other power to occupy any part of Tunisia and that she had better abandon her dreams of a new conquest of Carthage.[49]

The stage was set for French intervention by the Fall of 1878, before the famous series of clashes of French and Italian economic interests, sometimes said to be the reason France took Tunisia. French policy was ready-formulated long before Ferry came into office. To seize Tunisia, a favorable opportunity was still needed, both in France and in Europe, or lacking that, a determined man ready to run some risks. Not economic imperialism, but the workings of the European balance of power, together with certain French traditional aspirations, led immediately to intervention in the area.

The first trial of arms between the French and Italian consuls oc-

---

[44] *Ibid.*, No. 340. In *DDF*, No. 328, Waddington said he had it in mind to offer Tripoli to Italy as compensation. Now he felt that it might unduly arouse the Turks if two areas they claimed were taken from them at once, and he was casting about for other compensation.

[45] D'Estournelles de Constant, *La Politique française en Tunisie* (Paris, 1891), p. 81.

[46] Langer, *op. cit.*, pp. 74–75.   [47] *Ibid.*, p. 75.

[48] Broadley, *op. cit.*, I, 174.   [49] Lebon, *op. cit.*, p. 403; *DDF*, II, No. 352.

curred when the Bey, with the support of the English and Italian consuls, attempted to repossess an estate granted a French subject named Sancy on the grounds of an unfulfilled contract.[50] Roustan would permit no such loss to be suffered by a Frenchman. He posted a guard from the French consulate and prevented the seizure of the estate on December 9, 1878.[51] Waddington was alarmed at the bold confidence of the consul. Although he was uneasy about the wisdom of relying on Bismarck's good graces, he inquired whether Germany had encouraged the Italians in this case and also whether she would look favorably upon a French protectorate over Tunisia at this time.[52] Bülow gave Saint-Vallier immediate reassurance as to Germany's attitude, saying that she supported France fully. Then, when the French ambassador was visiting Bismarck at Friedrichsruhe, the Chancellor, on January 4, 1879, baldly stated that, "the Tunisian pear is ripe, and it is time for you to pluck it; the insolence of the Bey has been the August sun upon this African fruit which may spoil, or be stolen by another, if you leave it upon the tree too long!" Bismarck asserted that if the Italians appealed to him, they would be told that Tunisia was for France who had a free hand in the Mediterranean, as far as he was concerned. But he warned that the Italians would probably pay no attention to him. He further volunteered the information that he had already protested to England the actions of Wood in the Sancy case.[53]

With this assurance, an ultimatum was immediately dispatched to the Bey demanding that he leave Sancy alone and make reparations to him. Action by the French fleet was threatened if a satisfactory reply were not received.[54] The Bey accepted the demands and his minister made a public apology to Roustan.[55] Sancy got his lands back and then soon sold them for a comfortable sum to the *Société Marseillaise*.[56] The English consul, Wood, who had not followed Salisbury's changed policy, was retired shortly thereafter as a result of Bülow's suggestion to Lord Russell, the British ambassador to Berlin,[57] and Waddington's note on the matter to Salisbury.[58]

Encouraged by this success, Waddington tried once more to establish the projected protectorate over the Bey. He suggested to Roustan that he present to the Bey a proposal for a strict alliance between Tunisia

---

50 The estate had been granted in 1877 for stock-breeding purposes, and the Bey found that the contract terms regarding the number of animals on the farm at the end of a year had not been fulfilled. Broadley, *op. cit.*, I, 175. The Bey was also backed in this move by the International Debt Commission, including its French member. Staley, *op. cit.*, p. 341.

51 *DDF*, II, No. 364. 52 *Ibid.*, Nos. 366, 368. 53 *Ibid.*, No. 369.
54 *Ibid.*, No. 372. 55 Broadley, *op. cit.*, I, 178. 56 *Ibid.*, p. 179.
57 *GP.*, III, 388. 58 *DDF*, II, No. 375; Newton, *op. cit.*, II, 173.

and France without military occupation by the latter, but with France pledged to protect the Bey against all comers.[59] This suggestion was sent out on January 12 and was followed by a draft of the treaty on February 11, a draft which had been drawn since October, 1878.[60] Roustan found that the Bey was frightened by the suggestion that he needed protection against nations other than the French. The former reported as late as July 28 of that year that he had not found a favorable opportunity to present the proposal.[61] The matter was then dropped until the following May.

During the Depretis Ministry, Italy allowed matters to rest easily. England had informed her in January and February, 1879, that she was neutral in the matter.[62] The French position seemed to be improving.[63] Russia had actually sounded France in regard to a possible alliance, a suggestion which Waddington had refused to consider.[64] Italy was isolated. Nevertheless, the Cairoli ministry, upon its return in June, 1879, undertook a renewed campaign in Tunisia.[65]

The first results of this policy were apparent when the French consul discovered on March 4, 1880 that an Italian, Commander Rubattino, was about to purchase the bankrupt Tunis-La Goletta line.[66] The consul wired home that the road could be bought for four million francs.[67] The information was passed along to the Bône-Guelma Railway Company. While the secretary of the English rail company bargained in Rome, the Bône-Guelma Company bought the concern's holdings from an English agent specially invited to Paris.[68] The Italians were furious, and, in the uproar, the fact that Rubattino had government backing in his venture became clear. Freycinet ordered Roustan to secure the Bey's approval of the transaction,[69] but the French had reckoned without English law, for the sale was disallowed and a public auction held.[70] At the July 7th auction, Rubattino bought the railroad

[59] *DDF*, II, No. 375.　　　　　　[60] *Ibid.*, No. 381.

[61] *Ibid.*, No. 449.　　　　　　[62] Langer, *op. cit.*, p. 78.

[63] The diplomatic energies of Europe were absorbed in executing the settlement arranged in Berlin. Concurrently Italy annoyed Austria by allowing her flaming patriots to continue their irredentist activity; she angered both Germany and England by her flirtation with Russia. Bismarck was worried about Russia who still sulked after her humiliation at Berlin, and he was consequently annoyed at the Italians. The Austro-German alliance was signed on October 7, 1879, but Bismarck made haste to assure Saint-Vallier that it contained nothing inimical to France. Langer *op. cit.*, pp. 251–253; *DDF*, II, Nos. 398, 440; E. Daudet, *La Mission du Comte de Saint-Vallier* (Paris, 1918), p. 171.

[64] Langer, *op cit.*, p. 251.

[65] It also renewed the irredentist campaign against Austria simultaneously. *Ibid.*, p. 253.

[66] *DDF*, III, No. 49.　　　　　　[67] *Ibid.*, No. 80.

[68] Staley, *op. cit.*, p. 344.　　　　　　[69] *DDF*, III, No. 89.

[70] Rubattino's lawyers cited a statute that forbade the sale of any British-owned railroad in Africa without court consent.

for 4,137,500 frs., about four times its real value.[71] It became evident how so uneconomical a purchase was possible when the Italian government on July 15 guaranteed earnings of six per cent on the purchase price and on whatever sum was needed to repair the road.[72]

This affair was probably one of the most important single factors in bringing about French military occupation.[73] It showed unmistakably what the Italian intentions were and that France had to deal not merely with private citizens but with the Italian government's policy of buying up the public utilities of Tunisia.

Even the gentle Freycinet, then Premier, was disturbed at the news. The day following the announcement of the Italian guarantee of interest, he sent a sharp warning to Italy that Tunisia was France's sphere of influence and that his country could not allow other governments to interfere there. Freycinet wrote Noailles that he had told General Cialdini, Italian ambassador to France, that,

> the great interests created by us in Algeria do not permit us to allow another power to establish its influence in opposition to ours in a territory like Tunisia, which is the natural annex and the military key to our African holding. . . . I then explained to him that in our view there were two very distinct categories of enterprises on which the activities of the nationals of the two countries could be expended, which I called enterprises of a private order and undertakings of public works or those which normally fall within the exclusive domain of the State. Among the latter I cited telegraph lines, ports, railroads, etc. . . . In the domain of private interest there is absolute freedom of competition between French and Italians. . . . But when it is a question of State enterprises, of the political direction of the Regency, we cannot admit this division, which would be a constant threat for us and an inevitable source of conflicts.[74]

Answering through Noailles, Cairoli protested that Italy had no intention of infringing on French interests in Tunisia, although at the same time in Paris, General Cialdini was vigorously upholding the equality of Italian rights.[75]

While the contest for the Tunisian railroad was in progress, Freycinet, in May, again sent Roustan a draft for a treaty giving France a rather

---

[71] F. Vatin, *Les chemins de fer en Tunisie* (Paris, 1902), pp. 65–68.

[72] *DDF*, III, No. 213.   [73] Staley, *op. cit.*, p. 345; Langer, *op. cit.*, p. 255.

[74] *DDF*, III, No. 214.

[75] Lebon, *op. cit.*, p. 419. This was not the first warning Italy received during that year that France would insist on the preservation of the *status quo* in Tunisia, for on the preceding May 20 a similar word of caution had been spoken.

vague and limited control over the Regency.[76] However, the French consul replied that he could not persuade the Bey to accept the arrangement unless some marines were landed to support his arguments.

It is possible that, given a little more time, Freycinet might have sent troops into Tunisia in the late Summer of 1880. He enjoyed the full support of Germany,[77] but was uncertain about England.[78] A new Liberal Cabinet had come into office with Lord Granville as Foreign Secretary. His attitude varied from grudging approval to outright objection concerning French ambitions in Tunisia. Freycinet was encouraged when in the early Summer after three French warships were sent to Tunis, concessions were made to the French to develop the port near there and two rail lines.[79] Freycinet claimed that he was about to follow up this success by moving troops into Tunisia, when he was overthrown in September to be replaced by Jules Ferry.[80] According to his memoirs, he urged Ferry to realize the French ambitions in Tunisia,[81] but the new Premier did not then take his advice.

Ferry's Inheritance

Since it was Jules Ferry who finally did take Tunisia for France, he has repeatedly been credited with primary responsibility for so doing by friend and foe, politician and historian. Actually, when he came into office as Premier in September, 1880, he had no intention of moving into the Regency. He had his hands more than full with the expulsion of the Catholic orders. This question and that of school reform absorbed all his energies for the balance of 1880 and into the early part of 1881. He not only had no plans for action in Tunisia, but there is no discoverable expression of his opinion on the problem up to and through 1880.[82] So far as we can tell, he took no part in the Cabinet's discussions

---

[76] *DDF*, III, No. 109. This was the same draft as that which was presented in February 1879. *Supra.*, p. 37.

[77] At the Madrid conference of May-July 1880, which provided for the protection of native employees of Europeans in Morocco, the German delegate gave full support to his French colleague on Bismarck's orders. *GP*, III, 398, 399; Hohenlohe, *op. cit.*, II, 281; Wienefeld, *op. cit.*, pp. 70-71.

[78] Langer, *op. cit.*, p. 255.   [79] *DDF*, III, Nos., 232, 238.

[80] Freycinet, *op. cit.*, p. 168.   [81] *Ibid.*

[82] By a curious coincidence, Ferry's old mentor and friend, Emile Littré, wrote a long article in his review setting forth the foreign policy he believed the Republic should follow and expressing the belief that an imperial program including expansion in Tunisia, West Africa and Indo-China was the only way in which France could avoid becoming a "secondary" power. Not markets, but prestige, made it essential for France to grow overseas. This represented a complete reversal of opinion on the part of Littré who earlier had opposed imperialism in all its forms. He stated that he had reasoned out his program as the best course for France to follow. Yet there is no evidence that Littré influenced Ferry in this instance, although perhaps it did make the latter more amenable to colonial expansion a year later. E. Littré, "La République Française et l'extérieur." *La philosophie positive*, XXIV (1880), 128–144.

on North African affairs while he was Minister of Public Education. The web of diplomatic adjustment, imperial ambition and French investment in Tunisia was spun long before Ferry became Premier. He did nothing one way or the other to affect the direction of policy. But if Tunisia were not to be taken by France, Ferry would have had to effect a reversal of policy and especially a removal of Roustan. That consul pursued his course for the most part as before, but in general, he enjoyed less support from Paris immediately after Ferry's Cabinet came into office than previously.

Ferry's Minister of Foreign Affairs, Barthélemy Saint-Hilaire,[83] had no more interest in Tunisia than his chief. He was to prove somewhat more receptive, as North Africa had held a certain attraction for him since his inspection tour in 1855 of the projected Suez Canal.[84] But in the Fall of 1880, he was primarily concerned with the problems of the Montenegrin boundary laid down by the Congress of Berlin.[85] As late as February 1881 he expressed his desire to make an arrangement with Italy to maintain the *status quo* in Tunisia.[86] We have the testimony of one of the chief officials in the Ministry of Foreign Affairs that until early 1881 neither Ferry nor Saint-Hilaire had any intention of sending troops against Tunisia.[87] Gambetta was still opposed to any action against the Regency,[88] and since Ferry's majority depended on Gambetta's support, the Premier could not have moved in this direction if he had wanted to do so.

However, French diplomacy and the activities of Roustan had already committed France in Tunisia. The pursuance of the same methods and ends by France and Italy was certain to lead to deeper involvement. In Tunisia there was a continuing battle for concessions being waged among the French, Italian and sometimes English interests. Italian activities were becoming more menacing. These struggles for concessions were not the handiwork of Ferry or Saint-Hilaire, but when difficulties in Tunis arose, they felt bound to support Roustan and the various French interests as a matter of upholding French prestige. It was simply

[83] He was by nature a rather weak and timorous person, a scholar of ancient languages and philosophy, who did not enjoy an especially brilliant political career. He had conducted himself well in recent Senate debates on behalf of the moderate Republican cause and had been chosen to please the Upper Chamber. Gambetta had a very poor opinion of his abilities. J. Reinach, *Le ministère Gambetta* (Paris, 1884), p. 400.

[84] Parker Moon, *Imperialism and World Politics* (New York, 1926), p. 46.

[85] Wienefeld, *op. cit.*, pp. 75–78.   [86] *DDF*, III, No. 376.

[87] A. Billot, *France et l'Italie* (Paris, 1905), I, 25. Billot was one of the most influential imperialists at the Quai d'Orsay and later played an important role in the Tonkin and Madagascan affairs, pushing France along the road to Empire. He was, in 1881, an assistant bureau chief.

[88] *Ibid.*

assumed that it not only was patriotic but good business to support French investors and traders. Given the situation that prevailed when Ferry became Premier, with Italian ambitions and a determination to uphold French prestige, France would almost have to take Tunisia in the very near future. The only alternative was to abandon it to Italy. Neither Ferry nor Saint-Hilaire could or would do this.

One of the first cases with which Ferry's Foreign Minister was confronted was a quarrel between a French banking group and the Bey over property rights. Early in 1880 a former Tunisian Chief Minister, Kheredine, sold his estate, known as the Enfida, to the *Société Marseillaise*. Roustan was delighted with what he called this "province." [89] However, the Bey bade his courts not to register the sale, contending that he had not given the land to be sold to foreigners. Roustan protested unavailingly.[90] The problem was then complicated by a Maltese English subject, named Levy, who invoked the *scheffa* right under Mohammedan law.[91] Levy had as his lawyer A. M. Broadley, a correspondent of the London *Times,* recently arrived in Tunis from India. Broadley proved to be a pillar of strength, for he not only aired his client's case in the columns of the *Times* and wrote a most entertaining book on the situation in Tunisia with special attention to the wiles and wickedness of the French,[92] but he also had the ear of several members of Parliament.[93] This happy chain of circumstances soon brought England back into the Tunisian diplomatic tangle. Roustan, of course, thought the whole affair trumped up to harass the French.

Saint-Hilaire, good patriot and bourgeois that he was, from the first news he had of the incident, upheld the "incontestable" right of the *Société Marseillaise* to the property. He fully sanctioned Roustan's most serious complaints against this "denial of justice." [94] The Foreign Minister experienced little difficulty with Lord Lyons over the question, for the latter was displeased with England's growing involvement. Strangely enough, he agreed with Roustan's contention that Levy was merely a tool of other interests.[95]

When the French company lost in the local courts and Levy's servants moved in on January 12, 1881, they were soon expelled by guards from the French consulate.[96] The English Government upheld Levy's rights,

[89] *DDF,* III, No. 100. The land was great in extent but would take twenty years of development before it could even pay interest on its purchase price of two millions. Constant, *op. cit.,* p. 102.

[90] *DDF,* III, No. 292.

[91] According to this concept, a contiguous neighbor had first rights to buy property offered for sale, and if his bid were equal to other bids, the land must be sold to him.

[92] Broadley, *op. cit., passim.*   [93] Constant, *op. cit.,* p. 104.   [94] *DDF,* III, No. 292.

[95] Newton, *op. cit.,* II, 239.   [96] *DDF,* III, No. 341.

having been prodded by pointed questions in the House of Commons. Saint-Hilaire was disturbed by the turn of events and tried unsuccessfully to arrange the matter in conversations with Lyons.[97] Despite his desire to avoid serious trouble over the case, Saint-Hilaire was determined to uphold French rights, and there were several sharp exchanges, in January and February, 1881, between London and Paris over the rights of their respective nationals.[98] France dispatched a warship to Tunis,[99] and England sent one to counterbalance it.[100] Lyons continued to tell his government how little he liked the affair, and the ships were shortly withdrawn.[101]

In the discussions with London, there was little mention of simple or abstract justice. The French cited arguments concerning their prestige and dwelt on the paramount importance of safeguarding French-interests in Tunisia. Saint-Hilaire reminded the English, not so much of the rights in the suit, as of Salisbury's promise to Waddington of a free hand in Tunisia. A free hand to Roustan meant the freedom to crush any interests conflicting with those of Frenchmen. Ferry himself took no active part here but must at least have authorized the general line of conduct taken by his Foreign Minister who had inherited the problem.

Another incident, not of Ferry's making, worried the Bey late in 1880. A group of French bankers brought forward a proposal to establish in Tunis an agricultural mortgage bank, or *Crédit Foncier Agricole*. The backers apparently intended to make mortgage loans to farmers, foreclose when the inevitable bad harvests came, and thereby build up some extensive land holdings.[102] A representative of the group, Léon Renault, who was also a deputy, was presented to the Bey by Roustan on December 21, 1880.[103] He asked the Bey to grant the *Crédit Foncier* the exclusive right of note issue to the value of the loans made and for a guarantee of the bank against loss.[104] Coincident with this visit were rumors of troop movements in neighboring Algeria. Roustan dropped some very broad hints that if the *Crédit Foncier* plan were adopted the troop movements would remain mere rumors, as the project in question would serve to consolidate the friendship of Tunis with France.[105] This is a good example of the kind of pressure Roustan exercised on the Bey. It was not a direct threat but its meaning was unmistakable. Yet the Bey made bold to reject the proposal on the grounds that in 1873 the

---

[97] *Ibid.*, note.
[98] *Ibid.*, Nos. 351, 364, 370, 375.
[99] *Ibid.*, Nos. 355, 363.
[100] *Ibid.*, No. 361.
[101] *Ibid.*, Nos. 366, 367. After France occupied Tunisia, the dispute was settled in court against Levy.
[102] Staley, *op. cit.*, p. 349.
[103] Broadley, *op. cit.*, I, 191.
[104] *Ibid.*, pp. 192–193.
[105] L. J. *Tunisie, 1870–1881* (Paris, 1881), No. 171.

French had objected to a similar English plan. When Ferry was later accused of allowing his agents to exercise unseemly pressure on a friendly power, he cited this refusal as evidence of the fact that no real pressure had been applied.[106] France was not yet ready to throw her full weight against Tunis.

The French had considered for a long time that they had an official monopoly of the telegraph lines of Tunisia under the 1859 grant.[107] The official Tunisian contention, probably under Italian influence, was that no such monopoly had been given,[108] and the Italians now attempted to capitalize on this view. Cairoli in November, 1880, instructed General Cialdini in Paris to open negotiations with France for a cable concession to link Sicily and Tunis. The action was undertaken against the advice of Cialdini who warned Rome that the French would be upset by such steps. He reported that nothing could persuade the French to yield, as they were determined eventually to move into Africa.[109]

Throughout the Fall of 1880 there was a series of quarrels of a similar nature in Tunisia. There were arguments about port rights, harbor improvements, and rights of French and Italian nationals.[110] None of these was very important in itself, but the sum of all contributed materially to worsening relations between France and Italy and France and Tunisia.

The foregoing series of incidents have formed the basis for the oft-repeated assertion that Tunisia was taken mainly for the personal profit of private French investors.[111] In the light of the latest documents, it is putting the cart before the horse to attribute the conquest of Tunisia to private economic interests. The private investors and speculators were more often the tools of political policy than the formulators of imperialistic projects. Yet, serving as the instruments of diplomacy, they did, nevertheless, urge diplomacy forward.[112] In the confusion of power politics and national prestige, private economic interests were able to take advantage of diplomatic policy for their own profit-making purposes.

Nearly all the French diplomatic corps was urging the Ferry Ministry to take Tunisia at once. When Noailles visited Paris he pressed for a strong course to stop the Italians from seizing the prize,[113] and repeatedly thereafter his dispatches besought Paris to act. Saint-Vallier wanted to end the "deplorable weakness" toward the Bey.[114] Challemel-Lacour from London; General Chanzy, ex-governor of Algeria, then ambassador in St. Petersburg; and Tissot in Constantinople all begged Saint-Hilaire

106 *J. O. C.*, 11/9/81.   107 *Supra*, p. 33.
108 Broadley, *op. cit.*, I, 184–185.   109 Langer, *op. cit.*, p. 269.
110 *L. J. T.*, Nos. 201–210; *DDF*, III, Nos. 243, 292, 297, 298, 315.
111 Woolf, *op. cit.*, p. 104.   112 Staley, *op. cit.*, p. 328; Schuman, *op. cit.*, p. 62.
113 *DDF*, III, No. 286.   114 *Ibid.*, Nos. 345, 349, 406.

to move against the Regency.[115] Roustan kept up a running fire of requests for permission to act more energetically with the full support of his government against the Italians and the Bey. When a raid of a Tunisian tribe into Algerian territory in February was allowed to pass without reprisal, that consul was in despair about the French future in Tunisia.[116] All these advisors advanced arguments setting forth considerations of French prestige and position. National honor rather than profits of any individuals or groups was at stake so far as they were concerned. It was the Italian pretensions that had aroused a patriotic fervor in the diplomatic corps.

At every moment on the eve of the move against Tunisia, France enjoyed the support of Bismarck. As before, she had to contend with the grudging acquiescence of England and the opposition of Italy. Following up his earlier advice to Italy to concentrate on Tripoli,[117] the German Chancellor, in November 1880, twice warned Cairoli that he disapproved of Italian activities in Tunisia.[118] Not only did he give full diplomatic support and encouragement to France but he even tried to push her into more prompt action in North Africa.[119] Bismarck was quite frank to admit that he wanted to distract French attention from the "hole in the Vosges." [120] But the lost provinces always remained the ghost at the table. Not even Saint-Vallier, who worked so amicably with the Chancellor, fully trusted the German intentions.

Despite France's request, Granville refused to warn Italy that the latter could expect no help from England because Tunisia was ear-marked for France. Indeed, Challemel-Lacour warned Barthélemy Saint-Hilaire that England was the "real adversary in Tunis" and the inspirer of Italian resistance. He made this remark when the Foreign Minister expressed a desire to come to an agreement with England on the Tunisian questions.[121] Italy continued to encourage the resistance of the Bey. Maccio, the spearhead of the anti-French forces, had warm encouragement from the Italian press.[122] The Italians did not take seriously the repeated warnings of Noailles to desist in their provocations. They were encouraged by the unwillingness of Saint-Hilaire to act and

---

[115] *Ibid.*, Nos. 376, 381, 386, 406, 418, 421.   [116] Constant, *op. cit.*, p. 109.
[117] *DDF*, II, No. 369.   [118] *Ibid.*, III, Nos. 294, 307; *GP.*, III, 399–400, 535.
[119] *DDF*, III, Nos. 418, 422.   [120] *Ibid.*, Nos. 294, 307.
[121] *Ibid.*, No. 375. The following Spring Bismarck told the French that while Lord Dufferin was in Berlin in August 1880, he sounded the Chancellor on behalf of Granville on a proposal for a European intervention in Tunisia. This Bismarck refused to entertain. When the French asked Granville for an explanation, he emphatically denied any connection with such an incident. Saint-Hilaire and Challemel-Lacour were of the opinion that Granville had permitted such an inquiry but that Bismarck had exaggerated its importance in reporting it. *Ibid.*, Nos. 495, 526.
[122] *Ibid.*, Nos. 258, 266.

by Gambetta's known opposition to the affair.[123] As late as February 15, 1881, the Foreign Minister told Saint-Vallier that he intended to preserve the *status quo* because the situation at home and abroad would not then permit France to undertake and carry through any action in Tunisia. Determined to exhaust all diplomatic means, he advised Roustan neither to retreat nor to advance there.[124] Gambetta was most displeased by the furor over Tunisia. He still wanted to concentrate French energies on her continental and domestic problems. He tried to smother the affair by sending to Rome as his personal agent Baron Robert de Billing, a bizarre character who had been French consul in Tunis, to arrange a settlement outside the normal diplomatic channels.[125] Early in January 1881, De Billing had arranged the simultaneous retirement of Roustan and Maccio. Such a solution casts an interesting light on what Gambetta thought was the root trouble in the Regency. De Billing moved on to Tunis where, without consultation with Roustan, he tried to persuade the Bey to sign a treaty of protectorate for Roustan's recall.[126] Not to be outdone, the consul apparently tried to induce the Bey to sign a treaty with him instead, and matters went from bad to worse at the court. De Billing claimed to have secured preliminary consent from the harassed Bey, only to find that Gambetta had decided meanwhile to support French action against Tunisia. Events had moved past a stage where such stratagems would solve the problem.

At the beginning of the New Year, Signor Maccio led a delegation, including the Bey's nephew and the leading Italian residents of the Regency, to Palermo in Sicily to greet King Humbert of Italy who was touring the island. The French were worried by the news of this junket, and Saint-Hilaire warned the Italian government on January 5th not to try to compromise the French position in Africa.[127] In the Palermo reception a number of exuberant speeches were made about Italian destiny and plans. Maccio himself pointed toward Tunisia in an unmistakable appeal to Italian imperialist dreams.[128] The expedition caused Roustan great concern, especially the enthusiastic reception shown the delegation on its return to the Regency.[129] The Tunisian prince had been decorated by the King and duly impressed with Italian strength. To the French the incident was one of the clearest indications of the unceasing Italian ambitions in this quarter.

Maccio was more aggressive than ever upon his return to Tunis. He

---

[123] Lebon, *op. cit.*, p. 412.   [124] *DDF*, III, No. 376.
[125] De Billing's account of his mission appears as an appendix in Luigi Chiala, *Pagine di Storia Contemporanea* (Turin, 1895), II, 366–376.
[126] Both Noailles in Rome and Roustan in Tunis were greatly discomfited and somewhat mystified by De Billing's actions, *DDF*, III, 362.
[127] *Ibid.*, No. 327.   [128] Broadley, *op. cit.*, I, 194.   [129] *DDF*, III, No. 347.

unearthed a lapsed Italian concession to hinder the French construction of the Tunis-Sousse railroad. Even anti-French writers admitted that his objection was unjustifiable.[130] The fabrication of obstacles was contemporaneous with Italian subsidization of an Arabic paper, *Mostakel*, printed in Sicily, violently anti-French and widely circulated in Tunis.[131] Subsidizing the press was a game at which two could play, and French commercial interests reportedly backed French papers to stimulate a demand to take Tunisia.[132]

This combination of incidents was the turning point for the French attitude toward the Regency. The clear indication of Italian intentions, the successful currying of favor with the royal household, the violent anti-French campaign among the Arabs, together with the dangers for Algeria inherent therein and the increasing ambitions of the Italian consul finally convinced the Ferry Government of the need to act.[133] At the time these were not the reasons given, but Ferry, in the contemplation that came with retirement, admitted in 1892, that the provocations of Italy hastened the move on Tunisia.[134]

However, in early March, 1881, Jules Ferry was not yet persuaded of the desirability of taking Tunisia. When Saint-Hilaire in a Cabinet meeting suggested it, Ferry retorted, "An affair in Tunis in election year, my dear Saint-Hilaire, don't think of it." [135] Within three weeks Ferry had changed his mind and was preparing to send troops into the Regency.

Ferry's Foreign Minister had been swung over to this decision as a result of the intervention of Baron de Courcel, Director of Political Affairs in the Ministry of Foreign Affairs.[136] Courcel, a career diplomat, holding then the most important post in the bureaucracy at the Quai d'Orsay, had long been an active and vocal proponent of French intervention in Tunisia. Like his friend Noailles in Rome, he bemoaned the failure to act decisively in the matter.[137] He talked with Saint-Hilaire following the most recent Italian moves, and after some time persuaded him that France should take Tunisia as soon as possible. At least by March 13, the Minister was won over.[138] But besides Ferry there were also opposed the Minister of War, General Farre; President Grévy and his son-in-law Wilson, under-secretary of finance.[139]

Nothing daunted, Courcel went directly to the seat of power and talked with Gambetta. In two long interviews he expounded the French

130 Broadley, *op. cit.*, I, 203.   131 *Ibid.*, p. 195.   132 Schuman, *op. cit.*, p. 65.
133 Langer, *op. cit.*, p. 259.   134 *Discours*, V, 532.   135 Hanotaux, *Histoire*, IV, 633.
136 *Ibid.*, p. 650. The account of Courcel's intervention is based largely on his unpublished memoirs quoted in Hanotaux, *Histoire*.
137 *DDF*, III, Nos. 384, 396, 401.   138 Hanotaux, *Histoire*, IV, 633.
139 Général C. Mangin, *Regard sur la France d'Afrique* (Paris, 1924), p. 84.

position and interests in Tunisia and succeeded in winning over Gambetta to consent to a French move.[140] His arguments dwelt on French prestige and French national honor which would presumably be vastly enhanced by the acquisition of this Regency and correspondingly diminished if the Italians acquired it. The taking of Tunisia would be, he argued, a brilliant victory for the Republic. So far as we have a record of these conversations, no mention was made of the opportunity for commercial advantage nor of the interests of French investors in Tunisia.[141] Neither then nor in his later career as ambassador to Berlin, was Courcel much concerned with such matters. After Gambetta's conversion, the cause of French intervention in Tunisia prospered, for he swung his followers into line. General Farre, Minister of War, was one of the first of these and other members of the Cabinet followed. Even the President's brother, General Grévy, Governor of Algeria, who at first had been opposed when he thought the intention was merely to punish marauding tribes, supported the plan when he learned it was intended to take over all of Tunisia.[142]

Jules Ferry was one of the last of the Cabinet to be persuaded that France should act against Tunisia at that time.[143] It was, after all, his administration that was running the risks both on the political front at home and on the military front abroad. Sometime late in March he changed his mind and decided to move into the Regency. He was not the instigator of the intervention; he did not act upon the urging of any commercial or financial interests; he had no stake in Tunisia himself, nor had he at this time any thought of systematically building a French colonial empire. Although he was friendly to business interests, he made the decision after all the striking "affairs" of French financial penetration had been satisfactorily settled in favor of the French. But the Italians were then more annoying and threatening than before, and the threat they presented was used to persuade the Ferry Government that it should move. The leader of that Government decided to act when it appeared politically feasible and necessary to do so. Behind-the-scenes pressure in Paris persuaded him to take a step that could materially increase the prestige of the Republic and of the moderate Republicans whose leadership Ferry shared with Gambetta. Although Ferry was slow to commit himself, once started, he soon became one of the greatest exponents of French imperialism. His conversion was to be especially marked in his second Premiership a few years later.

Apparently quite without knowledge of the support he was receiving from Courcel and Gambetta, Roustan was still busy in Tunis trying to

140 Hanotaux, *Histoire*, IV, 651.   141 *Ibid.*
142 *L. J. T.*, No. 87.   143 Hanotaux, *Histoire*, IV, 651.

persuade his Government to act. About March 20 he sent home a lengthy petition from the French residents of Tunis—a petition which he himself doubtless inspired.[144] It complained of the unfriendly attitude of the Bey, besought the Government to force him to respect French rights, and asked that the threatened French predominance be upheld. At about the time this petition reached Paris the Government was ready to act in Tunisia: all that was lacking was a convenient excuse.

A raid of the Tunisian Kroumir tribe into Algeria, of which Paris heard on March 30, provided the desired *casus*. This particular fracas, in the course of which some property damage was done and half a dozen French subjects were shot, was only one of many such raids along an unsettled border inhabited by nomadic, semi-civilized tribes.[145] Governor Grévy was able to produce a list of 2379 crimes committed along that border by Tunisian tribes between 1870 and 1881.[146] However accurate the list may have been, it was a good indication of the endemic nature of such disturbances.[147] Even French historians have admitted that the Kroumir raid, in retaliation for which the French moved into Tunisia, was merely an excuse.[148]

The day after news of the raid was received, General Farre wrote his opinion that the Kroumirs had to be severely punished.[149] One of Gambetta's supporters, he had been convinced for several weeks that French influence in Tunisia had to be increased.[150] His Premier did not long delay putting such a decision into effect.

Jules Ferry came before the Chamber on April 4 to announce that troops were to be sent to Tunisia to prevent a recurrence of these border raids.[151] He made no lengthy statement or justification and in a matter-of-fact manner asked for an appropriation of six million francs to pay for an expeditionary force. There was no hint of his intention of taking Tunisia. The appropriation was quickly approved by a unanimous vote.[152]

On April 11 Ferry was questioned in the Chamber on the extent of the preparations against the Kroumirs. He then admitted enlarging the scope of the contemplated move, saying that the intention of the Government was to prevent the renewal of such raids in order to protect Algeria.[153] The expedition was to be not only therapeutic but preventative.

---

[144] Broadley, *op. cit.*, I, 207. [145] *Ibid.*, p. 206. [146] *L. J. T.*, No. 112.

[147] French opinion was more easily upset by stories of Arab disturbances since an expedition headed by Colonel Flatters, while exploring in the Sahara desert, had recently been massacred by the Touaregs; disturbances in the Algerian hinterland were also current.

[148] Seignobos, *op. cit.*, pp. 343–344. [149] *DDF*, III, No. 416.

[150] Hanotaux, *Histoire*, IV, 652. [151] *J. O. C.*, 4/5/81. [152] *Ibid.*

[153] *Ibid.*, 4/12/81.

The Premier was immediately attacked by three Bonapartist members of the Right for extending his field of action. For the first time the accusa-tion was made in the Chamber that the expedition was intended to pro-tect French financial interests in Tunisia. Ferry rose to deny that the affair of the Enfida estate, bought by the *Société Marseillaise* and con-tested by Levy, had any influence on the decision to act, as charged, but that the essential purpose was to make secure the boundaries of Algeria. Full confidence in the Ministry was voted by 322 to 124—a good margin for the Cabinet at the time, being about the same as its usual plurality on domestic questions.[154] After this vote, the Chambers adjourned for the Easter recess. Ferry hoped to carry off the whole affair before Parliament reconvened.

However, the Premier and his Foreign Minister were still not fully decided as to the extent of their action. They were uneasy about forcing a protectorate on the Regency by force of arms. Once more it was Cour-cel who came forward and persuaded them that this was the only thing to do now that the opportunity was at hand. It was Courcel who drew up detailed orders for the expedition for Ferry and Saint-Hilaire to sign. According to these, the commander of the force was to surround the Bey in his palace and ask him to sign a treaty of protectorate. If he should refuse, another ruler was to replace him.[155] An army of 30,000 men was gathered to carry out these orders.[156] The important influence and close collaboration of Courcel was attested to in later years by Ferry.[157]

After Ferry had announced French intentions of sending an expedi-tion to Tunisia, considerable diplomatic negotiation was necessary to assure the nation's position. General Cialdini received assurances from Saint-Hilaire that no permanent military occupation or annexation of Tunisia was contemplated. He said nothing about establishing a pro-tectorate, however.[158] Cairoli, still indulging in wishful thinking, did not tell the Italian Chamber about the warnings received from Paris, thereby giving the erroneous impression that the French had no in-tention of staying in Tunisia. He definitely stated that there had been no agreement between England and France regarding the Regency in 1878, although he must have known that this was not true. Cairoli as-sured the Chamber on April 6 that France had given her "word of honor" that she would not seize Tunisia.[159] Saint-Hilaire on the fol-lowing day sent Rome a dispatch in which he denied that any limits had

[154] See Appendix.
[155] Hanotaux, *Histoire*, IV, 662. Again quoting from Courcel's memoirs.
[156] *Ibid.*, p. 657.   [157] *Discours*, V, 532.
[158] *DDF*, III, No. 427.   [159] Langer, *op. cit.*, p. 261; *DDF*, III, Nos. 430, 433.

been set to French action. The Italians were very clearly told that France would consult her own interests in the contemplated expedition.[160] Even more explicitly was Depretis told by Noailles, on May 5, that the French were annoyed at the actions of the "insufficiently controlled" Italian agents in Tunis whose duplicity the French blamed on Cairoli himself. The Paris Government considered matters to have gone far beyond a question of boundary infringements or the Bey's attitude, he continued. The Italian-inspired anti-French propaganda among the Arabs endangered France's position in Algeria, so she felt she must take Tunisia [161] to put an end to it for "the defense of civilization in Africa." Nevertheless, the Italians always claimed that they had been misled by the French into thinking that the latter would allow Tunisia to remain independent. As Ferry said later, "Cairoli was frustrated, surprised, but not misled." [162]

The Italian government hoped to the last moment to undertake a joint action with England against France. England, however, refused to cooperate [163] as did the other European powers.[164] Since Italy was not willing to go to war over the issue, she could only sit by in a rage at successive French steps. The Cairoli Ministry was upset by the French announcement of intentions and a Cabinet crisis lasted for ten days before the same Ministry was returned to office on April 18.[165] Several months later when Tunisia had definitely been taken by France, the Cairoli Government finally fell, the victim of a situation it could not avert and would not frankly recognize.[166]

Across the Channel, Granville was unfriendly to the whole proceeding of the Ferry Cabinet, yet he aptly described himself as "barking" not biting. He did not push his opposition hard, although he did try tentatively to resurrect the Porte's sovereignty over Tunisia. He was tempted to join the Italians,[167] but Gladstone and Dilke restrained him. Granville was thoroughly checkmated when Saint-Hilaire released to Blowitz, correspondent of the London *Times*, the Salisbury-Waddington negotiations of 1878. When these were printed on April 11 the opposition in England was crushed.[168] Granville next sounded the French on the question of mediating the problems,[169]—a suggestion which was quickly rejected. The British Foreign Secretary was content to let the matter rest after he received French assurances that they would

---

[160] *DDF*, III, No. 434.
[161] *Ibid.*, No. 502.
[162] *Discours*, IV, 533.
[163] Lebon, *op. cit.*, p. 428.
[164] The Italians sounded Germany, Austria and Turkey in the hope of arousing opposition to France—all without success. Langer *op. cit.*, p. 262.
[165] *DDF*, III, No. 468.
[166] Lebon, *op. cit.*, p. 436.
[167] Newton, *op. cit.*, II, 241–242.
[168] *Ibid.*, 242, 250.
[169] *DDF*, III, No. 515.

not occupy Bizerte or Tripoli, strategic points for control of the Mediter-ranean.[170] On May 10, through a statement of Dilke to Challemel-Lacour, England declared herself uninterested in the question.[171]

The Sultan threatened to send a naval squadron to the aid of the Bey. Saint-Hilaire dispatched a blunt warning from the Cabinet on May 7 that the squadrons would not be allowed to reach Tunis.[172] The French had previously rejected all claims of the Turks to an interest in the matter.[173] The Sultan told Hatzfeldt, German ambassador to Turkey, that he was going to send a force to Tunis to assert his authority. Bismarck, when informed, gave the same reply as his ambassador, strongly warning the Sultan not to attempt any such move.[174] Thereafter the Porte subsided into the helpless anger usual when it was despoiled by the Western Powers.

It was the firm stand of Bismarck that prevented the formation of a coalition against France in April and May of 1881.[175] He gave France complete and full assurance of his backing. On May 2 he told Saint-Vallier that France could annex Tunisia if she so desired, for Italy "didn't count" and had been warned by him not to interfere. On his own initiative he had also warned England.[176] Unquestionably he did all this because it was useful for his own purposes. He wanted to divert French attention from the lost provinces, and he wanted to avert a Franco-Russian alliance which was his own constant dread. Contrary to the suspicion of some French nationalists, he was not primarily concerned with splitting France and Italy apart.[177] Bismarck's efforts were appreciated in France and copious thanks were sent for his constant aid and support by Saint-Hilaire and President Grévy.[178] Ferry himself, in later years, frequently attested to the value of German aid during that critical Spring.

Conquest

The actual conquest of Tunisia proved to be quite easy. The expedi-tion, crossing the Tunisian frontier on April 24, quickly swept away the Kroumirs and even more quickly brushed aside the protests of the Bey against this unsolicited intervention.[179] The French columns moved on

[170] Newton, *op. cit.*, II, 252. Bizerte was occupied by the French soon after the ex-pedition was under way, much to English annoyance.
[171] *DDF*, III, No. 526.   [172] *Ibid.*, Nos. 507, 510.
[173] *Ibid.*, Nos. 457, 500. Saint-Hilaire did not share the earlier cóncern of Wadding-ton over what the Turks might do if Tunisia were attacked. *Supra* p. 37.
[174] *Ibid.*, No. 513.   [175] Langer, *op. cit.*, p. 263.
[176] *DDF*, III, No. 495; *GP*, III, 399–401.   [177] Langer, *op. cit.*, p. 263.
[178] *DDF*, III, Nos. 402, 513, 521.
[179] The Bey had proposed to reduce the tribes with his own forces but his suggestion was discarded. *L. J. T.*, No. 112.

Tunis and on May 12 presented that monarch with a treaty by which he should place himself under French protectorate. He was allowed two hours to deliberate and then, surrounded by French troops with fixed bayonets, he signed.[180] This treaty, known as the Treaty of Bardo from the name of the Bey's palace, did not actually use the word "protectorate" but it was that in all but name.[181]

The Treaty contained only ten articles but they destroyed the independence of Tunisia. The conventions already existing between the Bey and the Republic were renewed. The French government guaranteed the execution of the treaties which existed between the Regency and various European powers (Article 4). France was bound to lend its constant support to the Bey against all dangers threatening his person or possessions (Article 3). But, to balance this guarantee, the Bey was to conclude no international treaties without the consent of France (Article 6). The French government was henceforth to be represented before the Bey by a resident minister (Article 5), and power was reserved to the French government to settle, with the agreement of the Bey's government, the basis for a new financial organization of the Regency (Article 7). France was to occupy all points which she thought necessary to hold (Article 3), and was to put down the rebellious tribes along the Algerian frontier and the littoral (Article 8).

Almost incidental were the provisions to settle the alleged problem in Franco-Tunisian relations—the invasions of Algerian territory by Tunisian tribes. Article 2 authorized the temporary occupation of Tunisian territory until "the local administration is in a position to guarantee the maintenance of order." The French government was also authorized to prevent contraband of arms on Tunisian territory, in the interest of the security of Algeria (Article 9).[182]

The French Parliament had reconvened after the Easter holidays on the same day that the Treaty of Bardo was being signed. There was no news of what was going on in Africa upon the opening day, Ferry contenting himself with reporting good progress in Tunisia. He glowingly described the skillful conduct of the army in its first trial since Metz. He hinted at the imminence of a new treaty with "some lasting guarantees" from the Bey. But he said that no annexation of Tunisia would take place.[183]

The following day the Treaty was announced, and simultaneously

---

[180] J. Reinach, "Le Traité de Bardo," *Revue politique et littéraire, 3e sér.*, XXI (1881), 641–646.

[181] The term "protectorate" was first used in the Treaty of Marsa of June 8, 1883. *Infra*, p. 69.

[182] Text in *DDF*, III, No. 523.

[183] *J. O. C.*, 5/13/81.

a *Livre Jaune* was released containing the· documents justifying the French action. The theme of this collection was that French action in Tunisia was necessary in order to safeguard Algeria. It indicated the economic potentialities of the Regency, but the point was stressed very lightly.[184]

Parliamentary Debate on Tunisia

The Treaty came before the Chamber of Deputies for ratification on May 23, 1881. Technically it was not necessary for such a treaty to come before Parliament under the terms of Article 8 of the French Constitution.[185] Politically it seemed desirable to secure parliamentary approval. Acceptance of the Treaty, if there had been any doubt about it, was made certain by Gambetta's declared support. On the day that Ferry announced the conclusion of the Treaty, Gambetta wrote him a congratulatory note enthusiastically acclaiming this feat.[186] The opposition came from the extreme wings of the Chamber, both Left and Right. Especially virulent was the criticism of the Right already bitter against Ferry for his anti-clerical legislation then being discussed and applied.

Clemenceau led the criticism from the Extreme Left. He charged the Government with violating the constitution by waging an undeclared war and with exceeding the intentions of Parliament in Tunisia. The Government's immediate reply was that there had been no war in Tunisia since diplomatic relations had not been broken off.[187] This fine point was to be used time and again by statesmen of the Third Republic [188] to justify colonial aggression. The Third Republic was merely typical of all European imperialist powers in this regard.

Only the arch-germanophobe, Clemenceau, referred to Germany during the debates. Yet it was undoubtedly the unnamed power to which other deputies referred when discussing the dangerous situation in Europe. The "Tiger" believed the supposed benevolence of Germany to be "dangerous." With memories of the late war still rankling, he "feared their gifts" and insisted nothing could be intended for France's ultimate good if it had approval from beyond the Rhine.

Although the effect of the Tunisian expedition on the European balance would seem to have been one of the most important considerations for the French, it was never threshed out in open debate in Parliament. Always there were veiled references to its implications, but sel-

---

[184] *L. J. T., passim.*
[185] A. Esmein, *Eléments de droit constitutionnel français et comparé* (Paris, 1928, 8th ed.), II, 201.
[186] *Lettres de Gambetta*, ed. E. Pillias and D. Halévy (Paris, 1938), No. 474.
[187] *J. O. C.*, 5/24/81.   [188] Schuman, *op. cit.*, pp. 336–341.

dom any elaboration. The argument figured largely in the nationalistic press, however.

Highly significant in any attempt to discover the nature of the opposition to colonization was the limited extent of the discussions on the value of colonies for France. Throughout the whole period of the debates over the acquisition and pacification of Tunisia, the question was considered but once, on May 24. Through days of debate filled with much examination of the causes of the invasion, the legality of Ferry's moves, and the conduct of operations, there was scant indication of any real opposition to colonial ventures as such. Yet the press was filled with articles describing or decrying the value of colonies. Many times opponents of this particular venture admitted that they thought colonies, *per se*, were valuable and a worthy goal for French policy. Some there were who, like Clemenceau, were cool toward colonization, but they did not make an issue of imperialism in parliamentary debate.

Such discussion could scarcely be expected before May since, when the deputies voted the credits to punish invading Kroumirs, they certainly had no idea that they were embarking on a colonial program. Now, with a treaty establishing a protectorate in all but name, the Chamber had ample reason to think that France was on the perilous road to overseas expansion. In November, after the summer's expedition, this could be seen clearly. That little was said to prevent the development of a colonial policy is good evidence that the question of Tunisia was not one essentially of anti-colonial feeling. It was rather part of the struggle for power between the Republicans and Monarchists and, within the Republican ranks, between the supporters and opponents of Gambetta, the dominant Republican figure.

Jules Delafosse, a Bonapartist, voiced the single wholly anti-colonial statement:

> The extension of our colonial possessions is not for France an advantage, an element of greatness and of strength. I believe that the colonial system is not successful, and, consequently, is suited only to people who have an excess of population. France has no, or only a very few, emigrants. Every colony is a cause of weakness during war and an expense during peace.[189]

He cited the preface, written by the Foreign Minister, of the *Livre Jaune* on Tunisia in which mention was made of building railroads, lighthouses, and harbor improvements, as well as of developing French industry and commerce in Tunisia. He demanded to know, "With

[189] *J. O. C.*, 5/24/81.

what money?" and "For whose benefit?" He drew applause from the Right, but did not stir the rest of the Chamber with this query.

Despite his reservations on the value of colonies, Delafosse stated that he would vote for ratification of the Treaty, because it was "a diplomatic success" and a "positive advantage" to France. Somewhat paradoxically, he wanted only to point out the "heavy responsibilities and even the eventual dangers" that it entailed.[190] His anti-colonial sentiments did not constitute very deep convictions.

The *rapporteur* of the bill, Antonin Proust, by way of answer, flatly contended that a colonial policy was "desirable" and "profitable to our interests." This bold-faced admission by the Government that it supported a policy of colonial expansion despite previous denials of such intentions was greeted by cheers from the benches of the majority. Amid the jeers of the Right, Proust maintained that the Government would and should protect French private interests abroad. He emphatically denied that public money was intended for the commercial development of Tunisia. He did not dwell on the economic possibilities of the Regency, however. The main reason still advanced for the Treaty was the necessity of protecting Algeria.

Unwilling to ratify the Treaty and desirous of opening new negotiations was the obstreperous Cuneo d'Ornano. A consistent opponent of the Government, this Bonapartist was noted for noisy interruptions that did not endear him to the majority. He now endeavored to affirm his sincerity by avoiding "any digression on the form of actual government or on the persons of the ministers."

He reminded the Chamber that border invasions in the African desert were endemic. From the *Livre Jaune* he read dispatches to show that raids had been committed "as much by our Algerian tribes into Tunis as by Tunisian tribes on our Algerian territory." He came to his main charge as he cited again the preface of the *Livre Jaune* to prove that the exploitation of Tunisia was the real purpose of the expedition. Whether this exploitation was for good or evil, he did not judge but went on to say:

> . . . these are private interests: . . . if the benefits, instead of going into the vaults of the Treasury, go into the purse of certain promoters, is it legitimate, is it just to guarantee these individuals benefits by the cooperation of our army and taxes? There is my whole objection.

Once again came cheers from the Right and hostile silence from the majority. He pointedly asked the Left why it did not "protest in the

190 *Ibid.*

name of the rights of man" and "defend these African populations against the invasion of a nation which comes to hamper them in the exercise of their political liberty." He proposed to eliminate the clauses giving France a voice in Tunisian affairs. The Government, amid the taunts of the Right, decided not to answer his attack, and the proposal was defeated, 344–113 votes with 78 members abstaining.

Ferry spoke only briefly in this debate to refute some assertions of the opposition. He contented himself with saying that the Tunisian debt was not guaranteed by the Treaty and he maintained, with tongue well in cheek, that the Bey had not protested against the arrangement.[191] This was, of course, simply not true. The Treaty was then passed by the Chamber, 431–1. Talandier of the Extreme Left was the sole negative voter. Those who had spoken in opposition refrained from voting. It was passed unanimously by the Senate without discussion.[192]

Another installment on the bill for the expenses of colonial expansion, to the extent of 14,266,000 francs to pay for the cost of occupation through July 10,[193] was presented to the deputies by the Minister of War on July 9. Little opposition could be offered to the request since many of the expenses had already been incurred and the rest were tacitly authorized by the approval of the Treaty of Bardo. In the brief discussion of June 14, one Bonapartist, Janvier de la Motte, protested that the appropriation would still not be sufficient and that the affair would be very costly as he had warned the Chamber from the beginning. To the applause of the Right, he criticized the Government's refusal to say how far it intended to go in Tunisia. The credits were voted 429–0.[194] The Senate passed the bill the same day with 244 votes and no opposition.[195]

Matters were not going as well in Tunisia as the Cabinet would have liked. The country had been incompletely pacified and a series of uprisings broke out, beginning with one at Sfax on June 28. These were in large part made possible by the fact that in order to protect the French troops from the rigors of the African summer, the army had been too quickly withdrawn before full French control was established. Revolts against the new protectorate in the southern and eastern parts of Tunisia required a new expeditionary force to quell them. The Ferry Government was then in a weak domestic position. It had just divided on the question of the *scrutin de liste*: its refusal to support that measure before the Senate and the defeat of it on June 9 had alienated the Gambettists.[196]

191 *J. O. C.*, 5/24/81. 192 *J. O. S.*, 5/28/81.
193 *J. O. C.*, 6/15/81. 194 *Ibid.*
195 *J. O. S.*, 6/15/81. 196 *Supra*, p. 24.

When the Government was interpellated on the question of weakening French garrisons in order to send men to Tunisia, it had a narrow escape. The vote of confidence it demanded passed only by a 249–219 vote.[197] Whenever the Government seemed to be endangering French continental security it encountered trouble. But the fact that on July 22 the Chamber quietly voted credits for an expedition to Tonkin [198] lends proof to the contention that the close vote on Tunisia did not reflect a great sentiment against colonies *per se.*

Ferry nearly came to grief over a domestic issue on July 25 when he was questioned about changing the election dates. On that day the votes of the Cabinet itself were all that saved it.[199] Three days afterwards Parliament adjourned for the summer recess.

A quick and fortunate campaign in Tunisia would have materially aided the fortunes of Ferry during the elections.[200] His hope of such a campaign was frustrated by the continued risings and unsettled conditions there. These went on during July and needed more and more troops. No longer could the expedition be presented as an easy operation capable of quick fulfillment, and in consequence the Government could gain no support at the polls from a successful Tunisian expedition.

If, at the time, there had existed in the ranks of the deputies any considerable sentiment against the Tunisian affair or against a policy of colonial expansion, it is reasonable to suppose that these issues would have been important during the campaign. That they were scarcely raised may be taken to indicate that the opposition was not fighting Ferry's Tunisian expedition on grounds of general policy or anti-colonial principles.

The Commission charged with tabulating the electoral platforms of all candidates for the Chamber did not consider the Tunisian question important enough to deserve a separate tabulation. Under the general heading "Peace," the Commission cryptically remarked that a number of candidates "contented themselves with denying that peace had been attained by the events in Tunisia; others, on the contrary, blamed the Government for having violated it in Africa." Quite typically none of the deputies made the question of Tunisia a major consideration of his campaign,[201] for campaigns rarely centered upon the conduct of foreign affairs.[202] Similarly, there were no statements made for or against a policy of colonial expansion.[203]

[197] *J. O. C.*, 7/1/81.   [198] *Infra*, p. 158.
[199] *J. O. C.*, 8/26/81; Supra, p. 24.   [200] Constant, *op. cit.*, p. 183.
[201] *J. O. C., Documents Parlementaires, Annexes, 1883, Annexe* No. 808.
[202] Joseph Barthélemy, *Démocratie et politique étrangère* (Paris, 1917), p. 87.
[203] *J. O. C., Annexes, 1883, loc. cit.*

After the Treaty of Bardo, the campaign of ridicule and insult in the Paris papers aimed at the Ministry continued. Henri Rochefort in the *Intransigeant* contended that the Kroumirs did not exist and offered a reward for the capture of one such allegedly mythical being. The Kroumirs became a joke in the Parisian cafés, in popular songs and on the stage.[204] During the campaign all the charges heard in the Chamber were poured forth with venom in the opposition press.

But in the very calm elections, the Republicans gained new strength in the enlarged house, with 457 seats against 90 for the Right.[205] The Extreme Left had actually lost strength in the election before the more moderate candidates. Since they, like the Extreme Right, were ardent critics of the Tunisian venture, we may judge that public opinion was not strongly behind the opponents of a colonial policy. In politics it is highly important for the right people to do the wrong things. The unpopular political parties were those standing against the expedition. Those favoring colonialism could not have asked for weaker opponents.

If the elections were a triumph for the Republican elements, they were not a triumph for the incumbent Ministry. It was Gambetta who, with added supporters, was to form a new Government.[206] Ferry was doomed before Parliament opened and "there only remained for him to choose the way to die." [207] But he wanted before resigning to justify himself and secure approval for the Tunisian venture. He announced he would resign immediately following the debates on Tunis, whatever might be the outcome of the discussion.

Meanwhile the pacification of Tunisia had been completed. During the month of August troop movements in France had been suspended in order not to disturb the electorate. A renewed campaign in September and October put down all the rebels whose last stronghold was Kairouan, the holy city of Tunisia. When it was occupied on October 26, military resistance to the French came to an end. But 30,000 troops were necessary to carry out the task. They were not led with especial brilliance, were not equipped for desert warfare and were generally poorly supplied, for military ordnance had been caught in the midst of a reorganization. Despite all these handicaps, the losses only amounted to 782 killed. The casualties were made much of by the opposition press, however, both during and after the electoral campaign. To the above criticism was added another impugning Ferry's refusal to call an early meeting of Parliament. He was in a dilemma, for the mandate of the old Chamber ran through October. There was some doubt as to whether

---

204 Constant, *op. cit.*, p. 188.   205 *Supra*, p. 25.
206 *Supra*, p. 26.   207 Constant, *op. cit.*, p. 259.

this lame-duck Chamber or the new one should be called. Delay decided in favor of the new.

The press attacks on the Tunisian policy reached their height in Rochefort's tirades against the Cabinet in his *Intransigeant*. On September 27 he stated the whole affair to be a swindle, arranged by Gambetta and Roustan to line their own pockets. Roustan was accused, moreover, of taking bribes from various French interests. Upon the advice of Barthélemy Saint-Hilaire, he brought a suit for libel against Rochefort. At the trial in December the defense could show no direct evidence to support its charges that personal profit had accrued to anyone in the government from French intervention in Tunisia. A set of wild rumors was aired, but proof was altogether lacking. The accusations had not been specifically brought against any member of Ferry's Cabinet, but Saint-Hilaire was involved by implication.[208] The trial succeeded in showing only that Tunis was full of a number of shady characters who were intriguing for their personal profit and that Roustan had had many contacts with them. Roustan could fairly say that the situation was typical of such Oriental courts in those days and that he had to deal with whatever persons might surround the Bey. Nevertheless, Rochefort was acquitted by the jury on the grounds that he had believed his information true when he printed it.[209] As Gambetta remarked when explaining why he refused to bring any suit, this was usual in political cases in which conviction was rare even when guilt was well proven.[210]

Parliament convened on October 27. On that date Ferry read a telegram from Tunis to the Minister of War stating that the town of Kairouan had been occupied on the 26th of October and that the last of the rebellious tribes had retired. Bursts of laughter from the deputies, who had so often been told of an approaching end of hostilities, greeted his announcement. Especially to the deputies on the Right the expedition was now a huge joke. The ridicule of the Paris papers and cafés had penetrated the Chamber.

Ferry took the initiative on November 5, after the Chamber had completed the routine work of organization. He was answering the charges hurled outside the halls of the Chamber against the Ministry and anticipating three demands for interpellations.[211]

He emphatically denied that he had been waging an unauthorized war in Tunisia. The Chamber and Senate, when they had approved

208 *Le Temps*, December 11–15, 1881.
209 *Ibid.*, December 16, 1881.   210 Hohenlohe, *op. cit.*, II, 323.
211 These demands had been put forward by Naquet and Amagat of the Extreme Left and the Comte de Roys, a member of the Center and a supporter of Ferry.

the Treaty of Bardo, had given the Ministry, "a very clear mandate . . . which makes us henceforth responsible for the tranquility of the Regency." Amid the vehement denials of the Right, he stated that the Chamber had given the Ministry a "blank cheque" to handle affairs during the summer recess. This meant that the credits voted had been an "instalment" but not a "limit" on the cost of the necessary expedition. Had the Chamber not so intended, it would have objected more vigorously to the dispatch of troops during July, he contended.

Ferry reiterated his statement of April that the expedition was not for the support of private interests but for the suppression of invading tribes to make safe the glorious legacy of Algeria. He castigated the polemics on Tunisia as the political machinations of his opponents on domestic questions: "Today the campaign conducted by the Right has found some unexpected reinforcements on the Extreme Left. The Intransigents have replaced the Monarchists." Thus, "the question of Tunis has become an electoral platform for the people who have not found another." He ended with a cry, "Don't touch France, don't set your hand on the army." [212] His eloquence drew from Clemenceau the sarcastic remark, "You are not France!" [213]

Although often cheered from his own benches, Ferry was continually heckled during his speech by the members of the Left and Right. Charges of waging war, misappropriating funds, disorganizing the military machine, and fighting for private interests were continually flung at him.

On November 7, Naquet, from the Extreme Left, bitterly assailed Ferry for deceiving the Chamber about the nature and extent of the operations he had undertaken. He quoted Ferry's April speeches that claimed the operations were merely to protect the Algerian borders. "Never for a single moment did the Chamber know, in voting the credits . . . that you were planning to annex Tunis." [214]

Ferry had seriously compromised himself on November 5 when, seeking to justify the autumn operations in Tunisia, he claimed that he had foreseen the need of such operations as early as the previous Spring. The opposition seized with glee upon his confession as proof of deliberate lying. "If you knew then that there would be an insurrection in the month of October, your duty was to make known to the Chamber what you knew," shouted Naquet. Now his opponents had confirmation from Ferry himself that the charges of deceiving the Chamber, which they had so long maintained, were true.

Naquet professed that he was not opposed to colonies as such: he thought they were desirable for France. "We would never reproach you for having had a colonial policy. What we do reproach you for is having lacked confidence in this Chamber." Naquet charged Ferry with a failure to consider the true interests of France in the expedition. He claimed it was undertaken and directed purely with an eye to domestic political advantage.

Ferry's contention that he had received a blank cheque from the Chamber and could proceed to spend whatever funds he wished, disturbed some of his staunch supporters. For a parliamentary government to follow such a doctrine was dangerous. Memories of past despotism were evoked by his declaration.

Le Faure, the *rapporteur* of the June bill for credits, rose to challenge the Premier's interpretation of his powers. He asserted that it was the understanding of the Committee that hostilities would end on or about July 10, as the Minister of War had stated to the Chamber and the Committee. Even he, a loyal supporter of the Ministry, maintained that when further funds had been needed, Ferry should have called the Chamber to approve them. Instead, he had spent more money than had been appropriated and had transferred funds intended for use in France to the Tunisian expedition's account.[215] Here was dissension among the ranks of the majority. It was not motivated by the problem of colonial expansion, but by the high-handed actions of the Premier.

One of the most bitterly contested questions during the November debates was the handling of the army. This was an especially sensitive point due to France's fear of becoming militarily weak in the face of an arming Europe.

Inevitably, as always in extensive military operations, the service of supply came in for criticism. Charges had been hurled in the press about the poor condition of the clothing and food furnished the troops. Lengthy and detailed accusations and denials filled the debates during November. Most of the trouble may be laid to the unusual conditions of terrain and climate for which continental troops were not adequately prepared. Changes were slow, as usual in so tradition-bound an organization as an army. The difficulties were aggravated to some extent by an incompleted reorganization of the ordnance branch. There was no doubt that many men suffered hardships thereby, but there was no justification for claiming a national catastrophe such as that the opposition tried to picture.[216]

More important were the charges concerning the effect on the European military balance of collecting some 30,000 men to send abroad. France at the time had no Colonial Army. So, in addition to 8,000 men

---

[215] *Ibid.*, 11/8/81.   [216] *Ibid.*, 11/9/81.

from Algeria, there were, both for military and political reasons, no large units that could be sent to Tunisia. Regiments, companies, platoons, and even individual men had to be gathered from points all over France.[217] The apparent confusion from such a continual shifting of forces, made the expedition seem to the public larger and more poorly organized than it really was. The French army depended upon a skeleton organization with a staff into which reserve troops could be fitted in time of mobilization. If a mobilization were to go off smoothly, it was necessary to keep each *cadre* intact. But some 25,000 to 30,000 men were drawn from these *cadres* in April and May and thereby "100,000 to 150,000 men had been directly compromised at the possible time of mobilization." [218] In his November 5 speech, Ferry explained the shifting of troops during the Summer as having been necessitated by the reestablishment of the *cadres*. He thus admitted that in the Spring he had weakened the defense of France.

Naquet cited the figures on the army strength to show that where France's army should have been 171,000 men in 144 infantry regiments, there were actually only 30,000 to 40,000 men in the French army in Europe during the late Spring and Summer. He cited companies that had from two to a dozen men in their ranks. Such charges made a deep impression on the Chamber.[219] The Ministry could, and did, claim in defense that a large part of the army's weakness in numbers was due to the gap between classes of conscripts and to the leaves granted men advanced in their training. The irrefutable fact remained that France's military strength had been very seriously impaired during many weeks.

The opposition made it very clear that they were in no way attacking the army itself. When the unimpressive and unpopular Minister of War was ineffectively defending himself, he tried to upbraid the deputies for attacking the brave French army.[220] He was cut short by interruptions and denials. Le Faure hurled back at Ferry his concluding words of November 5, "You have laid hands on the army!" [221]

The next day, the chief speaker of the Intransigent group on the Left, Clemenceau, agreed with and reiterated the main points of the previous speakers. He ran over the charges of waging an unauthorized war, misusing funds, weakening France in Europe and conducting the expedition unwisely. He attacked Ferry's argument that the invasion of Tunis simplified the defense of French borders, because, he said, France now had larger boundaries to defend, and had traded a weak neighbor for a stronger one when she became contiguous with Turkey.

---

217 *Ibid.*, 11/8/81. General Farre's defense. 218 *Ibid.*, Naquet.
219 Henri Brisson, the presiding officer, remarked that these charges, "had made the most profound impression of all." *Ibid.*
220 *Ibid.* 221 *Ibid.*

Clemenceau's great quarrel with the Government, however, concerned what he claimed were the real motives behind the expedition. He held that it was a scurrilous attempt to support French financial interests with the money and troops of France. "It is not that I wish to protest against the idea of such a program (as the development of national interests abroad); what I criticize especially is the way in which you have undertaken and carried it out." Commercial development he did not object to, but that taxpayers should have been made to carry the expenses of it, he deplored. Clemenceau again referred to the *Livre Jaune,* which the Government had already found embarrassing, to support his contention that France had been dragged into Tunisia largely by the speculative activities of various financial interests. He reviewed the cases of the Bône-Guelma railroad, the Enfida dispute, and the Crédit Foncier.[222] He did not claim that these incidents were the sole cause of the invasion of Tunis but he did point out that the irritation produced by these and the unfriendly acts of Roustan aggravated the crisis from which war resulted.

As an indefatigable advocate of *revanche,* Clemenceau could not approve any scheme that led France across the sea. Not only did Tunisia weaken the army at that moment, but it always would be "a military liability for freedom of action on the continent." He demanded an inquiry,

> because we have no confidence in you (the Government), because you lightly embroiled yourself in an affair with which you were not acquainted, because you have let yourself be led by events without knowing where you were going, without having a plan laid down, without sight of the future.[223]

With his back to the wall before the array of facts and the logic of the opposition, Ferry defended his policy on November 9. He denied that the expedition was essentially a *coup de bourse,* as the radicals insisted. Roustan had been acting patriotically to maintain legitimate French interests when he fought for the railroad and the telegraph monopoly in Tunisia. It was essential for the security of Algeria that Tunisian public utilities be kept in French hands. He pointed out that all the "affairs" Clemenceau cited had been settled before France had moved in.

Following this line of thought, he shifted his ground when stating the reasons for the invasion of Tunisia. He read the petition from the French residents of Tunis, under date of March 14, reciting the obstacles placed before Frenchmen there and the advantages of French penetration.[224]

[222] *Supra,* pp. 40, 44, 45.   [223] *J. O. C.,* 11/9/81.   [224] *Supra,* p. 51.

It asked that the French government should "make the government of the Bey of Tunis respect the interests of the colony and the legitimate influence" of France. The opposition burst into immediate protest at this change of grounds. Here was a tactical error on Ferry's part. No longer were the Kroumirs, as he had often sworn, the reason for invading the Regency.

The Premier admitted, to the unconcealed joy of his opponents, the necessity of occupying some points in Tunisia permanently. It was to be a "limited occupation," a protectorate still, without the name or formal approval by Parliament. He maintained that he had not deliberately concealed the facts of the situation from Parliament. In explaining his reticence he took the stand: "that in regard to foreign policy, there are some moments when the Government should know how to act without announcing what it wants to do." Clemenceau retorted that such a theory could lead to "the suppression of the Republic, for that would be the life, the very existence of France abandoned to the hands of an irresponsible Cabinet."

The charges of misappropriating money Ferry denied. Funds had been shifted from the military budget for home expenses of the troops to the Tunisian expedition. He claimed that the budget appropriation and the supplementary appropriations had not been exceeded. This was a deliberate lie, for more credits were needed at the moment and were to be passed on December 1.[225]

The Chamber had already bound itself to carry out the Treaty of Bardo. Now he appealed to it to do so "with firmness" and not to allow the revolting tribes to imagine that dissension within France was going to allow them to run unchecked.[226]

Neither then nor in a justification written in 1892 [227] did Ferry dwell on the economic potentialities of Tunisia. Nor did he in this debate mention the important role that fear of Italian interference had played. This factor, the crucial one in deciding the moment of French action, was lacking in the official justification. Later, however, Ferry admitted its importance.[228]

The Chamber now had before it the arguments of both sides, fully presented. Although Ferry had been forced to shift his ground and even to contradict himself, he had put forward his defense cleverly. Nevertheless, his opponents had made use of all that had gone before to show great gaps between some of the Premier's statements and his actions. The accidents of warfare and French inexperience in colonial operations were blamed on him. Certainly many of his actions had been

[225] *J. O. C.*, 12/2/81.
[227] *Discours*, V, 530 ff.
[226] *Ibid.*, 11/10/81.
[228] *Ibid.*

highhanded and Parliament had been misled. But France had gained a fine new colony.

When the deputies turned to voting, they showed themselves to be in a complete and utter quandary. The defeat of Ferry, if not his policy, was a foregone conclusion. Gambetta delayed asserting himself, so the Chamber was leaderless. There ensued a tumultuous scene in which the lower house seemed to have gone collectively and wholly mad. For two hours in one of the most amazing sessions in its history, the Chamber tossed on the horns of a dilemma wanting neither to destroy the work of Ferry nor to give him a vote of confidence. It rejected Clemenceau's order for an investigation, 328-141 and another demand for an inquiry couched in slightly different terms. Swinging to the other side, it rejected the Order of the Day, pure and simple, asked by the Minister, 312 votes to 176. Still the Chamber would not pass a vote of censure on the Government, twice voting down motions to bring it to trial. Some sixty Orders of the Day were proposed criticizing and praising the Ministry on every ground that had been discussed during the long days of debate. All were defeated. A motion for closure went down, 267–184. The suggestion to commit to a committee failed, 331–89. Unprecedented confusion reigned during this avalanche of motions. The *Journal Officiel* could not keep up with them: some thirty-three Orders of the Day were recorded; the rest were lost in the tumult.[229]

Finally, Gambetta, the real leader of the majority, took charge of the situation and arose to address the confused, bewildered, and exhausted Chamber. Only an appeal from him could save France her newest territory. He calmly told the deputies,

> France has set her signature on the Treaty of Bardo, and without entering into quarrels which are only personal quarrels, I ask that the Chamber by a clear vote, and in a way to make it clear at home and abroad, should say that the obligations which figure in this treaty over the signature of France shall be loyally, prudently, but wholly, executed.

Amid the applause of the Center and Left, he proposed this Order of the Day: "The Chamber, resolved upon the full execution of the Treaty signed by the French nation May 12, 1881, passes to the Order of the Day." This was passed, 365 votes to 68, with the Extreme Left still voting against the measure.[230]

[229] *J. O. C.*, 11/10/81. The "Order of the Day" was the term for the motion put to the house at the end of an interpellation of a minister and his answer. The motion might express the sentiment of the chamber as it "passed to the Order of the Day" i. e. the regular calendar of business.

[230] *Ibid.*

Tunisia was saved by the prestige of the next Premier of France. Ferry was defeated, although his plan had succeeded. The following day, as he had promised, he resigned to be replaced by Gambetta on the 14th of November. The crisis was over, the Government was in a strong position, and little more discussion on the subject was desirable or possible.

Gambetta did not mention Tunisia in his opening ministerial declaration,[231] but on December 1 he came before the Chamber to demand supplementary funds to pay for the Summer and Fall campaigning. He reiterated his stand of November 9, accepting the Treaty of Bardo and all it implied. He pledged himself to pacify the country and then come before the deputies with further plans. Meanwhile, he would pursue the policy of "neither annexation nor abandonment." The Chamber supported him with 395 votes of the 444 cast.[232]

During his second term as Premier, Ferry had an opportunity to continue the French reorganization of the Regency which was being ably conducted by Paul Cambon. Here as elsewhere, he was a strong believer in the protectorate as the best form of colonial government for states with cultures alien to the French. He preferred to make use of their already established religious, tribal and political organizations, and perhaps most important of all, he also believed that this was the most economical manner for France to rule Tunis.[233]

In March, 1883, a law was passed creating French courts in Tunisia with provision for the European states thereafter to yield their rights for consular courts. After some negotiations, and with the aid of Bismarck, the various foreign consular courts were closed.[234] The most difficult problem in this connection was presented by the English courts because negotiations for their closure happened to coincide with Granville's displeasure over French action in Madagascar and Indo-China. But on November 18, 1883, he agreed to close the courts effective the following January.[235] The other powers followed suit.[236]

A financial convention was concluded between Ferry's second Government and the Bey on June 8, 1883.[237] Under this arrangement, approved by Parliament in April, 1884, France guaranteed a loan intended to finance the conversion and part payment of the Tunisian debt. The Financial Commission, which had been receiving half of the Regency's

---

[231] *Ibid.*, 11/16/81. [232] *Ibid.*, 12/2/81. [233] *Ibid.*, 4/2/84.
[234] Constant, *op. cit.*, pp. 374–375. [235] *DDF*, V, No. 136.
[236] There had been consular courts in the Regency for Italy, Germany, England, Belgium, Denmark, Spain, Greece, Sweden, the United States, Austria-Hungary, Portugal and Russia as well as France.
[237] This was the Treaty of Marsa in which the word "protectorate" was used for the first time. Text in Constant, *op. cit.*, p. 466.

revenues, was dissolved and thereafter the finances of Tunisia were in a much sounder condition.[238]

Summary

No simple, easy explanation can account for the French acquisition of Tunisia, for the causes are obscured by a complicated web of nationalistic, economic, and diplomatic considerations and rivalries. No single motive can be ascribed to the large number of men who contributed to forming French policy. Once it was formed, statesmen like Ferry, who came later, could have changed it only with the greatest difficulty and the danger of so losing face that they would have been repudiated by a nationalistically inclined Parliament. Ferry and his compeers could procrastinate, but they could hardly avert a move against Tunisia by 1881.

Nationalistic rather than economic forces really set in motion a chain of events. French political and economic influence in Tunisia had old roots and had become a national tradition. But the diplomatic trading of 1877–1878 really assured France an opportunity to secure control over the Regency. French ambitions there were known, and England used them in taking Cyprus for herself. Although the arrangements were presented to them ready-made, French statesmen accepted the offered freedom of action for use at a more convenient date.

Economic motives for moving into Tunisia were of secondary importance. A series of incidents, clashes of interests were used as convenient tools by a broader diplomacy. In the whole range of French economic life these interests and stakes were quite small. Railroads, telegraphs, harbor works, and agricultural developments in Tunisia needed a great deal of government support to keep going: without a subsidy there would have been no profits.

Italian ambitions and pretensions in Tunisia, wherein economic penetration cloaked political designs, precipitated French action. A strikingly important role was played by the permanent officialdom in the French Foreign Office and by the career diplomats. Eager imperialists like Courcel in the Foreign Office, Roustan in Tunis, De Noailles in Rome, General Grévy in Algeria and Saint-Vallier in Berlin could successfully use the argument that French prestige demanded action before Italy could move. With such arguments, hesitant Republican leaders were swung over. Much of the planning and the important action in Tunisia thus was undertaken by men not directly responsible

[238] Rambaud, *Ferry*, p. 306.

to the people or by ministers who did not consult with the elected representatives of France.

Certainly Tunisia was not taken in response to any popular agitation. But France was uninterested rather than opposed to the venture. The protectorate was accepted as an accomplished fact. Such protest as there was came from those groups already opposed to all the actions of the moderate Republican Government. Their previous attitude toward Ferry and his colleagues determined their attitude toward Tunisia.[239] The votes on the measures dealing with the Regency showed that the Government had for these about as good pluralities as for domestic measures voted on at the same time.[240] The value of a colony or colonies *per se* was hardly mentioned. Of course, there was uneasiness about the losses in manpower, the expense of an expedition and national security. But that was to be expected from a popular assembly sensitive to public criticism.

It has been maintained mistakenly that the supposed furor stirred up by the Tunisian venture in 1881 was due to a definite anti-colonial sentiment in France, variously attributed to the loss of the first colonial empire, to the desire to concentrate on a policy of *revanche* and to the temperament of the French people. A "Little France" movement has been fabricated to explain the opposition to Tunisia and other colonial undertakings. It is based chiefly on the fact that Ferry was defeated on the question of Tunisia in 1881.[241] But as set forth above, his defeat was primarily due to considerations of domestic politics. Tunisia was merely an excuse, the first question to be introduced after the elections of the Summer of 1881, in which Gambetta clearly became the predominant leader. After Ferry left office, Tunisia was not abandoned; no group seriously broached such a suggestion.

Until early 1881 Jules Ferry was not the arch-imperialist that might be supposed in view of his later career. As he afterwards admitted himself, he was in reality heir to a policy to which he added little. When he became Premier he had no personal plans for action in the colonial sphere: he was completely absorbed in domestic political questions. The role of an imperialist was almost thrust upon him. Conversion, which only later assumed deep conviction, came when the leaders of his coalition had been persuaded that the prestige of France demanded that she forestall Italy in taking Tunisia; then he had assurance that his parliamentary majority would hold together through

---

[239] In all of the debates on the subject, twenty-one deputies spoke against the expedition. These were divided: Right, twelve; Center and Left, four; Extreme Left, five.

[240] See, *Appendix*.   [241] Roberts, *op. cit.*, I, 265–266.

vigorous action there. But to the members of that coalition full knowledge of his plans was not granted. He could act because the diplomatic arrangements had already been made and Bismarck continued to hold the ring clear for France. Once Ferry decided to act, however, he brought energetic determination to the problem. He was persistent and firm in carrying out his policy even though it did not always go as smoothly as he would have wished. Once embarked on a policy of imperialism in Tunisia, he soon began to reinforce French control in other theaters, and when, in two years, he again became Premier, he entered on an extensive program of overseas expansion.

Chapter Three

HARVEST WITHOUT SOWING IN
OCEANIA AND WEST AFRICA

In two widely separated parts of the world, the islands of the South-western Pacific and the river valleys of West Africa, the French had been active before Ferry came into office. Their work in both theaters was carried on and their control extended during both his premierships, for the most part without his intervention. When, in the early 1880's, other European powers threatened to encroach on her sphere of influence, France strengthened her grip on her Polynesian islands where the annexation of various archipelagoes, in part initiated by local officials, needed only Ferry's encouragement to bring about its successful culmination. The Polynesian holdings do not bulk large in the French Empire, but their acquisition was symptomatic of the new spirit of colonial development.

In West Africa and in the Pacific, French expansion was undertaken by governors and officers of the existing French colonies. Neither action was communicated to Paris until it was well under way. In West Africa modern French expansion, begun by ambitious officers as a matter of military conquest, was then linked to the railroad-building program. Both the spirit of conquest and the concrete plans for a railroad ante-dated Ferry's assumption of power.

Once in office and after his decision to move into Tunis, he encouraged the growth as much as he could with the resources at his command. Although neither field of action was of primary importance in the history of French imperialism, both demand some consideration, if only as part of Ferry's program of empire-building.

Oceania

The most important of the Pacific island groups in the French sphere were the Society Islands (or the Isles of the Wind), the chief of which was Tahiti, held by France as a protectorate since 1842 when she had assumed control after a quarrel between English and French missionaries. The governors of these small volcanic possessions held virtually complete authority, although nominally operating through the native king.[1]

English influence remained strong, however, partly because the English had a large share in the colonies' trade, but more because the larger part of the natives had been converted by members of the London Missionary Society before the advent of the French.[2] The latter exposed themselves to sharp criticism from their English rivals by their very poor government.[3] The colonial officials were sunk in tropical lasciviousness, inefficiency, and corruption: the islands were overrun with petty incompetents[4] whose administration was condemned even by French writers.[5] In 1880 and until the present day, they provided perhaps the worst example of French colonial rule.[6]

Hand and hand with poor administration went a failure to develop the commercial possibilities of the islands. The most important traders, as usual in the South Seas, were Germans from Hamburg, followed in importance by Americans from California.[7] Tahiti had a population of only 10,000, but French trade there was slight even for that number.[8] French merchants handled only about one tenth of it in 1879[9] and, despite support lent by their government, had managed to gain only one half of the total trade five years later.[10] They were handicapped by the fact that there was no regular shipping service to France: occasional sailing vessels provided the only direct commercial contact with the mother country until after 1890.[11]

Two events served to revive French interest in the Polynesians. With the consideration of the project for a Panama Canal, Tahiti suddenly acquired a new potential importance as a base for ships sailing between the proposed Canal and Australia or New Zealand.[12] Coincidentally, the French were alarmed by the accession of a new native ruler in 1877, for his wife was the daughter of an Englishman and a Tahitian prin-

[1] A. Rambaud, *France Coloniale* (6th ed., Paris, 1893), p. 631.

[2] *Ibid.*, p. 638.

[3] G. Hanotaux *et* A. Martineau, *Histoire des colonies françaises* (Paris, 1933), VI, 458.

[4] National Archives: State Department Archives (hereafter, SDA), *Consular Letters, Tahiti*, Vol. VII, January 1, 1875–December 31, 1886, No. 179.

[5] F. Soulier-Falbert, *L'Expansion française dans le Pacifique Sud* (Paris, 1911), Chap. V.

[6] S. Roberts, *op. cit.*, II, 516.

[7] SDA, *Tahiti, loc. cit.*; E. Levasseur, *Histoire du commerce de la France* (Paris, 1912), II, 545.

[8] Imports from France consisted chiefly of wines, brandies, and luxury goods intended for the 1,000 or more white inhabitants.

[9] SDA, *Tahiti, loc. cit.*

[10] *Ibid.*, No. 203.

[11] Rambaud, *op. cit.*, p. 149.

[12] SDA, *Tahiti*, No. 154.

cess. It was feared that this infusion of English blood might one day lead to English claims upon the island.[13]

The Commandant of Tahiti was ordered by Paris on September 9, 1879 to open negotiations with the King and local chiefs for the establishment of full French sovereignty. Shortly thereafter a new Commandant experienced little difficulty in persuading them to transfer to France full powers of government in the Society Islands and their dependencies, thus bringing the lagging talks to a successful conclusion on June 29, 1880.[14] Besides Tahiti and Morea, the arrangement included approximately eight small coral islands to the East, known as the Tuamotus or Low Archipelago, which had a fishing population of about 5,000 persons.[15]

This treaty lay on Ferry's desk when he came into office, but he did not present it to Parliament during his whole first term. Although the agreement was considered, in the islands, to have been in effect from the beginning of 1881,[16] there is no evidence to show that Ferry felt any interest in the affair. The treaty was passed in the Chamber by a voice vote on December 19, 1881.[17] Neither Gambetta nor any of his ministers took part in the discussion as the Chamber accepted the favorable report of the Commission. Similarly, there was no discussion or recorded vote in the Senate's approval a few days later.[18] A pension of forty-six thousand francs was awarded the royal family, and the matter passed off the parliamentary scene as quietly as it had come on. When the new arrangement was announced, the American consul wryly reported that it inspired no enthusiasm among the island population, despite glowing accounts in the local French newspaper of the realization of French destiny.[19]

On the other hand Ferry did play a part in securing a protectorate over the Leeward Islands, about one hundred miles Northwest of Tahiti, which had been the object of some Anglo-French rivalry before the middle of the century. A joint declaration of 1847 had pledged both governments to preserve the independence of these nine islands.[20] French commercial interests there were very slight; the Australians and the Germans handled most of the small trade.[21]

French eagerness to control the Leewards was aroused by the voyages in 1878-1879 of the German warships *Ariadne* and *Bismarck* when they went through the islands signing commercial treaties with the chiefs.[22]

[13] Rambaud, *France Coloniale*, p. 632.
[14] *Ibid.*, p. 633.   [15] *Ibid.*, p. 660.   [16] SDA, *Tahiti*, No. 166.
[17] *J. O. C.*, 12/20/81.   [18] *J. O. S.*, 12/27/81.   [19] SDA, *Tahiti,* No. 166.
[20] L. J., *Nouvelles-Hébrides et les Iles-sous-le-Vent* (Paris, 1887), No. 1.
[21] SDA, *Tahiti*, No. 150.   [22] *Ibid.*

Apparently the French would have had cause for alarm if the German traders could have persuaded Bismarck to move. Commercial circles in Berlin were calling for German annexation, citing claims that German officers and nationals had been frequently mistreated by French consuls in the South Seas. Saint-Vallier in Berlin urged his Government to restrain the French agents *vis-a-vis* the Germans to avoid trouble.[23]

A few months after the *Bismarck* appeared, Waddington asked England to reconsider the declaration of 1847 in view of the changed conditions.[24] Salisbury agreed to reopen the matter in November, 1879.[25] Talks with the English progressed satisfactorily as Salisbury indicated his willingness to make an adjustment in return for French consent to revise some boundaries on the West African coast.[26] Then the overzealous Governor of Tahiti upset the plans of the Quai d'Orsay.

Governor Chessé had landed on Raiatea, chief of the Leeward Islands in May, 1880, and extended a French protectorate over the inhabitants upon the "solicitation" of the chiefs.[27] He made proper reservations for the later settlement of international agreements, but that was not enough for the English. London made inquiries and was told that the Governor had been formally censured for his act, which Freycinet admitted was a flagrant violation of the 1847 agreement. He promised England satisfaction. However, he did not neglect to point out "the difficulties that the withdrawal of our flag would present from the point of view of the common prestige of all the European powers in those waters." [28] The English navy was little concerned about French prestige. A British warship removed the French flag from Raiatea and assured the chief that he was not bound by his recent agreement.[29]

This was the situation that Ferry faced when he became Premier in the Fall of 1880. Shortly afterwards England agreed to accept Freycinet's suggestion that the Leeward Islands problem might be adjusted by a *quid pro quo* on the Newfoundland Fisheries dispute.[30] In the meantime the protectorate was to be provisionally recognized. From Berlin, Saint-Vallier urged the Cabinet to authorize a move into the Leeward Islands, at the same time urging it to take action in Tunis.[31] Vice-Admiral Cloué, then Minister of Navy and Colonies, had decided by December, 1880, that Saint-Vallier's advice was good, but the rest of the Cabinet had not yet decided to support the cause of colonial expansion.[32]

But shortly after Ferry had been persuaded that French troops should be sent into Tunis, he undertook energetic action in this other

[23] *DDF*, III, No. 321.   [24] *L. J. Nouvelles-Hébrides*, No. 4.
[25] *Ibid.*, No. 5.   [26] *Ibid.*, No. 216.   [27] *Ibid.*, No. 6.   [28] *DDF*, III, 218.
[29] SDA, *Tahiti*, No. 158.   [30] *L. J. Nouvelles-Hébrides*, No. 8.
[31] *Ibid.*, No. 9.   [32] *DDF*, III, No. 321.

less important theater of empire-building. While England protested against the slow progress of the talk on the Leewards and Newfoundland,[33] the Cabinet ordered Chessé to consolidate the French position in the Leewards. Accordingly a new treaty of protectorate was signed on May 25, 1881. The natives' request for such protection had succeeded a free distribution of wine, rum, pork, and hardtack from three French warships lying at anchor off Raiatea.[34] The protectorate still received only a provisional recognition from England pending the outcome of the talks on the Fisheries. Many more provisional extensions were given,[35] for agreement could not be reached on Newfoundland.[36]

There is no available evidence to show what part Ferry or his ministers may have played in the acquisition of the Gambier Islands, which were taken at about the same time. These six little islands, inhabited by a few hundred pearl fishermen, lying southeast of Tahiti's dependency of the Tuamotus, were acquired by the enterprising Governor Chessé on February 21, 1881. France had held a nominal protectorate here since 1844 but, although French missionaries had been working on the spot for a long time, no effective political control had been exercised.[37] When both the American and German governments inquired, upon the prompting of their nationals trading there, about the French claims to these islands, the French soon reinforced their position.[38] Chessé sailed over from Tahiti with a frigate and obtained from the native rulers a demand for French annexation, which was forthwith granted. This was approved by the President of the Republic the following January 30th.[39] The juxtaposition of the American and German inquiries makes it seem likely that Paris had a hand in this matter. But in any case, Chessé was a man who needed no encouragement to add to the French domain.[40]

Although French expansion in Oceania took place in part during the Premiership of Jules Ferry, he had relatively little to do with it. After he had decided to move against Tunis, he did authorize his colleagues in the Navy and Foreign Office to intervene actively to protect French interests in the Leeward Islands. His Foreign Minister carried on some desultory negotiations with England concerning them.

---

[33] L. J. Nouvelles-Hébrides, No. 10.   [34] SDA, Tahiti, No. 168.

[35] DDF, IV, Nos. 113, 195, 310, 558.

[36] In 1887 a protectorate was finally recognized by Britain in return for French consent to a proposal for setting the New Hebrides under a condominium. L. J. Nouvelles-Hébrides, No. 48.

[37] SDA, Tahiti, No. 146.   [38] Ibid.   [39] Rambaud, France Coloniale, p. 655.

[40] Chessé was also instrumental in annexing the Tubais or Australes Islands, dependencies of Tahiti three hundred miles to the South of that island, on the request of the natives in March, 1882. Thus nine hundred islanders and 145 square kilometers were added to the Empire. Ibid., p. 656.

But this problem was dwarfed by the Ministry's more pressing concern with the acquisition of Tunis. The expansionist moves had been under-taken largely to forestall action by other European powers, especially Germany. To a certain extent the hand of the central government was forced by the colonial administration in Tahiti. Since Paris was 10,000 miles or more away and was not vitally interested in these unimprotant islands, the officers on the spot could gratify their desire for national prestige by annexing them and securing consent later. As with Tunis, Ferry found matters well under way and he had merely to lend his con-sent once he had decided to act in the colonial sphere. Thereby France's empire in the Pacific was increased.

West Africa

During the ministries of Jules Ferry the French Empire in West Africa grew, but its growth was due only in small part to the initiative of that great Republican. Without his help, military conquest and railroad building were already materially enlarging the colony of Senegal and opening up the French Sudan when Ferry came to power. During his second Premiership, he took some steps to aid the process but, with the limited resources he had at his disposal, he could do little, as the hard-ships experienced in the tropics discouraged Parliament from granting funds for further French penetration. The developments in West Africa and in Oceania are roughly comparable since France's holdings in both areas grew while Ferry was Premier, but not because of him.

The first colonial expansion under the Third Republic was along the upper reaches of the Senegal River, setting out from the old French city of Saint Louis at its mouth. Carrying forward work begun under the Empire,[41] the energetic Governor Brière de l'Isle greatly enlarged the colony during his tenure of office from 1875 to 1881. Acting without fanfare and without authorization from home, he began a military conquest of the river valley and the adjoining Fouta country. Several hundred square miles were added to French territory during his gov-ernorship, partly by outright annexation and partly through protec-torates.[42] Notable public improvements including harbor works and aqueducts were made. He founded the port of Dakar as an outlet for the colony since the capital, Saint Louis, was accessible by boat only during the two months of flood water. He financed these measures by

[41] The real founder of the Senegal colony had been a General Faidherbe who, during two terms as governor, 1854–1862 and 1864–1866 pacified and organized the region. His work was actively carried on by Admiral Jauréguiberry, governor during his ab-sence. P. Monteil, "Contribution d'un vétéran à l'histoire coloniale," *Revue de Paris*, Année 30 (1923), 104.

[42] Hanotaux *et* Martineau, *op. cit.*, IV, 164; Monteil, *loc. cit.*, p. 98.

imposing local port duties and so avoided control and interference from Paris.[43]

The inauguration of a plan for railroad building in the colony, under the Freycinet Plan of public works undertaken in 1879, gave new impetus to the growth of Senegal. Brière de l'Isle had already been surveying railroad routes before Admiral Jauréguiberry, the former Governor, now become Minister of Colonies, asked for such plans.[44] In February, 1880, a bill was introduced to construct railroads firstly, from Saint Louis to Dakar; secondly, from the last navigable point on the upper Senegal, Kayes or Medina, to the Niger River; and, thirdly, from Kayes directly West to Dakar. Construction of the Dakar-Saint Louis line was approved at once. The proposal to build the Senegal-Niger road was passed only in February, 1881. Although this occurred during the Premiership of Ferry, there was no discussion of the bill in Parliament at that time. Construction of the third line was postponed for many years.

Surveying and arranging for these railroads added materially to French holdings. A Lieutenant Monteil negotiated protectorates over the remaining independent tribes on the Dakar-Saint Louis route.[45] Two expeditions of Captain Joseph Galliéni, later to become famous as the defender of Paris in 1914, secured the territories along the upper Senegal, and between the Senegal and the upper Niger, thus acquiring the foundations of the French Sudan. From 1879 to 1881 he explored the area, signing treaties with some of the chiefs and waging war on others.[46]

Jules Ferry came on the scene while Galliéni was out on his second expedition and railroad plans were moving forward. He did little to affect the projects one way or the other, leaving West African affairs to continue as before. Just a few days before he assumed office a new administration was created to govern the newly acquired areas, called the Upper Senegal. It was intended to push further into the Sudan. The first commander here, Colonel Borgnis-Desbordes, appointed January 1, 1881, established his capital at Kayes to get a deep-water town on the river. He energetically started work on the road to the Niger, and the construction of a fort at Kita, about fifty miles from the Senegal, was begun on February 7, 1881.[47]

[43] Monteil, loc. cit., p. 101.
[44] Ibid., p. 112. The Inspector-General of Naval Works, Legros, was also an ardent supporter of the project. Joseph Galliéni, Voyage au Soudan français (Paris, 1885), p. 6.
[45] Monteil, loc. cit., p. 118.
[46] Galliéni, op. cit., pp. 2–8, 150 ff.; Hanotaux et Martineau, op. cit., IV, 175.
[47] Levasseur, op. cit., II, 504.

During the Spring of 1881, Ferry encouraged this colony by sending out a new expedition, intended to strengthen the forts along the Senegal above its navigable portion and as far as Kita. Such encouragement ceased, following events in Tunisia in the Summer of 1881, as insurrection flared in that incompletely pacified colony, absorbing all French energies. The colony of Upper Senegal was ordered not to undertake any further military engagement.[48]

The railroad builders in West Africa had to cope with terrible problems. The climate and malaria took its toll of the whites and decimated the Moroccan and Chinese laborers. There were not yet adequate safeguards against either yellow fever or other tropical diseases. Moreover, they were faced with hostile tribes in a little-known country more that five hundred miles from the coast. The major part of each appropriation had to be used to equip and supply the forts along the route. In the interim between Ferry's premierships several more forts were built. The last of them, on the Niger at Bamako, about 250 miles from Kayes, was established just as Ferry returned to office in 1883. Despite the forts' protection several native chiefs were constantly harassing the French. A leader named Ahmadou, whose lands covered much of the upper Niger valley, was long a thorn in the French side. But the worst was a chieftain named Samory. The French began their struggle with him in 1881 and almost annually from 1884 to 1898 campaigns were waged against him. He actually defeated them in the 1884–1886 campaign.[49] Only after a gunboat had been transported overland to the Niger were the blacks effectively quelled.

French engineers had had little experience with building railroads in the tropics and therefore made costly mistakes. Transportation was so poorly coordinated that, when the 1880 building materials arrived, they were too late, for the river was at low water. The material had to be dropped on the bank below its destination where it deteriorated for lack of proper storage facilities. By the end of 1881 there were only 700 meters of track laid down. By the end of the first year of work, one kilometer of roadbed and less than 800 meters of track had been laid.[50]

Because of these difficulties the bills for construction ran high. The first appropriation for the Kayes-Niger line, presented in a bill of February 5, 1880, was for 1,300,000 francs to build forts, telegraph lines and to make a topographical study of the route.[51] In February, 1881, during the Premiership of Ferry, the Chamber voted 8,500,000 francs for the Medina-Kita section of the line with a provisory terminal at

48 Hanotaux *et* Martineau, *op. cit.*, IV, 175.   49 *Ibid.*, p. 202.
50 R. Godfernaux, *Chemins de fer coloniaux* (Paris, 1911), p. 180.
51 *J. O. C.*, 2/6/80.

Bafoulabé where the Bakhoy and Bafing rivers join to form the Senegal. Although the bill was passed while Ferry was in office, he did not personally take part in the discussion. Another appropriation of 7,500,000 francs was voted 363–17 on March 13, 1882. Although it was supposed to cover the extension of the line by 23 kilometers and lay 74 kilometers of roadbed as well as strengthen the forts, only sixteen kilometers of track were laid, and even this section was not well ballasted.[52]

During his second Premiership Ferry had to come before Parliament to ask an additional appropriation of 4,677,000 francs for the railroad in the Senegal valley. In one session in July, 1883, he was questioned sharply on the huge cost and the small progress that had been made. Until then, for an expenditure of sixteen million francs, France had obtained only sixteen kilometers of railroad. This inadequate result exposed the Ministry to attack and Clemenceau was quick to press the advantage. Ferry frankly admitted that the situation was unfortunate, but appealed to the Chamber's patriotism not to withhold supplies from French troops in the Senegal jungles. He could point to the forts as concrete gains and to the construction of a telegraph line to the Niger at Bamako. He merely mentioned in passing that the region had commercial possibilities, but neither went into detail nor emphasized the point. He promised that results would show from the use of the funds. The bill was then passed 273–101.[53] During the succeeding year material previously left lying on the banks was carried up to Kayes and surveying was done for an additional seventy kilometers.

But the Chamber refused the Government further credits for this railroad in December of 1883. The project was again attacked on the grounds of heavy expense and poor results. The charges were obviously true even though the difficulties involved provided some extenuating circumstances. How the Ministry felt about the matter is evident from the fact that neither Ferry nor the other ministers replied; indeed most of the Cabinet was not even present for the discussion of the bill. The task of answering the Government's critics was left to Felix Faure, the Undersecretary of Navy and Colonies. Although he promised to produce better results with the new money, the appropriation was defeated by 234 to 197 votes.[54] Such a vote did not indicate a general aversion to all colonies on the part of the deputies since, on the following day, the Chamber granted twenty million francs for the Tonkin expedition by a 327–154 vote. What the Chamber objected to was the expense of the Senegal venture, not the principle of expansion.

In order to secure the funds for this railroad, intended to link the Senegal and Niger, Ferry took advantage of the fact that under French

[52] Godfernaux, op. cit., p. 181.   [53] J. O. C., 7/14/83.   [54] Ibid., 12/18/83.

constitutional law a money bill may originate in the upper Chamber of Parliament. The bill's passage was aided by a letter to the Senate from General Faidherbe urging it not to abandon the promising French colony, sanctified by the blood and toil of so many heroes. This same appropriation to cover the 1884 expenses by a grant of 3,300,000 francs was then brought back to the Chamber which passed it on March 31, 1884, by a vote of 311–84. But the money was voted only after Admiral Peyron, then Minister of Navy and Colonies, had told the Chamber that the sum asked for was needed for contracts that were already signed. He also promised that no new railroad construction would be undertaken nor would funds for such even be asked in the future.[55]

By 1885 only 54 kilometers of rails and 110 kilometers of roughly laid roadbed were done. This had cost 13,745,571 francs between 1881 and 1884: 260,000 francs per kilometer.[56]

Ferry little needed to concern himself with the construction of the second of the two railroad lines in Senegal, which was more successful than the first. The line from Saint Louis to Dakar, part of the Freycinet Plan, had been let out as a concession, with interest guaranteed by the State. In June, 1882, an 88-year concession was given the *Compagnie de chemin de fer de Dakar à Saint Louis*. It required two military campaigns, one in the Spring of 1882 and one in 1883 to put down the hostile tribes along the route.[57] With the submission of Cayor in August, 1883, the way was cleared of unfriendly natives.[58] The construction was then able to proceed with a minimum of delay and without the great difficulties of terrain confronting the line to the Niger. Its 264 kilometers were built at a cost of 70,000 each.[59] Opened in sections, the whole line was in operation on May 1, 1885.

The railroad construction and opening up of the Senegal hinterland had some stimulating effect on French trade. However, merchants were slow to move into this poorly pacified region whose native populations offered rather unsatisfactory markets. French trade with the Senegal in 1878 was twenty-five million francs; by 1888 it had risen to sixty-two million. The average from 1887 to 1896 was forty million while the average for the succeeding decade was seventy million.[60] Despite the increase in the total picture of French trade, the colony was not very important.

The history of French expansion in the Senegal and Sudan regions

[55] *Ibid.*, 4/1/84.
[57] Hanotaux *et* Martineau, *op. cit.*, IV, 166.
[59] Hanotaux *et* Martineau, *op. cit.*, IV, 164.

[56] Godfernaux, *op. cit.*, p. 181.
[58] Levasseur, *op. cit.*, II, 503.
[60] Levasseur, *op. cit.*, II, 509.

during this period is a story of conquest started and developed largely by military men in the colony rather than by statesmen in Paris. Merchants are conspicuously lacking. The officers were motivated by considerations of military prestige and a desire to extend French influence because that was thought good in itself. They were vaguely interested in opening markets for French products but much more concerned with empire-building for the sake of national glory. Paris, at first unconscious of the expansion, showed interest when a former governor was able to work Senegal into Freycinet's railroad building plan. It was this that opened the French Sudan. The story of Senegal is also a story of a struggle for African rivers. It was the French hope to win the whole course of the Niger from the British by approaching it from the Senegal. Here they were disappointed, although they did secure its upper half.

Although Jules Ferry was in office during a period of French expansion in West Africa he contributed little to its advancement. What developments he found already under way, he nevertheless encouraged with some energy, but his real interest did not lie in this field. Here imperial conquest was hampered, as we have seen, by factors of climate, topography, and tropical disease beyond his control. Moreover, an economy wave was in progress at home owing to falling revenues in a business depression and the Chamber forced the Government to call a halt, objecting not to expansion *per se*, but to the cost in men and money of the railroad designed to link the Senegal and the Niger.

At the same time, the French were exploring and slightly expanding their holdings along the coast of West Africa between the Senegal and the Gabun colonies in areas which they later acquired; for example: French Guinea, the Ivory Coast, Dahomey, and in Gabun itself. Again, Ferry himself was neither active nor even interested in any of these fields. It was on the initiative of the Senegal Governor, Brière de l'Isle, that the site of Conakry was taken, a protectorate established over the Fouta Diallon which lay behind French Guinea [61] and certain claims along the coast of French Guinea itself made good.[62] During Ferry's second Ministry, points along the coast of Dahomey were occupied.[63] Exploration enlarged the Gabun colony even before it became the base from which Savorgnan de Brazza made his epochal discoveries. All these were, at best, but feeble beginnings and merely provided some bases for the new burst of French expansion in the succeeding decade. There is no evidence to show that Ferry had any connection with these events. He was engaged in much more important projects.

[61] Hanotaux *et* Martineau, *op. cit.,* IV, 259–264.   [62] *Ibid.*
[63] M. Dubois *et* A. Terrier, *Les colonies françaises* (Paris, 1928), p. 527.

Chapter Four

EQUATORIAL AFRICA: THE STRUGGLE
FOR THE CONGO

Discovery and Exploration

France's acquisition of a large part of Equatorial Africa in and near the Congo River basin was made possible in great measure through the work of Jules Ferry. Of all the colonies acquired or enlarged during his premierships, this was the one for which Ferry personally was most responsible from start to finish. He early gave the explorer Pierre Savorgnan de Brazza subsidies to open up the area, and then with considerable skill he waged a diplomatic struggle with the Portuguese, English and Belgians to win, with Bismarck's aid, a great colony larger than France itself.

Until late in the nineteenth century, the heart of Africa, the great Congo basin, was completely unknown to Europeans. Closed by rapids in its lower course, this river with nearly two thousand miles of navigable waterway remained buried in mystery. After many men had tried unsuccessfully, to reach it, Darkest Africa was finally opened by the explorations of two men working from opposite coasts: Henry Stanley from the East and Savorgnan de Brazza from the Atlantic seaboard. Brazza was operating with the encouragement of the French Ministry of the Navy and from a base in the French colony of Gabun.

Brazza,[1] then a young ensign in the French navy, petitioned the Minister of the Navy in 1874 to be allowed to conduct an expedition to explore the Ogowé River in Gabun. Aided by his personal acquaintanceship with the Minister, Admiral de Montaignac,[2] he secured approval for his project. His first expedition was fitted out on a very modest scale. A private venture, some of the expense was born by the

---

[1] Brazza was the younger son of an Italian noble family of Rome. Educated in Paris, he entered the French naval school in 1868. He served with the North Sea squadron in 1870 and in Algeria against the Kabyle tribe a year later. In 1872 he visited Gabun in the course of duty and sailed a short distance up the still-unexplored Ogowé. His curiosity was aroused and he determined to try to discover the river's nature. First, however, he became a French citizen which compelled him for a brief time to serve as a simple sailor before passing his ensign's examinations. Comte Jacques de Chambrun. *Brazza* (Paris, 1930), pp. 1–37.

[2] *Ibid.*, p. 41.

explorer himself and some by the Paris *Société de Géographie*.[3] From the Ministry of the Navy he obtained an official blessing, a year's salary in advance, a force consisting of a medical officer named Ballay who was experienced in Ogowé exploration, a quartermaster, seventeen African sailors, and a small quantity of instruments, arms and general supplies.[4] From his family he received some financial assistance and the Rouen Chamber of Commerce presented him with a quantity of goods to use in trade.[5]

In the Spring of 1875 he started up the Ogowé which had been partly explored by Compiègne and Marche. He succeeded in parleying his way past the hostile natives on the lower reaches of this river, a barrier hitherto insuperable.[6] His expectation that the Ogowé was the road to Central Africa proved illusory, for he discovered that it divided not far from its mouth and that neither branch was navigable.[7] Nevertheless, he pushed on overland, despite tremendous physical handicaps.[8] His party reached the Alima River which flows East in the region behind Gabun. Supposing that the Alima flowed into a great interior lake, they went down the river in dugouts until attacks by the natives forced them to turn back. Brazza did not realize it at the time, but he was on a tributary of the Congo only five days' travel from the great river itself. The hostility of the natives was due to their experiences with Stanley who had passed that way not long before on his epochal journey across Africa.[9] All this Brazza learned only upon his return to Gabun where he heard of Stanley's exploit. That journalist had reached the Atlantic in April, 1877, to reveal for the first time the nature and size of the Congo.

While Stanley and Brazza were struggling through African jungles, Leopold of Belgium had set afoot an enterprise designed to build an African empire for his country.[10] To avoid international complications and persuade his own countrymen to acquiesce in his plans, he promoted the foundation of the International African Association.[11] This was organized at a Congress of African explorers and geographers called by Leopold at Brussels in September, 1876. The King of the Belgians talked at great length about opening Africa to the fruits of European civilization and commerce and ending slavery both along the Zanzibar coast and in the region about the mouth of the Congo.[12] An Interna-

---

[3] *Ibid.*, p. 45.   [4] *Ibid.*   [5] *Ibid.*, p. 46.
[6] Hanotaux *et* Martineau, *op. cit.*, IV, 388.   [7] Chambrun, *op. cit.*, p. 389.
[8] Porters for the expedition were too few and precious supplies were lost. Before long the expedition was without shoes and other vital supplies. *Ibid.*, p. 390.
[9] Hanotaux *et* Martineau, *op. cit.*, IV, 393.
[10] Robert S. Thomson, *Fondation de l'état indépendant du Congo* (Brussels, 1933), pp. 57–59.
[11] *Ibid.*   [12] *Ibid.*, p. 58.

tional Committee was established, heading a series of national ones for the direction and control of the activities of their nationals and for making their plans and discoveries known to the public. Leopold, as president of the International's executive committee, was able to dominate the proceedings of his organization.[13]

The International African Association nearly foundered on the rock of nationalism. The National Committees were a fiasco.[14] Only when Stanley was enlisted in November 1878, after he had failed to secure English backing for further exploration, did the African Association make headway. Then progress was made only after Leopold founded the Committee of Studies of the Upper Congo on November 25, 1878. This organization, still preserving a flavor of internationalism, was largely Belgian in its capital and plans.[15] In its articles of organization it set forth no political goals and claimed to be only philanthropic and scientific. But it also proposed to establish a chain of trading posts to open new outlets for trade and industry, and to determine the best means of linking the Upper and Lower Congo.[16] Stanley was dispatched with secret instructions to set up the Committee's posts and to sign treaties with the natives to secure the land for and between these posts.[17] He rejected the suggestion made by Leopold's agent that he attempt to form an independent Negro state in the region.[18] Leaving Belgium early in 1879, he went first to Mozambique to collect his expedition and arrived at the Congo in August, 1879. His heavy supplies were slowly transported around the rapids in the lower river on the way to the Stanley Pool where the Congo becomes navigable. When he reached the Pool he was surprised to find a French post under a Senegalese sergeant already there.

In France Jules Ferry had lent a receptive ear to Brazza's fears of Belgian designs on the Congo and his plans to forestall them. After Leopold had unsuccessfully attempted to hire Brazza to work for the Association,[19] the French explorer turned to his own government for aid. Both Ferry and Gambetta accepted his proposals.[20] As Minister of Education, Ferry had control over the Office of Scientific Missions which subsidized exploration.[21] On August 16, 1879, Ferry introduced a bill to

---

[13] *Ibid.*, p. 55.   [14] *Ibid.*, p. 57.

[15] *Ibid.*, p. 71. There was some Dutch money invested by a trading company with posts on the Congo estuary, but the firm went bankrupt before Stanley reached the Congo.

[16] *Ibid.*, p. 66.   [17] Henry M. Stanley, *Congo* (New York, 1885), I, 52–54.

[18] *Ibid.*   [19] *Ibid.*, p. 78.   [20] Chambrun, *op. cit.*, p. 86.

[21] The first evidence of Ferry's interest in remote lands is his active program of subsidization of exploration while he had control over the *Office des Voyages et Missions Scientifiques*. From 1879 to 1885, while he was Minister of Education or Premier, appropriations for exploration in West Africa, Indo-China and Madagascar as well as

subsidize the French Committee of the International African Association to the extent of 100,000 francs. The professed plan of the Committee was to have Brazza found stations for it, one on the Ogowé and one on the Upper Congo. These were declared to have primarily a civilizing mission, to bring the natives French culture, Christianity, and the abolition of slavery. Mentioned to Parliament, too, was the fact that the Committee would be able to open Central Africa to French trade.[22]

Brazza's real intention was to plant the French flag on the Congo. A secret agreement was made between the French Committee and the Government that the French flag should fly over the stations.[23] Brazza wrote the Minister of the Navy that if he succeeded, France would possess the lower river.[24] For the present, the French Committee served to give Brazza a certain immunity. None of these plans for territorial aggrandizement were revealed to Parliament by Ferry. There was no opposition to voting the appropriation.[25]

In addition to this grant from the government, Brazza received his personnel from the Ministry of the Navy, a small subsidy from the *Société de Géographie*, 50,000 frs. from the French Committee,[26] and 40,000 frs. from the International African Association itself.[27]

Four months after Stanley had arrived at the mouth of the Congo, Brazza left France, in December, 1879. Like faithful Achates, Dr. Ballay was again with him. Travelling with light equipment and a small force, for the sake of speed, they retraced their steps up the Ogowé and founded Franceville on its upper reaches. The French flag now flew 815 miles from Libreville, the capital of Gabun. Brazza went down the Alima in search not only of the Congo but also of the native suzerain of the region. Ascending the Lefini, a Congo tributary, he successfully completed his quest by meeting Makoko, chief of the Batékés. The Frenchman was received in a friendly manner, for he had established a good reputation among the natives.[28]

The Congo basin between the Lefini River and the Stanley Pool was given France by a treaty signed between Brazza and Makoko on September 10, 1880. Brazza went down to the Pool and in a second pact the

---

South America and the Near East rose sharply. During the first several years most of these ventures, with the exception of Brazza's, appear to have been inspired by scientific rather than political considerations. Brazza received another 100,000 frs. from this same office in 1880.

[22] *J. O. C.*, 8/17/79.   [23] Thomson, *op, cit.*, pp. 80–81.

[24] Napoléon Ney, *Conférences et lettres de P. Savorgnan de Brazza sur les trois explorations dans l'Ouest Africain de 1875 à 1886* (Paris, 1888), pp. 414–415. Cited in Thomson, *op. cit.*, p. 79.

[25] *J. O. C.*, 8/17/79; *J. O. S.*, 8/25/79.   [26] Hanotaux *et* Martineau, *op. cit.*, IV, 101.

[27] Thomson, *op. cit.*, p. 80.   [28] Hanotaux *et* Martineau, *op. cit.*, IV, 402.

assembled vassals of Makoko affixed their names to what was a nearly identical agreement on October 3, 1880.[29] Thereupon Brazza took formal possession of the ceded territory. A post, which was later named Brazzaville in his honor, was founded on the Pool.[30] A Senegalese sergeant and three men were left stationed there and it was this outpost of France that Stanley found on his arrival. France had triumphed in the first race.

The expedition continued down the river and met Stanley coming up some distance above Vivi.[31] The American was always contemptuous of the French explorer and their relations were very cool now as on other occasions.[32] Brazza returned to Libreville, stopped only for a day, and started back around the circuit to consolidate the French holdings. He first began the organization of the route between the Ogowé and the Alima, freeing the slaves wherever he established a French post.[33] After returning to the Pool, he set out on the very important task of finding the best alternative land route to the sea since the direct Congo valley route was preempted. He discovered the desired exit to lie North of the Congo through the valleys of the Niari and Kouilou rivers.[34]

Brazza found himself a great and popular hero on his return to Paris. The ensign had captured the city's imagination when he returned with treaties in his pocket conferring on France a fantastically described and mysterious tropical colony.[35] A tremendous public reception was held for him at the Sorbonne: he was feted by learned societies and hailed by cheering Paris crowds. He was decorated and laden with honors by public and private groups.[36] There developed a Brazza cult, complete with medals, pictures, parades and songs. It was this public enthusiasm that made Jules Ferry's task of consolidating Brazza's gains an easy one within France.

In high spirits, Parliament accepted Makoko's holdings in the Congo basin as a French possession in November, 1882. Not the slightest opposition was expressed in the legislative halls to the annexation. Government spokesmen lauded its commercial possibilities as being very rich and great. Repeatedly emphasized and praised was the peaceful

[29] Texts in *J. O. C.*, 11/19/82. Actually "Makoko" was the title of the chieftain but this was not known until later and the French persisted in referring to him as though this were his proper name.

[30] Hanotaux *et* Martineau, *op. cit.*, IV, 402.

[31] Stanley had been several times warned by his employers of Brazza's intentions but had rejected the warnings that he would be outdistanced in the race for the Congo. Thomson, *op. cit.*, p. 82.

[32] Stanley, *op. cit.*, I, 231–234.   [33] Hanotaux *et* Martineau, *op. cit.*, IV, 405.

[34] These two rivers are really one, the Niari being a large upper tributary of the Kouilou which flows into the sea. This route much later was followed by the railroad constructed by the French from the Congo to the Atlantic.

[35] Hanotaux, *Mon Temps*, II, 112.   [36] Chambrun, *op. cit.*, p. 113.

nature of the acquisition.[37] The Government for the moment, claimed only the right bank of the Congo.[38] A few days later, the French Committee of the International African Association presented to the Republic its stations, including Franceville, Brazzaville, and those on the Alima.[39]

Jules Ferry embarked on a vigorous and far-flung program of colonial expansion within a few weeks of his second accession as Premier in February, 1883. Important among his projects was the third Brazza expedition to organize and extend the new colony in equatorial Africa which was in preparation at the time. Ferry lent Brazza his full support as he had done even before becoming Premier.[40]

The expedition now needed no committee to hide behind. For the first time, Brazza, promoted to lieutenant and officially designated as "Commissioner of the Government of the French Republic in West Africa," headed an official French expedition. It was jointly financed by the Ministries of Education, Foreign Affairs, and Navy. The division of responsibility was due to the fact that Brazza's exploits were not well received in the Ministry of the Navy which felt it was being burdened with too many expeditions.[41] In the first month of Ferry's Ministry the navy was charged with expeditions to Tonkin and Madagascar as well as to Africa. Significantly, the Ministry of Education, then headed by the Premier, bore 980,000 frs. of the 1,275,000 frs. which Parliament appropriated for the new venture, the bill being presented to the Chambers by Ferry. It was frankly designed to pay for holding and expanding the French position. There were a few vague generalities about ending slavery and bringing civilization to Africa. Parliament heard from its Premier that it should approve the measure because it would enable new cubits to be added to the stature of France, her glory and prestige would be vastly enhanced by the equatorial African holding. The prospect of commercial gain to be found here was also set forth. Specifically, the measure provided the means to found eight French stations and some dozen forts both in the Ogowé-Alima and the Niari-Kouilou valleys. It was easily passed by the Chamber, 441-3.[42]

A sizeable expedition departed from Gabun on April 25, 1883 to protect and extend the interests of France [43] in an all-out race with the King of the Belgians for the Congo basin and its exits. Leopold had dissolved his Committee of Studies when he was faced with the threat of Brazza's activities and had formed the International Association of the Congo. This was merely a cloak for his designs to found a political

[37] *J. O. C.*, 11/19/82; *J. O. S.*, 11/29/82.
[38] *Ibid.*
[39] Hanotaux *et* Martineau, *op. cit.*, IV, 409.
[40] Chambrun, *op. cit.*, p. 119.
[41] Chambrun, *op. cit.*, p. 112.
[42] *J. O. C.*, 12/12/82.
[43] Hanotaux *et* Martineau, *op. cit.*, IV, 409.

state on the Congo.[44] From late in 1882, the King of the Belgians pursued an avowedly political end in Central Africa.[45] But even before Brazza set forth for the third time, his subordinates had been busy. Dr. Ballay had been dispatched to negotiate additional treaties with the tribes along the Alima River in July, 1882. The explorer De Chavannes was engaged in a similar mission in that area. Ensign Mizzon had, meanwhile, found a new route from Franceville to the Kouilou.[46]

Ferry's instructions to Brazza were to assure the French possession of the Niari-Kouilou route from the Congo to the shore. The towns at Loango and Pointe Noire were to be taken to accomplish this end.[47] It was the French hope to secure all the land from Gabun to the Congo but especially they considered it important to have the territory as far south as the Kouilou.

Leopold's Stanley won the race for the Niari-Kouilou valley, however. Thereby he evened the score with Brazza for beating him to the Stanley Pool and the surrounding area. Stanley was working hard to head off both Portugal and France, driven on by what was the very real danger that the Belgian Association would be cut off from the sea.[48] The Association dispatched expeditions to establish posts along the Niari-Kouilou Rivers and these were set up from January to March of 1883.[49] When Brazza's associate, Cordier, arrived at Loango on March 8, he found the Belgians already installed.[50] Although the Association held a treaty with the natives there, Cordier took possession of the place in the name of France, a purely formal procedure, before he sailed away. The Association still had two more posts between Loango and the Kouilou mouth,[51] so that Cordier's action could have little actual significance. Nonetheless, it was later used by Ferry in negotiations with the Association.

Brazza's men founded a score of small posts along the coast not far from Loango. Most of these were very unimportant and could hardly be considered as valid a claim as the fifteen posts established by the Association in the Kouilou valley. The French Commissioner was under strict orders not to enter into any quarrels with Stanley, for Ferry was worried lest a conflict break out in the field.[52] The problem of the exit from the Congo was to be settled by later negotiations. Stanley's victory proved to be a pyrrhic one, for Ferry was able to compel Leopold to

---

[44] Thomson, *op. cit.,* pp. 74–77. Leopold continued to use the name of the Committee when it suited his purpose in order to create confusion. For quite some time Stanley used the Committee's name in his work, apparently being appraised of the change only at a late date.

[45] *Ibid.,* p. 89.   [46] Hanotaux *et* Martineau, *op. cit.,* IV, 409.

[47] Chambrun, *op. cit.,* p. 136.   [48] Thomson, *op. cit.,* p. 94.   [49] *Ibid.,* p. 95.

[50] *Ibid.,* p. 98.   [51] *Ibid.,* p. 99.   [52] Chambrun, *op. cit.,* p. 149.

surrender the route. Both powers, however, secured an exit from the Congo basin.

Brazza returned to the Alima and, rejoining Ballay, went on to visit Makoko again in March 1884.[53] After losing the race for the Niari-Kouilou valley, the French Commissioner needed aid from his native ally to reinforce his position. The French position had been weakened because the post of Brazzaville had been unoccupied since 1882,[54] and Stanley was laying claims to both banks of the Pool and both banks of the river.

Originally Brazza had not specifically claimed both banks of the Pool. In 1881 he talked only of the left one. Now, however, he laid claim to both on the grounds that Makoko had given him all the lands under his sway, which he claimed included both banks, and secondly, that Malamine had for some time lived on the left bank and thereby made good French claims to that territory. Stanley, on the other hand, contended that Makoko had no longer any authority over the banks of the Pool and therefore was without power to bestow it on the French.[55] Both sides could produce agreements signed with various chieftains, agreements probably beyond the understanding of the natives and certainly accompanied with numerous gifts. In any event, the Association's Leopold-ville and other posts were already on the left bank of the Pool.

On his second visit to Makoko, Brazza arranged that he should receive anew the submission of the chiefs of the region including those on the left bank as they were presented to him by Makoko. Having renewed his agreement, he reestablished Brazzaville in April, 1884.[56] The French now had a useful point for bargaining to secure the Niari-Kouilou valley. Brazza proposed to negotiate the questions directly with Stanley who was at that time toying with the idea of offering part of the Congo to England in order to ward off France.[57] Stanley, however, refused to negotiate with, or even to see, Brazza. The French Commissioner then turned the problem over to Paris to be settled by negotiation.

While Brazza continued organizing the colony, one of his aides, Dolisie, pushed up the Ubangi to sign treaties of protectorate with tribes as far North as the Equator. It was the unfulfilled hope of Brazza and his subordinates to push French claims all the way to Lake Tchad and to the Nile.[58]

A halt was called to the advance in the Summer of 1885 partly because the French were recoiling from colonial ventures after Ferry's

[53] Ibid., pp. 142–144.

[54] Thomson, op. cit., p. 116. Actually "Brazzaville" was a peripatetic post, moving where the Senegalese sergeant, Malamine, chose to live.

[55] Stanley, op. cit., I, 298.   [56] Thomson, op. cit., p. 118.

[57] Ibid., p. 109.   [58] Chambrun, op. cit., p. 152.

defeat and the timidity of the succeeding ministries. But it was also the result of the Berlin Conference of 1884–1885 that settled the boundary claims of the French and Belgians in equatorial Africa. Before the halt was called, Brazza had founded a colony of 460,000 square miles, more than twice as large as continental France itself. Its acquisition had been peaceful and very inexpensive and was due primarily to the energy of that great explorer, backed by Jules Ferry. The task of securing French claims against other states was left to Ferry's negotiations.

Anglo-Portuguese Attempts on the Congo

The race for the Congo was given a dramatic new turn in February, 1884, when an Anglo-Portuguese treaty was announced, giving the territory around the mouth of the Congo to Portugal and establishing an Anglo-Portuguese patrol to control the river. This arrangement upset the French and Belgian plans and threatened to nullify at a stroke years of arduous work.

Portugal, from her early explorations, had old, vague claims to the equatorial African coast. She maintained that all the coast North of Angola[59] to Gabun belonged to her although she had never effectively occupied it. For many years she had wanted to occupy the Congo coast but had been stopped by the standing orders given the English Slave Patrol in 1856 to prevent just such a move.[60] When Brazza's claims were made known, there had been a good deal of bitter comment in the Lisbon press.[61] However, the French ambassador believed in December, 1882, that Portugal was mollified when the French promised not to move South of 5° 12′, a point South of the Kouilou River. Duclerc, when he was Premier, gave many assurances that Portuguese rights would be respected.[62] Portugal chose to interpret these assurances as recognition of all her claims but Ferry refused to admit such an interpretation. No definite settlement of the question was reached.

At the time that Brazza's treaty with Makoko was before the French Chambers in November, 1882, Portugal began talks with England to make an agreement respecting Portuguese and English claims and rights in equatorial and East Africa.[63] Negotiations continued with varying degrees of harmony for the next year and a quarter.

During the first months of Ferry's Premiership, as the Anglo-Portuguese negotiations lagged, Portugal proposed in July, 1883, that France

---

[59] Angola extended from 8° to 18° South latitude.
[60] Thomson, *op. cit.*, p. 135.   [61] *DDF*, IV, No. 543.
[62] *L. J. Congo, 1884*, Nos. 3, 5.   [63] *Ibid.*, No. 15.

and Portugal appoint a commission to settle the boundary questions of Guinea.[64] Challemel-Lacour proposed to extend the scope of the talks to all the boundary questions of the African West Coast. Portugal would agree only if her claims from 5° 12' to 8° South were previously recognized.[65] This would give Portugal the Congo mouth and restrict France to the interior Congo basin.

Ferry rejected this proposal, for he still hoped to secure the mouth of the Congo for France.[66] The negotiations died. Portugal resumed her discussions with England, more amenable than she had been before.[67] Probably with English consent, she occupied Landana at 5° 12' on the following September 29.[68] It was only in early February of 1884 that the French received an inkling of how extensive the Anglo-Portuguese arrangements were to be.[69] Even then, Ferry was not prepared for the sweeping nature of the accord.

The Anglo-Portuguese treaty, provisionally signed on February 26, 1884, seriously threatened the French and the Belgian enterprises. It recognized Portuguese claims to the land at the mouth of the river as far as Noki on the left bank, along the Congo coast, and inland there as far as the sway of the coastal tribes extended. An Anglo-Portuguese Commission was given control and police power over the river's course. New taxes were levied on the trading posts held by foreigners in Portuguese territory.[70]

Ferry violently opposed the treaty from the very first news he had of it,[71] for although neither England nor Portugal had done anything to open the Congo, they were attempting to appropriate it. On March 7, Ferry made a strong official protest to the Portuguese ambassador in Paris.[72] On the 14th, Ferry sent Lisbon a stiff note in which he protested against the Anglo-Portuguese patrol of the Congo, the increase in the Portuguese colonial tariff rates, in violation of the Franco-Portuguese Treaty of Prado of 1786 which promised that Portugal would not interfere with commerce South of 5° 12'. He summarily and completely rejected the Portuguese claims to the whole West coast of Africa near the Congo mouth. He told Portugal that he feared the "execution" of the treaty, the workings of the Congo patrol and what it might lead to as much as he feared the actual terms as they stood.[73]

The treaty was soon found to be universally unpopular. Protests

[64] DDF, V, No. 9. [65] L. J. C., 1884, No. 7. [66] Ibid., No. 10.
[67] Thomson, op. cit., p. 133. [68] Ibid., p. 135. [69] DDF, V, No. 210.
[70] L. J. C., 1884, No. 12. England was also to police the East coast of Africa and receive preference on the Adjuda fort and the Gold Coast possessions of Portugal if these were ever alienated.
[71] Ibid. [72] DDF, V, No. 219. [73] L. J. C., 1884, No. 14.

from Belgium, the Netherlands,[74] and Germany—the latter on April 18 —followed the French representations. In Portugal the arrangement was disliked because it allowed the English to have a degree of control over Portuguese lands and because its terms reduced the fullest Portuguese claims.[75] In England it was unpopular because such extensive Portuguese claims were recognized. The Portuguese colonial administration had an unsavory reputation in England because it had permitted an active slave trade to continue until very recently.[76] The arrangement was also heartily disliked by English merchants engaged in foreign trade who highly disapproved of the high tariff policies of the Iberian kingdom.[77] The English Foreign Office, which had negotiated the treaty to insure its commerce against being shut off from the Congo basin by France and the Association,[78] paradoxically found its own Chambers of Commerce severely criticizing it for the new arrangement.

On March 31, Ferry sounded Bismarck on the German attitude toward the Anglo-Portuguese treaty, pointing out the threat inherent in it to German commerce in Africa. For his own part, he stated that he was anxious to preserve freedom of commerce and navigation on the Congo.[79] Hatzfeldt and Courcel discussed the matter in Berlin on April 18 and on that same day Germany's protest was dispatched to Lisbon.[80] The German Chancellor was being petitioned by numerous German Chambers of Commerce to refuse to recognize the treaty, meanwhile.[81]

Hohenlohe according to Hatzfeldt's orders, talked with Ferry and Billot on April 22 about the possibility of acting in concert with the other powers. Both indicated their willingness and accepted as a basis the principle of equal treatment. Billot suggested that an international commission on the model of the Danube Commission might control the river.[82] On April 29, Bismarck informed England of his opposition to the treaty.[83] He had previously sought the cooperation of Holland, Spain and Italy and they similarly protested.[84]

Bismarck decided on this step and supported France throughout the rest of that Spring principally because he was so angry with England over the Fiji Islands and the Angra Pequena questions. The English government had been inexcusably dilatory about replying to his inquiries on the status of Angra Pequena. The German Chancellor's wrath

74 There were several Dutch trading posts in the Congo estuary.
75 *DDF*, V, No. 218.   76 *Ibid.*, No. 214; Wienefeld, *op. cit.*, p. 141.
77 Thomson, *op. cit.*, p. 143.   78 *Ibid.*, p. 140.   79 *DDF*, V, No. 226.
80 Germany. Auswärtiges Amt. *Aktenstücke betreffend die Kongo-frage* (Berlin, 1885), No. 9.
81 *Ibid.*, Nos. 4–8.   82 *DDF*, V, No. 244.
83 *Aktenstücke*, No. 17; S. E. Crowe, *The Berlin West Africa Conference, 1884–1885* (London, 1942), p. 28.
84 *Aktenstücke*, Nos. 18–21.

mounted with each month that passed without an answer.[85] Angra Pequena was placed under German protection on April 24, but Münster, the German ambassador, handled the matter so badly that neither he nor the British government was aware that Bismarck had now embarked on a colonial program until Herbert Bismarck visited London in June 1884.[86]

Discussion of the treaty in the Portuguese Cortes was dropped in May, and Portugal began to talk about holding a European conference on the subject.[87] Bismarck refused to recognize the treaty on June 7 and soon turned to the idea of a conference. England abandoned the accord on June 26. Just five days before, the English Cabinet had at last learned the true intentions of Germany in regard to Angra Pequena and decided to offer no opposition to Germany's claims there.[88] Although England had been forced to retreat in the Congo question by the coalition against her, she had succeeded in making her original point that the Congo should be opened to commerce.[89]

Meanwhile Ferry, by diplomatic means, was busily assuring France of her rights on the Congo, just as his agent Brazza was making them stronger by founding forts and trading posts. Since the earliest days of rivalry in the Congo, Paris and Brussels had exchanged mutual expressions of good will. When the treaty with Makoko was before the Chamber, Duclerc had assured Leopold that no conflict with the Association was intended by France.[90] This assurance was repeated in January, 1883, when Leopold expressed worry over French designs on the Congo.[91] Both Stanley and Brazza were instructed in the Spring of

[85] Although the English were very slow about answering Bismarck's requests, there is no evidence that they were trying to deceive or overreach him. Bismarck had first inquired about the status of Angra Pequena, where there was a German merchant established, in February 1883. He gave no indication that he wanted to acquire this or any other colony, as he did not wish to do so at that time. The British laid claim to this part of the African coast in an answer in November, and, on December 31, 1883, Bismarck inquired on what basis the claim was laid. The matter was discussed in a very desultory fashion between the Foreign Office, the Colonial Office and the Cape Colony with no realization of the importance of the question. This lack of realization was partly due to Bismarck's own vagueness and partly to Münster's failure to grasp Bismarck's intentions. William O. Aydelotte, *Bismarck and British Colonial Policy* (Philadelphia, 1937), pp. 133–134; Crowe, *op. cit.*, pp. 50–54; Mary E. Townsend, *Origins of Modern German Colonialism* (New York, 1921), pp. 163–169.

[86] Aydelotte, *op. cit.*, pp. 43, 51, 94. There was, moreover, a certain amount of duplicity on Bismarck's part in this incident. Crowe, *op. cit.*, pp. 45, 57; Townsend, *op. cit.*, p. 166.

[87] DDF, V, Nos. 270, 273.

[88] Aydelotte, *op. cit.*, p. 97. But conditions were attached to the formal note sent on July 19 that were again annoying to Bismarck. On June 19 England had agreed to appointment of a commission on the Fiji Islands claims.

[89] Thomson, *op. cit.*, p. 145; Crowe, *op. cit.*, pp. 23–25.

[90] *L. J. C., 1884,* No. 1.   [91] *DDF,* IV, No. 591.

1883 by their respective governments to avoid conflicts with each other.[92] These orders were not always well observed in the field, however. Stanley was greatly annoyed at having been beaten to the Pool by Brazza in their race for territory and always considered the French to be interlopers on his preserve.[93]

The official French position regarding the Association was that it was a private organization and so did not possess the rights of sovereignty. Ferry continued to support this interpretation on such occasions as he thought it would prove convenient. However, such a stand was more difficult to maintain now that the Association had established a chain of stations in the Niari-Kouilou valley, France's best means of access to the Congo basin. After Ferry's negotiations with the Association that now followed, the position became even more untenable.

On April 23, 1884, Colonel Strauch, the President of the Association, wrote Ferry offering France an option on the sale of the Association's Congo possessions should that body dissolve. Ferry accepted on the following day.[94] No parliamentary authorization for the action was sought. Unfortunately we have no published documents to enlighten us on the negotiations that preceded this exchange of notes. Why the arrangement was accepted by France we do know.

Ferry had two reasons for accepting this option. Like Germany, he had been worried lest England acquire the Association's holdings.[95] More important, however, was the fact that he believed that the Association would soon die from financial malnutrition and that France would receive its lands.[96] This remained Ferry's belief for a long time, his hope for even longer, and explains much of his dealing with the Association. Bismarck was also convinced that the Association was a purely financial speculation on the part of Leopold and he would have to abandon it due to financial difficulty.[97] Both the French and German leaders proved to be mistaken.

It is not completely just to present this exchange of letters as an unmitigated triumph for Leopold, as the best historian of the Congo affair has done.[98] As it turned out, it was a move most helpful to Leopold's cause. Leopold had no intention of giving away or selling the Congo, and he had the Association give the option upon its own insistence,

[92] *Ibid.*, No. 16.
[93] *DDF*, V, No. 319.
[94] *L. J. C., 1884*, Nos. 17 and 18.
[95] Thomson, *op. cit.*, pp. 164–165.
[96] *DDF*, V, No. 457; SDA, *France, Dispatches*, Vol. 96, No. 698; Hanotaux *et* Martineau, *op. cit.*, IV, 419.
[97] *Aus den Archiven des belgischen Kolonialministeriums* (Berlin, 1918), pp. 74–76.
[98] Thomson, pp. 166–169. This is an excellent statement of the Belgian case but it overlooks the important factor that Ferry was convinced of the Association's certain death. Billot still expected this demise as late as the following January, *infra.* p. 110.

not that of France.[99] It served his purpose of checking Portugal and was a workable threat against England and Germany that he might yield his lands to France. The declaration also involved Ferry in a paradox in the event that the Association, contrary to his expectations, did survive. While he was denying, on the one hand, that the Association could acquire rights of sovereignty, since it was a private enterprise, on the other hand, he accepted its promise to give France an option. So he admitted implicitly what he denied, for if the Association was only a private venture, then its promises had no value among states and any state had the same right as France to occupy its holdings. These letters proved to be a long step toward French recognition of the Association as a state which Ferry in April, 1884 still hoped to avoid.[100]

Just before this exchange of notes, the International Association of the Congo had been recognized as a sovereign state for the first time by the United States on April 22. Thanks to the labors of Henry S. Sanford, former Minister to Belgium, this recognition gave it a standing in the company of nations.[101] Ferry was not at all pleased by this strengthening of the Association and continued to maintain that it could not attain sovereignty.

The Portuguese proposal for an international conference on the Congo problem was made in both Paris and Berlin in May.[102] When Bismarck inquired about Ferry's attitude on the question, he replied on May 28 that he was quite willing to take part in a conference to arrange free navigation and equal rights on the Congo for all nations. He expressed the opinion that some kind of an International Commission for the Congo might best be set up to insure such rights. However, he explicitly barred territorial questions from the agenda.[103] On June 5 Bismarck replied that such conditions were acceptable to him,[104] and exactly a month later he acceded to the French suggestion that the proposed conference should also discuss the question of free navigation on the Niger.[105] However, Ferry had informed Bismarck on June 10 that he believed a Congo conference should not be called until after the approaching parleys on Egypt.[106] Therefore, the proposal languished during the Egyptian Conference in London, June 28 to August 2. This failed to satisfy the French desires largely because the anglophile German ambassador, Münster, refused to support the French claims despite

[99] Archiven (1918), p. 70.   [100] Thomson, op. cit., p. 169.

[101] Ibid., pp. 147–162. This is the best account of the means by which this recognition was slipped through the Senate, the amazing ignorance of the facts of the case displayed by the United States in granting recognition and the skillful engineering of the affair by Sanford.

[102] Supra, p. 87.   [103] Aktenstücke, No. 24.   [104] Ibid., No. 25.

[105] Ibid., No. 30.   [106] Thomson, op. cit., p. 205.

Bismarck's orders.[107] Ferry was greatly annoyed and long remained suspicious of German overtures.

Despite this inauspicious start, a Franco-German entente on West Africa was gradually worked out in the late Summer of 1884. It was arranged largely because Bismarck was so annoyed at England. The British Ambassador delivered Granville's answer to the German dispatch of December 31, 1883 on July 19. This stated that England was prepared to recognize Germany's right to protect Angra Pequena as soon as Germany gave assurance that no penal settlement would be founded there.[108] Bismarck refused to accept any such obligations.[109] Moreover, on July 16 the Cape Colony Parliament had voted to annex the whole Southwest coast of Africa, including the part claimed by Germany. Although the annexation was never carried out and was never approved by London, the attempt was very annoying to the Germans.[110] Bismarck extended formal protection to the Southwest coast from the Orange River to 26 degrees of south latitude on August 7 [111] which was finally recognized by Great Britain on September 22.[112] The African colonial question drove Bismarck to cooperate more closely with France which already had disagreements with England over Egypt, Madagascar and Tonkin as well as West Africa. The fact that Germany and England had so many disputes was a stroke of good fortune for Ferry's plans and ambitions. Alone he could not have stood against England without dangerous complications. Now Bismarck gave France even more support in her overseas ventures than he had for many years.

Renewed German overtures were made early in August when Bismarck urged that France and Germany should work out in principle an arrangement to insure freedom of trade on the still-unoccupied portions of the West coast of Africa and invite other powers to adhere to it. This would enlarge the proposed Congo conference program. He told Courcel that it should make no difference whether England chose to adhere to the accord or not. He frankly intended to make this entente a combination against England.[113] Courcel reflected Ferry's sentiment when he thought that a working agreement with Germany to further their mutual interests should be forwarded, but he would have much preferred to reach an understanding on Egypt first.[114] Hatzfeldt told him that Germany wanted France to take the initial new step in Egyp-

---

107 *Infra.*, p. 143.　　　　　　　　108 Aydelotte, *op. cit.*, p. 106.
109 *Ibid.*, p. 115. Germany had no intention of founding such a settlement there.
110 *Ibid.*, p. 117.
111 *Ibid.*, p. 118. Walfisch Bay was also taken by Germany on August 23.
112 *Ibid.*, p. 122.　　　　　　　　113 *GP.*, III, 680; *DDF*, V, No. 361.
114 *DDF*, V, No. 372.

tian affairs but that Germany would look with a friendly eye on definite proposals concerning them.[115]

In elaboration on Bismarck's thoughts, Hatzfeldt frankly said that the proposed accord was intended to prevent England from expanding up the entire West coast of Africa from the Cape Colony.[116] Courcel, who continued to be suspicious that the French were being used by Germany to trick England, took this opportunity to warn the German Foreign Secretary that France wanted to maintain friendly relations with Great Britain. Germany, he pointed out, was unable to give France active support in the theaters of conflict with England.[117]

In Paris, Ferry showed his interest in the German overtures but he let Hohenlohe understand that the London Conference had made him wary of German promises.[118] Courcel returned home on August 18 to confer with Ferry, and upon his return to Berlin presented the Premier's reply to Hatzfeldt on August 25.

Ferry's comments showed that he was not entirely pleased with the German proposals to extend the scope of the conference on Africa. The Bismarckian proposal for complete free trade on the Congo meant that Germany would benefit by French and Belgian efforts and give nothing substantial in return. The suggestion to open the whole coast to free trade not only was designed essentially to defend German trade against tariff barriers, but also as a move against England. Moreover, if France signed such an agreement it would have to be ratified by Parliament as a commercial treaty and he could show no compensating gain for France. He maintained that occupying powers should be permitted at least to charge duties to defray the cost of developing public works of commercial value. He expressed his willingness to draw up some general rules on the formalities to be observed to make occupation of African territory valid, as Bismarck, fresh from his brush with England on this problem, suggested. Ferry stood by his earlier agreement to a conference on freedom of navigation on the Congo and Niger and free trade in the Congo estuary. But this was to be arranged in conjunction with England. In fact, England was to be a party to all these arrangements.[119] Thus Ferry substantially modified the anti-British nature of Bismarck's proposals. As a good French statesman, he also took a firm stand against free trade. At the same time, he tried to secure German support for France in the

---

[115] *GP.*, III, 681.

[116] Actually Great Britain did not have the territorial ambitions here which Bismarck attributed to her. This misunderstanding contributed greatly to the cool Anglo-German relations and was not cleared up for several months. Crowe, *op. cit.*, p. 63.

[117] *DDF*, V, No. 372.   [118] *GP.*, III, 684.   [119] *DDF*, V, No. 376.

Egyptian question which preoccupied him.[120] Although Bismarck was unwilling to do anything about Egypt now, in general, he was pleased by the answer.[121]

After Courcel presented Ferry's reply to Hatzfeldt, he went on to visit Bismarck at Varzin where they discussed the situation at length on August 28 and 29. Their conversations were courteous but rather cool.[122] Bismarck recognized that France was reluctant to undertake an anti-English policy for she did not fully trust Germany,[123] but he still was annoyed to find France so slow to move.[124] Although they found little agreement on Egypt,[125] they were able to reach substantial accord on West Africa. The Chancellor satisfied France by stating that he would not support any claims to the Ogowé region put forward by the German explorer, Nachtigal,[126] who was then founding the Togo and Cameroon colonies. Each expressed good will toward the project of Leopold. They agreed to make an arrangement providing for free navigation of the Congo and Niger Rivers similar to the 1856 accord on the Danube. They also would agree on the formalities to be observed to make occupations effective and to invite other governments to adhere to the program after France and Germany had drawn it up.[127]

Courcel asked Bismarck to prevent the German press from claiming that a wide Franco-German entente had been established in order to avoid giving ammunition to Ferry's enemies. Bismarck readily consented, but he made only an evasive reply to Ferry's suggestion that Article Eleven of the Treaty of Frankfort, which gave Germany preferential tariff rights in France, should be modified. However, the Chancellor did again assure France of a free hand against China, although he expressed the hope that the war going on there would soon end.[128]

The first draft of the accord embodying the above points was sent to Paris on September 13. As a mark of special consideration it was written in French by Bismarck.[129] Ferry agreed in principle to the terms on September 19, stipulating as before that free trade in equatorial Africa should not include the colonies of Senegal or Gabun, nor should it prevent the Powers from levying taxes to defray the cost of public works of commercial value. He also objected to Bismarck's reference to the Association as a "state" on the grounds that such recognition was "premature." [130] It was agreed that the conference should be held in Berlin.

Immediately afterwards, a meeting of the Emperors of Germany, Austria and Russia took place at Skierniewice. Courcel expressed some con-

[120] *Ibid.*, No. 377.
[121] Hohenlohe, *op. cit.*, II, 351; *GP.*, III, 687.
[122] *DDF*, V, No. 385.
[123] *GP.*, III, 688.
[124] *DDF*, V, No. 385.
[125] *GP.*, III, 689.
[126] *Ibid.*, 688.
[127] *Ibid.*
[128] *DDF*, V, No. 385.
[129] *Ibid.*, No. 395.
[130] *Ibid.*, No. 402.

cern in Berlin that this might have anti-French implications. Therefore, on September 21, Bismarck paid Courcel a visit to reassure him. The Chancellor told the ambassador that no discussions inimical to France had taken place. Again he expressed at some length his dissatisfaction with England [131] and said that although his son Herbert was about to visit there, he had been instructed not to see Granville even if invited to do so.[132] Bismarck angrily remarked that apparently England wanted to appropriate all the unclaimed parts of the globe.[133] He denied the rumor that he wanted to embroil England and France in a war, asserting that what he did want was to establish an equilibrium with the secondary naval powers against England, a coalition which France should lead. He also wanted England to realize that a Franco-German entente was not impossible.[134] Actually it was the possibility conceived by Bismarck of naval cooperation between the powers with second-rate navies that paralyzed British policy in late 1884.[135]

The final draft of the convention on the Congo problems was agreed upon by France and Germany on October 4 [136] and invitations were dispatched to the Powers.[137] Two days later Herbert Bismarck had an interview with Ferry in Paris. The former had just refused, on his father's order, to see Granville while he was visiting in England. The interview was quite successful since each was pleased by the manner of the other and by the foreshadowed agreements. Ferry still maintained that the Association was not actually a state and that its claims were extravagant.[138] There was little further discussion on West African problems since such substantial agreement had already been reached. They exchanged complaints about the unreasonableness of England [139] and Ferry was pleased at the more cooperative attitude of the elder Bismarck on Egyptian questions.[140]

The Berlin Congo Conference

The entente between Bismarck and Ferry dominated the course of the Berlin Conference on the Congo throughout most of its sessions from November 1884 to February 1885. There were some stormy days when

---

[131] England had not yet given her unconditional recognition to the German protectorate over Angra Pequena declared the previous April. England had offered to grant this recognition only if Germany would promise not to found a penal colony there. Bismarck refused to accede to any limitations, and only on September 22 was unconditional recognition granted.

[132] *DDF*, V, No. 405.   [133] *Ibid.*, No. 407.   [134] *Ibid.*

[135] Langer *op. cit.*, p. 302.   [136] *DDF*, V, No. 417.

[137] Invitations were sent to Great Britain, the Netherlands, Belgium, Spain, Austria-Hungary, Portugal, Italy, the United States, Turkey, Russia, Sweden and Denmark.

[138] Thomson, *op. cit.*, p. 259. This remark does not appear in the published documents on the interview but was seen by Thomson in the Berlin archives.

[139] *GP.*, III, 694.   [140] *DDF*, V, No. 421; *Infra.* p. 146.

the territorial claims of France, the Congo Association and Portugal came into conflict, and when Bismarck tried to enlarge the free trade area open to German merchants. The Chancellor also lent the Association a good deal of help, but in the end he yielded to most of the French demands. On several occasions it looked as though the French possessions were to be seriously whittled down, but through negotiations and pressure, Ferry obtained a safe and economically practicable means of access to the Congo basin from the Atlantic through the Niari-Kouilou valley. He was also able to stave off demands for complete free trade along the whole West African coast. His opposition likewise killed the proposal for an effective international control of the Congo river. Ferry's great disappointment was that he did not secure the complete holdings of the Association by its demise. But considering the multiple tasks with which he was then burdened, he did well to steer his way through the conference in such a manner as to make good the French claims to the lands Brazza had secured and more besides. All this success would have been impossible without the support of Bismarck. The conference was not, however, primarily concerned with French territorial ambitions, for it established a free trade and free navigation area in this newly opened region, provided for the protection of the natives and established rules for occupation formalities. During the period of the conference, Leopold gained European recognition for his Association so that it was soon able to take its place among the nations as a sovereign state.

The nations were represented at the conference by their ambassadors or ministers to Berlin who were aided by certain experts.[141] Courcel's delegation was controlled throughout the conference by Ferry who, from Paris, directed the French course. Bismarck took little formal part in the conference, appearing only for the opening and closing sessions.[142] Behind the scenes he was active. England came to the conference at a moment when she had many embarrassments from West Africa, through Egypt to the Northwestern frontier of India. Bismarck, at the outset, mistakenly believed that British and German interests were in direct conflict in Africa, and in October he refused to discuss the conference with the English ambassador.[143] However, soon after the first session,

141 Courcel's aides were Dr. Ballay, Brazza's colleague; Engelhardt from the Foreign Office and Desbuissons from the geographical section of the Foreign Office. Belgium was represented by Lambermont and Banning; England by Malet. The United States minister was Kasson, aided by Sanford, and the ubiquitous Stanley who had conveniently changed his allegiance again.

142 Hatzfeldt presided at the plenary sessions and Busch, Undersecretary for Foreign Affairs, presided at most section meetings.

143 *DDF, V*, No. 430. Lord Lyons, fearing an understanding between France and Germany, warned Ferry that England could be very disagreeable if her interests were threatened. Newton, *op. cit.*, II, 334.

Bismarck discovered that England did not really oppose his designs. England insisted only that she be left a free hand on the Niger where Germany had no real interest.[144]

Leopold's International Association of the Congo held an anomalous role at the time. A private corporation in law, a state in fact, it was not officially represented at the conference although its delegates were present. Its interests were handled by the Belgian delegates outside their official capacities.[145] However, the Association preoccupied all minds during the discussions. Concurrently it worked hard to gain European recognition as a state. Its great success came with German recognition on November 8 in an arrangement eminently satisfactory to both parties. German merchants were given rights of free trade in the Congo and the Association was materially strengthened by such a recognition especially since its claims to the Congo left bank were acknowledged.[146] Bismarck was satisfied to have so well protected the interests of the German merchants, for he had expected an imminent collapse of the Association and the succession of France to its lands. The terms were designed to protect German nationals in that eventuality.[147]

Thus Ferry's plans were considerably upset because he had so confidently expected that the Association would wither and die.[148] He had tried to disregard it as much as possible, but now that it was recognized by Germany, it could not be taken so lightly.

The Franco-German proposal was presented on November 15 and discussed until Christmas. Ferry had strictly enjoined the French delegation to discuss only the three problems posed in the preliminary accord: freedom of trade in the Congo mouth and basin; freedom of navigation on the Congo and Niger, and definition of the formalities necessary to make new occupations on the African coast effective.[149] No territorial problems were to be discussed in Berlin according to these orders. But avoiding such discussion proved a vain hope.

At the very first meeting of the conference, Ferry found that he had

144 Crowe, *op. cit.*, pp. 74–77. This excellent monograph has the best treatment of the Berlin Conference, being especially valuable in revising the inadequate treatment previously given England's role. Miss Crowe does not do full justice to the French position, however.

145 The position of the Association *vis-à-vis* Belgium was peculiar. Still a private venture of the King of the Belgians, it was not recognized as a state by his country. In fact, it was quite unpopular with the Belgian Parliament, especially with the members of the Left. There was considerable sentiment against sending Belgian delegates to the conference and the delegates only with difficulty won cabinet permission to take an active part in the Berlin discussions. Emile Banning, *Mémoires politiques et diplomatiques* (Paris, 1927), pp. 14-15. The author was a close advisor of Leopold, especially on African affairs which he urged on from his post in the Foreign Office.

146 *Archiven* (1918), p. 75.   147 Thomson, *op. cit.*, p. 181.

148 *DDF*, V, No. 457.   149 *Ibid.*, No. 446.

to face the Congo boundary problem. Bismarck's sweeping suggestions at the opening session advocated not only completely free trade and navigation on both the Congo and Niger, but also came out for a declaration of the neutrality of the Congo basin in time of war and proposed to set very broad boundaries for the conventional Congo basin.[150] These proposals were certainly in violation of the letter and spirit of the preliminary arrangements the Chancellor had made with Ferry. The French Premier stood his ground and refused to accept specific definition of the Congo basin at this point. He wanted it to be in broad and general terms only, to allow for the possibility of stretching the French holdings later. As in the preliminary negotiations, he did not want to give all nations completely free access to the river above its estuary nor extend free trade so far up the African coast that it would include the territory of Gabun.[151]

At this juncture the French Premier met with two disappointments. England firmly declared that she would keep the Niger open for free navigation, but that she would police it herself. This destroyed French hopes of securing the lower course of the river.[152] and restricted France to the possession of that part above the cataracts. At this moment, too, Germany chose to announce the recognition granted the Association earlier in the month.

Bismarck was annoyed when Ferry rejected his proposal to give an International Commission the task of supervising the river and exercising surveillance over its banks.[153] Although it was he who introduced the new proposals, Bismarck was much irritated by the French refusal to set the broadest geographical limits to the Congo, stating that it was better not to have called a conference at all if France took this attitude.[154] He had had ample warning of Ferry's stand, for during the preceding May the Premier had stipulated that he would not permit territorial questions to be discussed at a conference such as this.[155] Ferry was incensed by the proposal of Stanley and the English to define the "commercial delta of the Congo" as extending from the Ogowé to Angola,[156] thus cutting into Gabun and including the Niari-Kouilou route. Dr. Ballay countered with a proposal for limiting free trade to the area included in the natural outlet of the river. Although Bismarck professed astonishment that the French territorial claims should include the Kouilou and Niari valleys, those advanced were the most modest the French had

---

[150] *Ibid.,* No. 453.   [151] *Ibid.,* No. 455.

[152] *Ibid.,* No. 452. English companies had recently bought out the French posts on the Niger. Crowe, *op. cit.,* pp. 124–129.

[153] *DDF,* V, No. 455.   [154] *Ibid.,* No. 452.   [155] *Supra,* p. 97.

[156] *DDF,* V, No. 458; U. S. Senate, *Executive Document 196,* 49th Congress, First Session (1886), No. 37.

considered. The Chancellor chose this moment to talk of the conflicting French and German claims to Petit Popo,[157] which were dropped soon afterwards.

Ferry accepted a trade which Bismarck proposed, using an American suggestion, to settle the problem. In return for German recognition of French claims on the African littoral, France agreed to extend the free trade area from the Congo basin to the Indian Ocean, subject to settlement with the Sultan of Zanzibar and Portugal,[158] a concession which cost very little. Then France and Germany agreed to restrict duties in the Congo basin to export tariffs to pay for commercially useful public works.[159] Ferry yielded to German insistence that free entrance to the Congo basin be allowed for twenty years, after which the question should be reexamined. This proposal was designed to aid German merchants, and Ferry's acceptance of it soothed Bismarck's anger at earlier Gallic resistance.[160] The Commercial Convention was thus settled on December 1. Commercial equality in the Congo basin was given to all nations; no discriminatory tariffs could be imposed; no entry or transit dues charged; no monopolies or commercial privileges granted.[161] Three weeks later the protocol was signed providing for freedom of navigation for ships of all nations along the Congo coast, on the river, its tributaries and the Niger.[162] Navigation on the Congo was to be supervised by an International Commission whose powers were exceedingly weak. The Belgians had supported the plan for a commission when they were afraid that they would lose control of the river mouths.[163] However, the objections of Jules Ferry were responsible for the fact that the Commission was not sovereign like that of the Danube.[164] Despite the fact that he had suggested such a commission early in the negotiations, the French leader had no intention of weakening French sovereignty in the cause of international cooperation.

There was no disagreement over a protocol providing for protection of the natives and all religious, charitable and scientific enterprises and institutions in the basin. Freedom of religion, including Mohammedanism, was granted as well.[165]

Although all these problems were worked out satisfactorily early in December, a noticeable chill in Franco-German relations continued. Both Courcel and Bismarck had complained to their respective associates that their relations had perceptibly cooled in October when Courcel returned from Paris. Bismarck blamed the situation on what he thought was Courcel's discovery that he had exceeded his Government's

[157] DDF, V, No. 460.   [158] Ibid., No. 461.   [159] Ibid., No. 467.
[160] Ibid.   [161] L. J. C., 1885, Protocol No. 4.   [162] Ibid., Protocol No. 6.
[163] Banning, op. cit., p. 28; Crowe, op. cit., pp. 110–117.
[164] DDF, V, No. 455.   [165] L. J. C., 1885, Protocol No. 5.

desires in going so far with a rapprochement on West Africa.[166] Courcel blamed the Chancellor's coolness on the hostile attitude of the French press to the rumored entente with Germany and on the intrigues of England and Belgium.[167] The real point of discord, however, was the Egyptian question. If the entente with France were to grow, Germany would have to give more help to France in this matter.

Relations between the two countries were on the mend when Bismarck and Courcel had another interview on November 27. Significantly, this took place shortly after Germany had received from England new proposals on Egypt with which she had been dissatisfied. The Chancellor asserted that he was delighted with the recent protocols on free trade and navigation in the Congo. Bismarck then expounded the advantages of a closer entente between France and Germany. He told Courcel that he wanted France "to forgive Sedan as you forgave Waterloo." [168]

Courcel did not respond to this enthusiastic picture of the future, suspecting that Bismarck was trying to embroil France and England in a quarrel. Moreover, that French patriot did not believe that Waterloo should be pardoned, much less Sedan. Courcel had always made it clear, and he now repeated, that the question of Alsace and Lorraine should never be discussed—it was a *noli me tangere*.[169] No forgiveness for the lost provinces could be expected, for no French statesman could abandon them, no German could relinquish them. Both Ferry and Bismarck recognized the limits of their entente. Although Bismarck now would have liked to widen its scope, Ferry was determined to keep it limited and specific.

Despite this German overture, some friction between the two powers remained. A constant irritant for the congress was the problem of recognition of the Association and its territorial claims. These questions were outside the congress' agenda but had to be settled in order to make its decisions workable. France felt that Germany supported the Association in its territorial claims and, as a matter of fact, Germany usually did for the sake of obtaining as much free trade area as possible. In Paris, hostility in the press to making any concessions to the Association endangered the whole entente.[170]

A new apple of discord was thrown into the congress by an American proposal that the Association build a railroad from the Pool to the Lower Congo. This was a Belgian plan which they had succeeded in getting Sanford to introduce for them.[171] Bismarck and England gave the scheme their support.[172] But the territory over which this railroad

---

[166] *GP.*, III, 697. [167] *DDF*, V, No. 467. [168] *Ibid.*, No. 475.
[169] *Ibid.* [170] *Ibid.*, No. 477.
[171] Banning, *op. cit.*, p. 25; *Senate Executive Document 196*, No. 52.
[172] *DDF*, V, No. 483.

would run was still in dispute: France, the Association and Portugal all hoped to secure it. France and Portugal, therefore, proposed that the powers build the road in common. This unworkable plan succeeded in stalling the American suggestion until Sanford later withdrew it.

Ferry was indignant at the American delegation's other proposal, supported by Bismarck and England, that all territories where free trade was established should be declared neutral in wartime.[173] He flatly refused to entertain this plan which was presented as a corollary of free trade, for he thought it infringed dangerously on French sovereignty. In any case, the proposal was outside the scope of the preliminary accord.[174] On Ferry's orders, Courcel was adamant in his opposition, pointing out that in case of war, France would be compelled to renounce the assistance of an important colony which she had won and organized with great labor. There were a number of stormy sessions between Courcel and the Germans over this proposal. Bismarck was bluntly told that the idea was unreasonable and was rebuked for backing the railroad plan and the neutrality proposal in violation of the agreement preliminary to the conference. The Chancellor expressed discouragement about the entente. Courcel feared that this incident would provide Germany with an excuse for breaking with France at the conference, but he held to his position.[175] Ferry, meanwhile, cautiously observed that the differences between France and Germany were only "secondary" and produced entirely by Germany's attempt to stretch the terms of the initial accord.

Hatzfeldt complained to Courcel of France's "backwardness" in opening the Congo for free trade and commercial development.[176] But Courcel talked with Bismarck on December 13, and the latter yielded, somewhat grudgingly, on all points, dropping the railroad proposal and his insistence on the neutrality of the Congo. He maintained that he did this to avoid a breakdown of the conference.[177] But a more important reason for Bismarck's yielding was his annoyance at England's tactless proposal that a new Egyptian settlement be made in Paris with Hohenlohe acting merely as an observer, thereby rejecting Germany's proposal to add Russian and German members to the Debt Commission.[178]

On December 27, Courcel was able to report that relations with Germany were improving, but he observed that friendship with her was "tempestuous" and quite dependent on Germany's convenience. The German rapprochement, he felt, was due to her desire to make France forget Alsace and win her away from England. Despite his fears, Courcel

[173] *Ibid.*; Crowe, *op. cit.*, pp. 135–137; *Senate Executive Document 196*, No. 46.
[174] *DDF*, V, No. 482.   [175] *Ibid.*, No. 500.   [176] *Ibid.*, No. 482.
[177] *Ibid.*, No. 486.   [178] *Ibid.*, No. 500.

maintained that France must cultivate German friendship since his country had moved away from England over the Egyptian question.[179]

By Christmas, the conference was deadlocked awaiting a territorial settlement in the Congo basin. Ferry had postponed this matter as long as possible because he expected an early death for the financially embarrassed Association. He had even entertained the illusory hope that the Berlin congress could be concluded with the territorial claims still pending. He found this impossible after the Association had received recognition by numerous countries. Each recognition included a statement of the Association's territorial claims which were in conflict with France's.[180]

There had been some negotiations on territorial questions between the Association and France before the conference opened. Following the April exchange of letters in which each party agreed to respect the other's territory, there had been an effort to delimit those areas. Trouble arose at once when France claimed the left bank of the Congo where the Association had four stations besides Leopoldville.[181] Then France offered to renounce the left bank in return for the Niari-Kouilou valley which was vital for her access to Brazzaville and the French Congo.[182] The difficulty was that the Association was in possession of the rivers by virtue of its several stations there. France had only some claims to Loango on the coast near the river mouth. Therefore, her only hope was to make good her hold on the left bank of the Congo.

On the early negotiations, we have only the Association's version as presented to the German Foreign Office. The published French documents are silent on the preliminaries of arbitration that the Association asserts took place. According to the Association's version, it proposed that the conflict over the left bank be settled by arbitration, and Ferry accepted this idea. He was said to have stipulated that the differences must be settled in Europe. Accordingly, Colonel Strauch went to Paris early in November to arrange the details. He talked with Billot and Dr. Ballay. The negotiations were allegedly proceeding on the principle that all necessary information should be furnished the arbitration tribunal, when they were interrupted by the opening of the Berlin Conference. When the Association sought to reopen them, it found that France's attitude had changed. The latter now maintained that the

---

179 *Ibid.*
180 By the end of December, the Association had added to its recognition by the United States and Germany, that by Great Britain, Italy, Austria-Hungary, and the Netherlands.
181 *DDF*, V, No. 475.
182 Thomson, *op. cit.*, p. 247.

sessions of the tribunal should take place in Africa.[183] It seems not unlikely that the French had concluded that an arbitration in Europe would have gone against them after awhile. At any rate, the Association believed that the transfer to Africa was preliminary to a complete rejection of the arbitration.[184]

Early in December, England and Germany forwarded an Association proposal to Portugal giving the latter the left Congo bank only as far as the port of Kissanga in Angola and leaving the major part of the left bank of the Lower Congo for the Association.[185] It was presented to Portugal as an ultimatum by Malet who warned that this was Portugal's last chance. Bismarck was not party to the threat and did not care for it.[186] Portugal refused the settlement and drew closer to France,[187] encouraged by Ferry's assurance to the Portuguese Minister that he did not intend to recognize the Association at that time.[188] Lambermont and Malet believed that some sort of understanding existed between France and Portugal [189] but their belief is not confirmed in the French documents, nor in the subsequent action of Ferry. Bismarck did not think that such an entente existed and was reassured on that score by Courcel on December 17. The Chancellor soon after lessened his support of the Association partly because of the French protests and his concern that the entente vanish, and partly because the French now would agree to a tripartite division of the Congo region.[190]

There was some discussion of territorial claims between France and the Association in Berlin, outside of the conference in December, but no progress was made.[191] Finally, an interview in Paris was arranged for the last day of the year, between Eudore Pirmez and Banning, for the Association, and Ferry and Billot, the Director of Political Affairs in the Foreign Office. Ferry was not over-anxious to come to terms, for he thought even yet that the Association would go bankrupt and France might become its heir.[192] Ferry had grounds for his hope, as the King of the Belgians actually was hard pressed and greatly concerned over his finances, since most of his capital was already sunk in the Congo venture.[193]

The French Premier still tried to maintain that the Association did

---

[183] This account of the arbitration proposals is drawn from Thomson, *op. cit.*, pp. 246–247. He bases his findings on archival material in Berlin, consisting of the Association's account of the matter to the German Foreign Office.

[184] *Ibid.*, p. 247.   [185] Banning, *op. cit.*, p. 38.

[186] Thomson, *op. cit.*, p. 256; although both England and Germany were supporting the Association, Bismarck's aid was tempered by his desire to preserve his entente with France. Crowe, *op. cit.*, pp. 155–156.

[187] *DDF*, V, No. 480.   [188] *Ibid.*, No. 485.   [189] Thomson, *op. cit.*, p. 257.
[190] *DDF*, V, No. 483; Crowe, *op. cit.*, p. 163.   [191] *DDF*, V, No. 475.
[192] *Ibid.*, No. 494.   [193] Banning, *op. cit.*, p. xvii.

not have the right to acquire sovereignty.[194] After the number of recognitions accorded it, this argument could have little value save a psychological one. Ferry began by demanding for France the left bank of the Pool, the Niari-Kouilou valley and access to the Congo estuary at Vivi. In return, he offered the Association recognition as a sovereign power and promised assistance to her in negotiations with Portugal.[195] He declined to accept Pirmez' memorandum containing the Association's refutation of the French claims to the left bank of the Pool.[196] When the Belgians offered to cede the Niari-Kouilou valley for an indemnity of five million francs, Ferry refused on the ground he had no way of securing such a sum of money.[197]

A second interview on January 2 produced better results. Ferry made a considerable concession in accepting a frontier whereby France held the right bank above Manyanga, well above the falls, instead of Vivi. It was agreed that the boundary line then should run up the center of the river and the Pool. France should receive the Niari-Kouilou route, Ferry agreeing to purchase the stations there for 300,000 francs, which he said he could raise without asking Parliament for an appropriation.[198] The Association representatives suggested that they be allowed to conduct a lottery in France as part compensation and Ferry immediately assented. The Association was to be recognized, and Ferry again suggested that France could take the Association's part in the negotiations with Portugal. The discussions were then adjourned as the Belgians had to confer with Leopold who quickly agreed to the proposals.[199] Still unsettled were the boundaries in the interior, the neutrality of the Association's holdings and the Portuguese claims. The French agreement with the Association was to wait for the negotiation of an Association-Portuguese agreement. But Ferry believed that the Congo problem was about to be solved,[200] and the Belgians were also confident.[201] Nevertheless, as late as January 6, after the arrangements were made, Billot still expressed to the American Minister his expectation that the Association would soon collapse.[202]

Ferry had an interview with Carlos du Bocage, the Portuguese military attaché in Berlin, who was sent to negotiate in Paris, on the same day that the tentative agreement was made with the Association. Du Bocage went away with the impression that Ferry was taking Portugal's side—just as the Association thought Ferry was supporting it.[203] Ferry

---

[194] *Ibid.*, pp. 6–7. Banning is the best source for these conversations. Unfortunately, the published French documents have practically nothing on this incident.

[195] *Ibid.*, p. 40.   [196] *Ibid.*   [197] *Ibid.*

[198] *Ibid.*, p. 41.   [199] *Ibid.*, p. 42.   [200] *DDF*, V, No. 508.

[201] Banning, *op. cit.*, p. 42.   [202] SDA, *France, Dispatches*, vol. 96, No. 698.

[203] Portugal. Ministero dos Negocios Estrangeiros, *Documentos Apresentados As Cortes. Questão do Zaire* (Lisbon, 1885), No. 79.

was undoubtedly encouraging both sides in his attempt to enlarge French holdings, but in early January he was more favorable to the Association, whatever the Portuguese may have been led to believe.

Portugal remained as recalcitrant as ever, stubbornly clinging to claims that the Powers could only consider as pretentious, since she was not occupying the area she claimed. Portugal insisted on having Cabinda and Molemba on the coast north of the Congo, Boma on the right bank of the estuary and Noki on the left.[204] The Association insisted on having all the right, nearly all the left bank and the privilege of constructing a railroad on the left bank.[205] While this bickering continued, the Berlin Conference was at a standstill and Bismarck grew more and more annoyed even threatening to lock the delegates in a room until they reached a solution.[206]

Ferry was not much help to the Association in its negotiations with Portugal at this time. On January 6 he professed ignorance to the latter country of the Association's full claims,[207] not imparting the information until January 9. He shortly after refused Pirmez' request to transmit the Association's demands to Portugal.[208] The Belgians felt bitterly that they were deserted by Ferry,[209] and negotiations were temporarily broken off.

Portugal proved as unsatisfactory and as recalcitrant as ever despite Ferry's offers. He hinted to the Iberian kingdom that she should win herself some friends by liberalizing her tariffs as Bismarck had suggested to Courcel.[210] Portugal refused. Ferry then tried offering Portugal some minor boundary adjustments and threatened her with joint action of the Powers, but still he made no headway.[211] Therefore, he took up the interrupted negotiations with the Association again, for it had yielded on those points in which he was especially interested.[212]

Ferry attempted to enlist the support of Bismarck against Portugal. The Franco-German entente on the question of Egypt was moving along smoothly at the time, and on January 28, Bismarck told Courcel that he would like to arrange a personal meeting with Ferry.[213] Among the documents now available, we have no answer to this suggestion. However, Ferry did try to take advantage of his friendliness by asking Bismarck to join France in putting pressure on Portugal. Bismarck, however, refused.[214] Courcel meanwhile admitted that Ferry's efforts to move Portugal were a failure.[215] Ferry himself advised Pirmez to shift the negotiations to Berlin where Germany and England might be able to aid France against the Portuguese.[216]

204 *Ibid.*, No. 82.   205 *DDF*, V, No. 517.   206 *Ibid.*, No. 520.
207 *Zaire*, No. 82.   208 *Ibid.*, No. 85.   209 Banning, *op. cit.*, pp. 57–58.
210 *DDF*, V, No. 520.   211 *Zaire*, Nos. 80, 88.   212 Thomson, *op. cit.*, p. 269.
213 *DDF*, V, No. 530.   214 *Ibid.*, No. 545.   215 Thomson, *op. cit.*, p. 272.
216 Banning, *op. cit.*, p. 57.

In this situation the French decided to proceed with signing an agreement with the Association without waiting for an agreement with Portugal. Courcel in Berlin was suddenly worried lest the current impasse should cause the Association to collapse and reopen the scramble for the Congo. He had decided it would be better to support a weak claimant like Leopold than to have some major European power involved there.[217] Apparently he was no longer sure that France would inherit the Association's holdings without trouble. Moreover, rumors of Portuguese occupation of both banks of the Congo now caused uneasiness in both France and Germany.[218]

These considerations precipitated action and a treaty between France and the Association was signed on February 5 in Paris by Ferry and Borchgrave. This gave France the Niari-Kouilou route, recognized the Association as a state, set her boundaries with the French Congo, and promised that the Association's neutrality would be respected under a detailed arrangement to be drawn in Berlin.[219] At the same time there were a number of other agreements made. One was a convention to set up a commission to decide what France should pay for the ceded stations of the Association;[220] another was a letter binding France to authorize a twenty million franc lottery; a third pledged France to continue to support the Association's case before Portugal; and a fourth, renewed the option which France held on the Association's territory. This arrangement represented a real diplomatic victory for Ferry since he had acquired the essential route between the Pool and the Ocean for France in the Niari-Kouilou valley.

The Powers were increasingly worried over reports that Portugal was moving to occupy the Congo right bank. When Ferry demanded of the Portuguese chargé whether these reports were true,[221] Portugal denied them,[222] but this did not satisfy all those interested. Bismarck was concerned lest a naval clash be precipitated and destroy the results of his long-drawn-out conference.[223] Accordingly, when the Association showed itself conciliatory and Portugal remained adamant, the Powers took Leopold's side.

On February 6, Courcel, on behalf of the Powers, assured Portugal that it could have Malimba and Cabinda, but he said that this was the last concession that would be made; hereafter the major Powers would support the rest of the Association's demands.[224] Portugal asked that this be put in writing for the Cabinet wanted to make its position clear

217 *DDF*, V, No. 554.
219 Text in *L. J. C., 1885*, pp. 319–321.
221 *Zaire*, No. 89.
223 Banning, *op. cit.*, p. 60.

218 *Ibid.*, No. 557.
220 *Ibid.*, pp. 321–322.
222 *Ibid.*, No. 90.
224 *Zaire*, No. 92.

to the Cortes. The request was granted on February 7.[225] Then, Portugal, still talking of the Association as a purely private venture, asked Courcel to mediate between the Association and herself. He accepted the mission on the 9th.[226] But at once Portugal returned to her old claim to the whole Congo mouth, insisting especially on Banana.[227] This deliberate attempt to force the Powers to exert pressure on Portugal to excuse the Cabinet before the Cortes [228] succeeded, for on February 13 France, Germany and England sent Portugal identical notes rejecting the Portuguese claims to Banana and urging immediate acceptance of the Association's latest offer.[229] The Portuguese yielded on February 15 and on that day a treaty was signed between Portugal and the Association in the French embassy. This gave Portugal Cabinda and Malimba North of the Congo and the left bank up to Noki. The Association kept Banana, Boma and twenty kilometers of the Atlantic coast North of the river. The Association's neutrality was recognized; Portugal received most favored-nation status.[230] Actually, Portugal received very generous terms, for she obtained territories she had not occupied before the division of the Congo began.

Jules Ferry had not covered himself with glory in this mediation attempt. He had not backed it forcefully. Playing a lone hand, he could show little but a prolongation of the conference for his efforts.

While these negotiations continued after Christmas, the conference was moribund, with only four sittings of the plenary body from January 5 to February 23. The problems remaining to be solved were the rules for future effective occupation, an agreement on neutrality of the Congo, and the general form of the treaty. During the remaining debates, Courcel dominated the proceedings, Bismarck having allowed him a free hand.[231]

On January 7, the Powers readily agreed to end the slave trade and slavery in the Congo. There was no opposition to this English proposal, but neither were there any penalties provided, so that in later years Leopold was able to drive his subjects to forced labor.

The procedure to be followed to make new occupations effective was adopted on January 31. The new rules were to apply only to African coastal regions then unoccupied. Hereafter, notification must be given the Powers when new lands were taken, and sufficient jurisdiction must be established to insure peace to make effective the rights acquired. The rules were to apply only to annexations.[232] The procedure was originally intended by France and Germany to check English preten-

[225] *Ibid., Annexe* D., p. 119.
[226] *L. J. C.*, *1885*, pp. 333–335.
[227] *Zaire*, No. 93.
[228] Thomson, *op. cit.*, p. 278; Crowe, *op. cit.*, p. 173.
[229] *DDF*, V, No. 591.
[230] Text in *L. J. C.*, *1885*, pp. 327–331.
[231] Banning, *op. cit.*, p. 43.
[232] *L. J. C.*, *1885*, Protocol No. 8.

sions. Bismarck had advanced this proposal in the heat of the Angra Pequena dispute. Ferry had always been cool to it. But it was Great Britain who voiced strong objections and Bismarck yielded, perceiving no great conflicts with England. Thus the new procedure did not mark a change: there was no definition of the nature of effective authority; no time limit for notification and, above all, few important coastal points remained to be occupied because nearly all the rivers and good harbors of Africa had already been appropriated.

Although Bismarck no longer supported the demand that the Congo states be neutral in wartime, the proposition was still before the congress. Neither France nor Portugal favored the neutrality, wanted only by Leopold who thought that it would provide a good parallel with the Belgian position in Europe.[233] A compromise text provided that the colonies or states in the Congo basin could declare themselves neutral and that such declaration would be respected by the Powers. If, however, those powers owning Congo colonies here were at war elsewhere, they could claim the good offices of other powers to make the Congo holdings neutral by common assent.[234] This protocol was adopted on February 23, but, again, there was no instrumentation provided.

The whole act of the congress was signed on February 26, 1885. The Association, finally having been recognized by Belgium on February 23, signed the act.[235] The measure was ratified by the French Chamber on August 3, 1885, after Ferry's fall, by a vote of 251–96. It was criticized by the Extreme Left, but there was no serious opposition to it.[236] The plurality was a good one for the weak incumbent Ministry. The convention between France and the Association was ratified on the same day by a voice vote.[237]

France's colony of Equatorial Africa, created first from the French share of the Congo basin and the Gabun hinterland, is the one colony that Jules Ferry built himself almost from the beginning. It was also the first overseas area in which he showed an interest in extending the French Empire while still Minister of Education. He was early attracted by the plans of Savorgnan de Brazza which he furthered with subsidies. In these vast, unexplored regions he saw an opportunity for gaining great prestige for France and some future commercial advantage for the tropical products of the land.

During his second Premiership, he not only arranged for organizing the territory but, with considerable skill, staved off the attempts of Eng-

---

[233] Banning, *op. cit.*, p. 46.   [234] *L. J. C., 1885,* Protocol No. 11.
[235] The Association became the Congo Free State on the following August 1.
[236] *J. O. C.,* 8/4/85.
[237] On the same day the Chamber voted 624,750 frs. to organize the French establishment at Obock.

land, Portugal, Germany and the Association to curtail the new French holdings. He was aided by the fortunate circumstance of Anglo-German friction in destroying the Anglo-Portuguese plan for control. He secured an option on the Association's territory although his hopes for being able to make use of it were dashed. He negotiated and maintained a working agreement with Germany which was rather difficult to do, both with regard to Germany and his opposition at home. He steered a firm course through the potential dangers of the Berlin Conference, securing most of the points he desired. One of his most important achievements was securing the Niari-Kouilou valley for France which had nearly been lost by the early action of the Association. That route was absolutely essential for French exploitation of the new holdings. He could not secure a hold on the lower Niger, but he did succeed in limiting the conventional Congo basin and free trade in the area. In all these situations he was much aided by the fairly steady support of Bismarck. Without it he would have been unable to secure nearly as much as he did. In this eminently peaceful venture, in the days when Darkest Africa fired all imaginations, he had complete support at home which he could evoke by appealing to patriotism and the duty to civilize inferior races. Considering the manifold complexities of the Congo problem and the numerous others with which he had to cope concurrently, his action here was very ably conducted.

Chapter Five

MADAGASCAR AND THE AMBITIONS OF FRENCH COLONIALS

At the outset of his second Premiership, Ferry was persuaded to attempt the seizure of the huge island of Madagascar. Misled by the advice of the deputies from Réunion, pushed on by French officials in the Indian Ocean area, he gave strong support to a punitive expedition that was just setting out for Madagascar when he assumed office. For two years he waged war on the Queen of that island, his expedition dragging out to a dismal failure, as French resources were overtaxed in Indo-China and in West and Equatorial Africa.

France had some old, vague claims to Madagascar that had nearly lapsed by Ferry's time. On the route to India, near which lay the once-prosperous sugar and coffee colony of Réunion, it was temporarily held by the French in the seventeenth century and again assailed by them during the July Monarchy.[1] By pushing their rivals off the central highlands, the most valuable part of Madagascar, the Hovas had become the dominant tribe in the nineteenth century. However, except in the very center of the island their control was incomplete, the organization of their government rather crude. But in 1862 and 1868 Napoleon III signed treaties with the Polynesian tribe, abandoning French claims to Madagascar, thus healing a break of long standing between the island and France.

Advances against Madagascar stemmed from the several French possessions in the Indian Ocean. Here the most important French colony was Réunion, formerly known as Bourbon. As a sugar island it had been a valuable asset to the *ancien régime,* but was of rather slight importance in the nineteenth century. It was represented in Parliament by two deputies and one senator. The other French holdings in the area were in the Comores archipelago in the Mozambique Channel between Africa and Madagascar. There, on the small islands of Mayotte, Nossi-Mitsiou, and Nossi-Bé, the French had staked out a claim in 1843. Only Nossi-Bé was inhabited by Frenchmen and had a French governor.[2] Although

[1] Attempts of Cardinal Richelieu and Colbert to colonize the island had been in the end unsuccessful. Similarly, an expedition of 1845 had failed.
[2] Hanotaux *et* Martineau, *op. cit.,* VI, 286–287.

trade with these islands was insignificant, they proved useful as bases for operations against Madagascar.[3]

During Ferry's regime, action against Madagascar was founded on French claims to its Northwest coast where, in 1842, a series of treaties had been signed with the Sakalave chieftains, setting their territories under French protectorate. But no occupation of the area followed, and other European powers considered these arrangements to have lapsed.[4] Nevertheless, one Sakalave chieftain did continue to collect a modest pension from the French governor on the neighboring island of Nossi-Bé.[5] That the French thought little of their earlier claims is indicated by the fact that Napoleon's treaties, recognizing the Hovas as rulers of the entire island failed altogether to mention the 1842 protectorates.[6]

Merchants from Réunion handled the small flow of French trade with Madagascar.[7] There were no railroads on the island and commerce with the natives was of the simplest kind. The few French property owners there found themselves in a constantly precarious position because of the various anti-foreign and specifically anti-French movements that swept the kingdom after the middle of the century.[8] Nevertheless, it was they who managed to preserve a modicum of French influence in Madagascar.

As a matter of fact, the Jesuit missionaries from France were primarily responsible for keeping this influence alive. They had been especially active after 1861, had made converts variously estimated at from 60,000 to 80,000 and had held rather extensive properties.[9] But the establishments of the London Missionary Society held a decided advantage over the Jesuits; they had been entrenched in Madagascar for a longer time, were more powerful, claimed more converts and could boast a closer tie with the court.[10] Although Christianity had recently been declared the official state religion, in this case it meant English Methodism. The consequent rivalry was in large part responsible for the persistently

---

[3] France also claimed the little island of Sainte Marie, close to the Eastern Madagascan coast, but here there were no French inhabitants.

[4] SDA, *Consular Letters, Madagascar*, No. 101.

[5] *Livre Jaune, Madagascar, 1881–1883*, No. 1.   [6] *DDF*, III, No. 362.

[7] Louis Vignon, *Les colonies françaises* (Paris, 1884), p. 31.

[8] Chief among these was Jean Laborde who was shipwrecked on Madagascar in 1847, who won the good graces of the Queen, constructed modern roads, buildings and factories including iron works, ceramic plants and textile plants run by slave labor. He was involved in palace plots and had a stormy career, having once to flee penniless, but returning and being later appointed French Consul in 1868, which post he held for ten years until his death. He had a few French adventurers as his aides. Hanotaux *et* Martineau, *op. cit.*, VI, 148–154.

[9] *Ibid.*, p. 157; SDA, *Madagascar*, No. 84.

[10] Chase S. Osborn, *Madagascar* (New York, 1924), p. 57.

anti-French policy pursued by the ruling Queen that so annoyed the merchants of Réunion.

Ambitions of Réunion

What really caused France to become involved in Madagascar in the 1880's were the demands and ambitions of the Réunion colonists. The Creoles and the officials, including the Governor, tried to pick a quarrel with the Madagascan government from 1879 on.[11] They were seeking trading privileges and advantages that they supposed would flow to them after annexation. The unfriendly attitude of the Hovas infuriated them. The French paper at Tamatave,[12] edited by a Creole, constantly denounced the native government's deliberate disregard of French interests.[13] The Réunion newspapers constantly urged France to seize Madagascar and were seconded in their demand by the Jesuits on the larger island.[14] The colonists, too, exerted a good deal of pressure on French officials in that part of the world. They found the governor of Nossi-Bé sympathetic,[15] and the French Consul, Casas, was reported to Paris by the commandant of the Indian Ocean Squadron as a mere tool of the Réunion colonists.[16] Paris felt no interest in these grievances and tried to discourage them.[17]

Réunion's representatives in the Chamber of Deputies actively pressed their island's claims on the central government. François de Mahy, the more outspoken among them, quite important in Republican circles and several times a minister, has been justly named the man responsible for France's ultimate possession of Madagascar.[18] He zealously repeated in Paris the arguments advanced in Réunion for the annexation of its big neighbor. According to his account it was a rich, easy prize and he completely misled Ferry and his ministers as to the difficulties that might face them in the arena.

If the basic reason for France's involvement in Madagascar was the influence of Réunion's ambitions, several specific incidents offered an immediate excuse to act against the Hovas. When the heirs of the late French Consul, Laborde, wanted to sell lands to a mission in 1879, they found the sale disallowed by the native government.[19] The French were then confronted with a new law that forbade ownership of property in Madagascar by foreigners.[20] But this right had been guaranteed under the treaty of 1868. The French Consul, Casas, importuned his

[11] SDA, *Madagascar*, Nos. 98, 104; *DDF*, III, No. 64.
[12] Then chief port of Madagascar.
[13] SDA, *Madagascar*, No. 104.
[14] *Ibid.*, No. 156.
[15] *Ibid.*, Nos. 104, 105.
[16] *DDF*, III, No. 217, note.
[17] *Ibid.*
[18] Hanotaux *et* Martineau, *op. cit.*, IV, 156.
[19] *DDF*, III, No. 64.
[20] *L. J. M., 1881–1883*, No. 2.

government for a demonstration against the law [21] but was ordered in July, 1880 to avoid complications. Almost immediately afterwards he was removed by Freycinet.[22]

During his first term in office Ferry apparently did not concern himself at all with the Madagascan problem. It was not until the Spring of 1881 that he became interested in expansion and then he had quite enough to handle with Tunisia and such mild support as he gave French expansion in Oceania.

Affairs in Madagascar continued on their previous course with the new French Consul, Baudais, taking every opportunity to assert French rights.[23] Gambetta expressed his uneasiness about English ambitions [24] in Madagascar, but was in office too short a time to do anything about the problem. This consideration does not seem to have influenced the Duclerc Government in carrying out the rupture of relations with the Hovas kingdom that soon followed, although in Madagascar it was an important factor in determining the officials on the scene to act.[25]

The aggressive French Consul found an opportunity to start action against Madagascar over the unimportant claims to the Northwestern part of the island. In the late Spring of 1882 a mission of Hovas officials, together with some English missionaries, went there and, after visiting with the chieftains of the region, raised the Hovas flag.[26] The American Consul, Robinson, claimed responsibility for this Hovas attempt to reassert sovereignty over the Northwest part of the coast, inhabited by the French-protected Sakalave tribes. In connection with a new trade treaty between the United States and Madagascar, he had insisted that Hovas police power must be made effective over the whole island in order to guarantee security to American traders. For this purpose, he maintained, the mission had gone to the lands of the Sakalave tribes whom they had never thoroughly controlled.[27]

Baudais at once protested against such an infringement on the French protectorates and asked his government forcibly to intervene since the Hovas were intransigent.[28] The Madagascan government denied the French claims to the coast, citing the 1868 treaty which recognized their king as sovereign over the whole island, as well as the indemnity they paid for the 1882 incident on the Sakalave coast.[29] The natives

[21] *Ibid.*, No. 3.   [22] *DDF*, III, No. 217.

[23] The Hovas government was compelled early in 1882 to pay an indemnity for the death of some French Arabs in a fracas on the Sakalave coast. SDA, *Madagascar*, No. 164.

[24] *DDF*, IV, Nos. 230, 269.   [25] Hanotaux *et* Martineau, *op. cit.*, VI, 155.

[26] G. Grandidier, *Le Myre de Vilers, Duchêne, Galliéni* (Paris, 1924), p. 2.

[27] SDA, *Madagascar*, No. 101.   [28] *DDF*, IV, No. 362.

[29] *Ibid.*

were encouraged in their firm attitude by the American Consul and the English and Norwegian missionaries.[30]

Freycinet authorized Baudais to protest against the Hovas action,[31] which he did so energetically that he stirred up a violent anti-French demonstration. Early in May he judged it best to leave the capital, Tananarive, and retire to Tamatave on the East coast.[32] He received little encouragement from the new Duclerc Cabinet that came into office in July, 1882. The Premier informed his Consul that he was anxious to avoid all complications in Madagascar.[33]

The Hovas government dispatched a mission to Paris to discuss the whole problem of Franco-Madagascan relations, including property rights and protectorates.[34] This did not deter the French admiral in command of the Indian Ocean Squadron, working in collaboration with Baudais, from removing the Hovas flags where they had been planted on the Northwest coast.[35] The mission from Madagascar arrived in Paris in November 1882, adamant in upholding all Madagascan claims, as Baudais reported they would be.[36]

The three French negotiators were all adherents of a greater France overseas policy. They were Billot, at that time Director of Political and Commercial Claims of the Ministry of Foreign Affairs, later the staunch supporter of an aggressive policy in Indo-China against Annam and China; [37] Decrais, Director of Political Affairs at the same office, who had drawn the first two proposed treaties of protectorate for Tunis; and Vice-Admiral Peyron, chief of staff of the Ministry of the Navy.[38] As Minister of the Navy under Ferry later, Peyron was very active in support of colonial expansion in Indo-China.

The French delegates insisted on the recognition of their control over the Northwest coast and on the right of foreigners to own real estate in Madagascar. It soon developed that the Hovas did not want to discuss these matters.[39] Their greatest concessions were to allow foreigners to hold twenty-five year leases on property, leases that could be renewed only three times. They refused to consider any concessions on the Northwest coast. The Hovas envoys departed from Paris with precipitate haste, insisting that they had been insulted by Duclerc.[40] The French maintained that they had been fair and reasonable and that

[30] *Ibid.*, V, No. 243.

[31] *L. J. M., 1881–1883*, Nos. 6, 8.

[32] *Ibid.*, No. 12.

[33] *DDF*, IV, No. 506.

[34] *L. J. M., 1881–1883*, No. 17.

[35] *Ibid.*, No. 21.

[36] *Ibid.*, No. 25.

[37] *Infra*, pp. 163, 174.

[38] *DDF*, IV, No. 577.

[39] *L. J. M., 1881–1883*, No. 27.

[40] SDA, *Dispatches, France*, Vol. 91, No. 254. This is a dispatch of December 2, from Robinson who, on his way home, was in Paris at the same time as the Hovas. At their urgent entreaty he accompanied them in their hasty departure.

the Hovas had reneged after promising to give ninety-nine year leases to French subjects.[41]

The Madagascans went to London, and within a week England, whose cabinet was being harassed about Madagascar by some of the clergy and Bible societies,[42] offered her good offices to settle the dispute, but was at once turned down by France.[43] A commercial treaty giving Englishmen the right to hold ninety-nine year leases was concluded on January 17 by the delegates.[44] However, the latter were advised to make peace with France by the English government, which would not press their case.[45] Nor did they receive too warm a reception upon reaching Berlin. Hatzfeldt refused to help their Queen against the French. Bismarck demonstrated his coolness by requiring the delegation to pay its own living expenses while in Berlin,[46] although the Hovas did succeed in getting a commercial treaty with Germany. But while they were visiting in Berlin in April 1883, France had already undertaken action against their island.

Plans for military steps in Madagascar were drawn up by Duclerc immediately after the Hovas delegation left Paris in December.[47] He set forth as his chief reason for active measures, the Hovas encroachments on the French protectorates. The French demands for property rights were not mentioned. It is clear that Duclerc was motivated partly by anger against the behavior of the Madagascan delegation and partly by a desire to restore what he considered wounded French prestige. He was, of course, following the line pressed on him by the Réunion colonists anxious for their trading and property rights.

An expedition of a few hundred men was placed at the disposal of Admiral Pierre, who was ordered to the Indian Ocean. The Cabinet thought it would be quite easy to crush the Hovas resistance. By a coincidence, François de Mahy, deputy from Réunion, was then Minister of Commerce and *ad interim* Minister of the Navy. It was he who drew up the instructions for Pierre and gave him even stronger verbal recommendations.[48] Thus he was able to exercise an important influence over French policy in Madagascar by giving it an energetic start. In February 1883, Admiral Pierre left France with orders to insure

[41] *DDF*, IV, No. 577.   [42] *Ibid.*, No. 556.   [43] *L. J. M.*, *1881–1883*, Nos. 33, 38, 40.

[44] *Ibid.*, No. 38. The Hovas attitude on foreign property ownership found a more favorable reception in England since she had had, until shortly before, a statute forbidding foreigners to own title to land there.

[45] *Ibid.* Before leaving England the Hovas also negotiated a treaty with Italy and completed negotiations on a treaty with the United States.

[46] *DDF*, V, No. 23; E. Daudet, *La Mission de Baron de Courcel* (Paris, 1919), p. 25.

[47] *L. J. M.*, *1882–1883*, No. 1.

[48] *Ibid.*, No. 3; Hanotaux *et* Martineau, *op. cit.*, VI, 156.

French rights on the Northwest Madagascan coast with the Indian Ocean Squadron which he had been appointed to lead.[49]

Ferry and War

Jules Ferry became Premier for the second time just nine days after Pierre had received his orders. He was now a determined imperialist and, within a few weeks of his assumption of office, acted in fields as widely separated as the Congo, Indo-China, and Madagascar to impart new energy to French colonial expansion. Here is a typical case in the story of Ferry's imperialism: he gave vigorous execution to a project already under way with which he had no previous connection. He took care to see that Pierre immediately received more detailed and firmer instructions for action in Madagascar.

Three weeks after Ferry became Premier, Charles Brun, Minister of the Navy and Colonies, ordered Admiral Pierre to wipe out the Hovas strongholds in the North, Northwest, and Northeast parts of Madagascar; to seize the town of Majunga on the Northwest coast and hold its customs post. From there he was to proceed to Tamatave on the East coast and present an ultimatum to the Madagascan government. This was to demand that the French protectorate over the Sakalave tribes north of the 18th parallel be recognized and that the Madagascan government provide guarantees that the 1868 treaty provisions relative to the right of foreigners to hold property in Madagascar be put into effect. French nationals who had suffered loss through the action of the Madagascan government were to be compensated. In case his demands were refused, Admiral Pierre was instructed to seize Tamatave, if he thought such a move practicable.[50]

Such a procedure, of course, constituted an undeclared war, clearly in violation of the spirit of Article 8 of the Constitution of 1875. That fact did not worry Ferry or his Minister. No word of the intended action was given to the French Chamber of Deputies. Certainly Ferry himself had no realization of the consequences it would have.

The orders were rather easily carried out by Admiral Pierre. Majunga was taken on May 20.[51] In retaliation, the French missionaries were expelled from Tananarive and their other establishments in Madagascar. The Admiral presented his ultimatum to the Hovas, including a demand for an indemnity of one million francs for damages suffered by French citizens. It was rejected at once by Queen Ramavalo. Thereupon Tamatave was shelled and taken on June 10, 1883.[52] There was no resistance, for both the civilian population and the military garrison had withdrawn before the bombardment began.[53]

[49] *L. J. M., 1882–1883*, No. 3.   [50] *Ibid.*, No. 5.   [51] *DDF*, V, No. 39.
[52] *L. J. M., 1882–1883*, No. 14.   [53] SDA, *Madagascar*, No. 129.

The European complications in this incident arose from troubles with the English at Tamatave. When the attack began, the English Consul, Pakenham, was already mortally ill, but was nevertheless subjected to annoyance and humiliation by the overbearing French commander. The consular files in his house were forcibly removed by French marines. An English missionary, named Shaw, was arrested and placed aboard a warship on a charge of having attempted to poison French soldiers. Captain Johnstone of the English warship *Dryad* and Admiral Pierre exchanged harsh words and threats, nearly coming to a passage of arms over the treatment of English nationals. Pierre put a force ashore, declared martial law and Baudais installed a mayoralty to rule the town. All foreign consulates were closed.[54]

Back in Paris the Hovas delegation, on its way home, came to ask Ferry his terms. On June 20 he told them in an interview that the basic and all-important demand was for full recognition of the French claims to the Northwest coast. Until this was granted there could be no thought of changing the attitude toward Madagascar. Ferry told the envoys that he could not discuss the matter further, that Admiral Galiber at Tamatave had full powers to negotiate and conclude an agreement.[55]

Protest over the Tamatave incident soon came from England. France's position was complicated by the fact that the Madagascar problems coincided with the questions of Egypt and Tonkin. Granville asked on July 10 for an explanation of the French actions at Tamatave toward Pakenham, the consulate, Shaw, and the impoliteness shown Captain Johnstone.[56] This was apparently the first news Challemel-Lacour had of these events. The report from Baudais arrived only on July 20 and gave no account of the details about which the English had complained.[57] Only in the following month were they learned, and at once Challemel-Lacour censured Baudais for his over-zealous action, informing him that France had no intention of occupying Tamatave and that, therefore, the French mayoralty should at once be discontinued, and that all the consulates should be allowed to reopen. The instructions contained a very sharp rebuke to the Consul, for the affair was most vexing to the Foreign Minister.[58]

The English Methodists were much excited over the Shaw case.[59] That missionary was tried for poisoning French soldiers but acquitted since there was no real evidence against him.[60] Challemel-Lacour freely admitted that the Admiral had erred here, and he himself proposed that France pay a 25,000 franc indemnity, which was duly accepted.[61]

[54] *Ibid.*, No. 129.
[55] *DDF*, V, No. 52. Galiber had succeeded Pierre, who had fallen ill and who died shortly afterwards on his way home.
[56] *DDF*, V, No. 62.   [57] *L. J. M., 1882–1883*, No. 25.   [58] *Ibid.*, No. 26.
[59] *Ibid.*, No. 33.   [60] *DDF*, V, No. 84.   [61] *Ibid.*, No. 124.

The obligation to defend the French case forced Challemel-Lacour to make a justification of the French action to England on August 12.[62] But within a week he wrote a private letter to Ferry in which he admitted that the actions of Pierre and Baudais at Tamatave were completely unjustified, that the English captain, missionary, and Consul all had been badly mistreated.[63] In October Challemel-Lacour modified his official stand on the matter and expressed his regret to England for the attitude of the late Pierre, although he still held that his acts were legal, even if his manners were unfortunate.[64] England accepted these apologies after Granville had unburdened himself of a nasty summary of the case to the French Ambassador, Waddington.[65] The incident contributed to the cooling of Anglo-French relations that were then especially chilled by their disagreements over Egypt.

Challemel-Lacour had little taste for the whole Madagascan affair. In June he said that he did not like it and that it was both Ferry's idea and his work to date.[66] By August he was greatly discouraged. He was even more disheartened about the state of affairs in Tonkin which simply served to deepen his annoyance about Madagascar where French energies were immobilized. In a personal letter to Ferry he complained that the French agents in Madagascar had played them false. They had misinformed the Cabinet about the difficulties involved and the powers of resistance of Madagascar. He complained that the deputies from Réunion had also misled the Cabinet into thinking that the affair could be easily managed. The Foreign Minister averred that thenceforth he would distrust these deputies. He was worried about the English attitude and the intrigues of the English missionaries at the court of Tananarive. He also feared that the Summer's fevers would take a heavy toll of French troops in the unhealthful lowlands of the Madagascan coast.[67]

Challemel-Lacour had good grounds for disillusionment about the Madagascan affair, for the French found themselves in a stalemate there. The fleet was blockading the coast; Tamatave and Majunga were held by small forces. A new Hovas Queen had been crowned in July and Admiral Galiber held new talks from November 2 to December 7 with her envoys at Tamatave. The Hovas offered, on November 24, to settle the whole affair by paying the French an indemnity, but would not yield on the question of the Northwest coast. They continued to cite the 1868 treaty as justification for their stand. Galiber indignantly refused to consider an indemnity sufficient.[68] The Admiral and Baudais did

---

[62] *L. J. M., 1882–1883*, No. 30.   [63] *DDF*, V, No. 60.   [64] *L. J. M., 1882–1883*, No. 37.
[65] *Ibid.*, No. 40.   [66] *DDF*, V, No. 53.   [67] *Ibid.*, No. 80.
[68] *L. J. M., 1882–1883*, No. 46.

their best in these conversations to extend the scope of the French demands as far as they could.

When Ferry read the report of these unsuccessful negotiations he ordered his agents at Tamatave to modify their demands, on January 11, 1884. According to his terms, only the territory cited in the 1841 and 1842 treaties with the Sakalaves must be freed of Hovas troops, not the whole northern part of the island.[69] Three days later Ferry told Baudais to offer to leave Majunga.[70] Baudais replied that this would be interpreted as a fatal sign of weakness,[71] but the following March he reluctantly agreed.[72] New talks went on at Tamatave from February 21 to March 13.[73] Ferry ordered that the French demand for an indemnity be cut from Galiber's ten million figure to three million and that no territorial demands should be made on the Madagascans.[74] The officers on the spot, probably because of the urging of the Réunion colonists, were constantly trying to secure an outright annexation of territory for France.

Ferry's conciliatory course was reversed as a result of a debate in the Chamber on March 27. The Cabinet was interpellated by De Lanessan on the Madagascan policy with the purpose of driving it to take more aggressive action. One of the Réunion deputies, Vaulcomte, arose to assure the Chamber that Madagascar would really be quite easy to take with a small force, especially since the Hovas rule over many of the tribes there was not fully established. He dwelt at length on the unfriendly attitude toward France of the present native government and offered recruits from Réunion to help the regular French troops. He set forth Madagascar's great value as a naval base for France, pointing to the bay of Diégo-Suarez as the best harbor.

The Comte de Mun, outstanding legitimist spokesman and usual critic of the Government for its anticlerical policies, arose to urge that the Ferry Cabinet uphold France's historic rights in Madagascar with vigor. Only a few members from the Extreme Left criticized French action on the island.

Ferry assured the Chamber that he would uphold French claims in Northwestern Madagascar and demanded that France have as many rights and privileges there as did other European powers. He declared, however, that France had no intention of establishing a protectorate over the whole island. The Chamber then voted 437–26 to uphold French rights in Madagascar.[75]

The Madagascan was the most popular colonial venture of the Ferry Government because it had the support of the Right in Parliament.

[69] DDF, V, No. 188.   [70] L. J. M., 1884–1886, No. 2.   [71] Ibid., No. 3.
[72] Ibid., No. 7.   [73] Ibid., No. 5.   [74] Ibid., No. 6.   [75] J. O. C., 3/28/84.

The Monarchists viewed the attempt for control of Madagascar as a Monarchist tradition, as each of the Monarchist parties had had a king who tried to extend French influence there. Ferry was in the peculiar position of having to restrain the Conservatives' ardor to pursue French interests. He was deeply involved in Indo-China, having a war with Annam and with China on his hands, and simply did not have enough military strength available to strike boldly in Madagascar, which necessarily remained a sideshow for him.

After this mandate from the Chamber, new orders were sent to the recently appointed commander in the Indian Ocean, Admiral Miot. On April 7 Ferry and Admiral Peyron, now Minister of the Navy and Colonies, ordered that there was to be no more discussion of French claims on the Northwest coast, but that they were to be made effective by force. Hereafter, only the questions of indemnities and property rights were to be discussed. The indemnity to be asked was three million francs.[76]

The Chamber of Deputies voted Ferry 5,361,000 francs more for the Madagascan expedition on July 21, 1884. Bishop Freppel lent his strong support, and even Delafosse, the most intransigent of the Bonapartists, agreed with the Republican policy in this case. The Conservatives were still anxious to defend France's historic rights; their imperialist sympathies were chiefly stirred by considerations of prestige. Perhaps they had some intent of embarrassing the Government, too. The Premier promised to act firmly but prudently, and the appropriation was passed by a vote of 360–81,[77] a very large majority for Ferry's Cabinet at that time. The negative votes came mostly from the Extreme Left.

France enjoyed the good will and the active support of Bismarck in the Madagascan affair whose later course coincided with the close collaboration on the question of the Congo and Tonkin. From the very beginning Bismarck had discouraged the Hovas. In October, 1883, the German Consul at Tamatave had warned Baudais that a German ship was suspected of running arms to the Hovas.[78] In Berlin, Oswald, the most important German merchant in Africa, told Courcel that he would not attempt to go counter to French action and policy although it was costing him a good deal to follow this course. He urged the French to take even stronger measures against the Hovas but also cautioned them to restrict their territorial demands to the Northwest coast since only there had they any chance of success. Courcel's opinion was that this was simply an attempt to win the good graces of the French colonial officials.[79] Nevertheless, the German attitude did remove one possible source of great embarrassment.

76 *L. J. M., 1884–1886*, No. 11.   77 *J. O. C.*, 7/22/84.
78 *DDF*, IV, No. 147.   79 *Ibid.*, V, No. 243.

Stalemate

Out in Madagascar the officials were urging immediate and strong action. The Governor of Réunion recruited volunteers for an expeditionary force by posting notices stating that all Madagascar was to be put under French protectorate. He promised land in Madagascar to all those who would join the expedition.[80] Baudais, on August 2, wrote home that the situation was growing steadily worse and a large expeditionary force was needed at once.[81] Shortly afterwards he reported the discovery of gold on the island,[82] probably with the hope of stirring Paris action. When Baudais received his new and belligerent orders from home he wryly replied that they showed a fine spirit, but what was needed were more ships and men to put them into effect. Admiral Miot, similarly, reported that he had no forces at his command with which to strike anew.[83]

Actually, the French were bottled up at Tamatave and Majunga. They had only about eight hundred men in the one place and a handful in the other. Their Sakalave allies had been defeated by English-led Hovas and refused to fight again till real French aid appeared.[84] Meanwhile the Madagascan trade was going elsewhere. The East coast of the island is cut by countless bays and inlets and the simple trade could be easily carried on at any of these ports still open. American shippers in the area profited enormously by the dislocation of the trade at the expense of the French and Germans. The Hovas economy was not hurt. The needs of the island were quite simple and the French, who seemed to have imagined that they could starve out the natives as they might some European foes, were sadly disappointed.[85] The situation was not at all altered by the occupation of the port of Ambodimadio. The Hovas remained just as adamant as ever.

Baudais wrote to Ferry at length on October 25 to urge him to establish a protectorate over the whole island. He pointed out that the blockade was now ineffective and more decisive action was needed. He cited the Chamber's votes of the preceding March 27 and July 21 as affirming that body's intention of insisting upon French rights over the whole island. Such certainly was not the meaning of the vote, but Baudais was not limited by literal interpretations. At length he reviewed the French historical rights over the island. He said the only solution was to march to the capital, Tananarive, with a military force

---

[80] *J. O. C.*, 7/22/84.
[81] *L. J. M., 1884–1886*, No. 21.
[82] *Ibid.*, No. 22.
[83] *Ibid.*, No. 19.
[84] Hanotaux *et* Martineau, *op. cit.*, VI, 159.
[85] SDA, *Madagascar*, No. 154.

and seize the whole island, establishing a protectorate.[86] This letter was received on November 23. There is no answer to it in any of the official French publications. In fact, there is a complete gap in the official documents for the balance of Ferry's second term. He was very deeply involved in war with China and had no forces to spare for Madagascar whatever might have been his will. Baudais tried later to put his plans into realization without authorization from home.

From late 1884 to Ferry's fall in March, 1885, there was no real change in the situation in Madagascar. The town of Vohémar was occupied on October 6; the bay of Diégo-Suarez in December; and a few minor ports later. But in each case it was the same story: there were no troops to push inland. To make matters worse, the expedition suffered the loss of several ships in a February hurricane. Tamatave was a dead town, with only a hundred residents, no trade and therefore no customs receipts for the French.[87] By June, 1885 the blockade was effective only at those points held by French troops.[88] Meanwhile fever decimated the soldiers.[89] Ferry asked for an additional appropriation of twelve million francs on March 25 but had to resign on March 30 before the bill could be discussed. The money was finally voted on July 30.

Shortly after Ferry's fall, Freycinet supported by Admiral Galiber, now Minister of the Navy, and Admiral Miot in Madagascar decided to withdraw from Madagascar. They believed that further action would lead to a long, hard war which it was impossible to undertake now.[90] Freycinet no longer trusted Baudais whom Galiber described as an obstacle to negotiations with the natives.[91]

Ironically, on the day before Freycinet wrote of his lack of confidence in Baudais, the Consul had opened new negotiations with Tananarive through the Italian Consul to secure what he frankly called a "protectorate."[92] These overtures were unsuccessful, but Freycinet was informed of them only after their conclusion.[93] At once he recalled Baudais and on October 15 the Consul was dismissed for having exceeded his powers.[94] Unknowingly, Baudais had nearly spoiled a plan which Freycinet himself had been developing.

The Chamber had passed new credits of twelve million francs for the Madagascan expedition on July 30, by a vote of 277–120. At that time Ferry made an apologia for his colonial undertakings, chiefly devoted to justifying his Tonkin policy.[95] Madagascar he hailed not as a place for markets or a field for investment but as a useful naval base and an addition to French prestige.[96] Despite the vote, Freycinet ap-

[86] *L. J. M., 1884–1886*, No. 23.   [87] *Ibid.*, No. 24.   [88] SDA, *Madagascar*, No. 117.
[89] *Ibid.*   [90] *L. J. M., 1884–1886*, No. 26.   [91] *Ibid.*, No. 30.
[92] *Ibid.*, No. 36.   [93] *Ibid.*   [94] *Ibid.*, No. 41.
[95] *Infra*, pp. 190–192.   [96] *Discours*, V, pp. 172–220.

pointed a new negotiator, Patrimonio. His was to be a secret mission, concealed even from other French officials in the Indian Ocean theater.[97] It was this arrangement that Baudais had nearly spoiled and certainly handicapped with his own talks with Tananarive.

The outcome of Patrimonio's conversations was that a treaty was finally signed between France and Madagascar on December 17, 1885. France kept only the bay of Diégo-Suarez. The treaty established a most ill-defined "protectorate" over Madagascar. But an explanatory letter accompanying it gave the Hovas broad rights in foreign affairs which quite nullified the protectorate the French claimed. At a later date a good many conflicts arose over the interpretation of this treaty, and a costly military expedition was necessary to secure the whole island for France.

An analysis of the reasons for the French attempts on Madagascar must recognize several principal influences which, when they were joined under the guidance of Jules Ferry, accounted for the dreary struggle in which France found herself involved there. The first of these was the ambitions of the colonists of Réunion who wanted land and trading privileges on the island. French economic imperialism in this case stemmed not from the continent of Europe but from an old colony. Reinforcing material ambition was a missionary rivalry existing not only among various sects, but between English and French missionaries. To the support of these groups that wanted the mother country to take over the island were rallied key French officials in Madagascar. These men found excuses for action in quarrels over property rights and the encroachment of the native government on old French territorial claims. They were able to create an entanglement for France which was brought home to Paris by the visit of a native delegation. The actions of this group infuriated the incumbent Premier who was thus persuaded to send out an expedition to protect historic French claims.

Jules Ferry inherited this state of affairs on becoming Premier for the second time. The situation was clarified by his willingness to embark on empire-building. He had no particular economic ambitions here but was moved by appeals to French prestige and the defense of historic rights. Ironically this anti-clerical was defending a position brought about in large part by missionary rivalry. He was persuaded to act energetically by the deputies from Réunion who had had a large hand in launching the original expedition. Misinformed as to the difficulties that might be faced, he was further involved by the actions of the Consul and the Admirals on the scene. Before Parliament, which had not been consulted in the launching of the expedition, he justified his expedi-

[97] *L. J. M., 1884–1886*, No. 31.

tion on the grounds of upholding French historic claims and establishing naval bases. He experienced no difficulty with the Chambers, for he had the support not only of his own coalition but also of the Conservatives who saw Madagascar as a French colony by traditional right. Ferry's expedition was a failure, nevertheless, principally because his forces were so dispersed elsewhere that he could not muster enough strength to strike a telling blow against the rulers of the island.

Chapter Six

FRUSTRATION IN EGYPT

One of the keenest colonial rivalries of the last quarter of the nineteenth century was that between France and England for pre-eminence in strategically and commercially important Egypt. It was inevitable that Jules Ferry, when he sought to strengthen the French position abroad, should have taken an interest in this land, long an object of French cultural, military and economic expansion. For many years before Ferry, French governments had supported the claims of their Egyptian bondholders. During his first Ministry, France and England were amicably sharing control of Egypt and his interest was to keep that condominium intact thus ensuring payment of interest on the bonds. As fate would have it, he was out of the premiership during the critical period of the Nationalist uprising when France allowed England to assume the chief role in Egyptian affairs.

During Ferry's second Ministry, he persistently tried to take advantage of England's multiple embarrassments in Egypt and elsewhere to regain for France a considerable share in the control of Egypt through the device of European supervision. Bismarck, when he was annoyed at England, lent considerable support to the French Premier's designs, enabling him to curb England's attempt to enlarge her powers in Egypt. Ferry successfully preserved and extended international financial control there, but he did not succeed in establishing international political control of either Egypt or the Suez Canal. Such progress as he made toward those ends was undone by his successors. During the latter part of his second Ministry, these problems were ones in which he was most interested, if not most successful.

Egypt and the Bondholders

France's interests in the Nile valley ranged from the time of the Crusades, Napoleon's ill-fated expedition, the brilliant archeological investigations following the discovery of the Rosetta Stone, to the construction of the Suez Canal, and commercial and financial exploitation of Egypt. French cultural influences were the strongest from Western Europe, while French capital and skill notably improved Egypt throughout the nineteenth century, culminating in Ferdinand de Lesseps' construction of the Canal.

The Khedive Ismail,[1] reigning from 1863 to 1879, met his undoing in borrowing excessively from European bankers.[2] His ambitious modernization program greatly strengthened Egyptian commerce and improved the lot of many of his subjects.[3] However, his personal extravagance, antiquated tax system, chaotic fiscal methods and the poverty of the nation made payment of the ruinous interest rates impossible.[4] It was the imminence of bankruptcy that induced Ismail to offer a substantial block of Canal shares to the canny Disraeli who made his famous political investment in the road to India in 1875.[5] Naturally, England's interest in Egyptian affairs waxed stronger thereafter.

The continuing financial struggles of the Khedive, and the fears and demands of the bondholders led to the mission of Stephen Cave to investigate and report on the financial situation,[6] then to the establishment by the Khedive in 1876 of the *Caisse de la Dette Publique* to unify the debt and control revenue receipts and debt payments. On the insistence of the English bondholders, the Debt Commission became a joint French and English body with two controllers; this was the so-called Dual Control.[7] Essentially it established rule of Egypt by the bondholders. Throughout these investigations and negotiations, the Third Republic stood firmly and openly behind the French investors, while British support remained unofficial but powerful.

Continuing fiscal troubles, despite ruthless taxation and collection (bearing chiefly on the small peasants), led to another inquiry headed

1 Egypt was under the suzerainty of the Sultan of Turkey, but enjoyed a considerable autonomy.

2 For an excellent brief summary of the Egyptian question from 1870 to 1883, using recently published documents, see: Langer, *European Alliances*, pp. 251–280. A standard work favorable to the French by the Premier in office during this critical period of 1882 is: Charles de Freycinet, *La question d'Egypt* (Paris, 1905). A classic account by the great English administrator of Egypt, who was a British controller and subsequently Consul-General, is: Lord Cromer, *Modern Egypt* (London, 1908, 2 vols.).

3 Langer, *op. cit.*, p. 253.

4 On Egyptian finances see: Theodore Rothstein, *Egypt's Ruin* (London, 1910). The interest rates, allowing for the discounts and the bankers' commissions, ran from twelve to twenty-five percent.

5 *DDF*, II, Nos. 13 ff.; G. E. Buckle, *Life of Benjamin Disraeli* (London, 1920), V, Chapter 12; Rothstein, *op. cit.*, p. 8; Halford Hoskins, *British Routes to India* (New York, 1928), pp. 460–463. The Duc Decazes had let slip the opportunity to buy the shares despite the urging of Gambetta. Mitchell, *Bismarckian Policy*, p. 178.

6 Rothstein, *op. cit.*, pp. 12–17.

7 Neither French nor English statesmen were wholly pleased with this condominium, but it appeared the most practical solution for the investors and the nations at the moment. See Freycinet, *op. cit.*, pp. 154 ff.; Cromer, *op. cit.*, I, 12 ff.; Lady Gwendolen Cecil, *Life of Salisbury* (London, 1921), II, 331–334.

nominally by De Lesseps but actually by Charles Rivers Wilson.[8] His scathing criticism of Ismail's system of personal rule virtually forced the Khedive to establish a Ministry under Nubar Pasha with European Ministers in the persons of Wilson and De Blignières.[9] The chief aim of the Ministry was to ensure full and prompt payment of the European investors. A demonstration by unpaid army officers gave Ismail the opportunity to rid himself of the Ministry, only to have the powers, led by France, request the Sultan, as suzerain, to depose him and install his son Tewfik Pasha in June 1879.[10] The Dual Control was reestablished with the open backing of the French and English governments.

Egyptian nationalism now rose to plague the dominant European powers. Nationalist sentiment had been growing for some years in Egypt as a political and religious renaissance. At once anti-Turk and anti-European, it combined elements of Pan-Islamism and Western European political ideals.[11] The Controllers-General, who had scant understanding of the movement, heaped fuel on the fires by reducing the pay of the lower Egyptian army officers, while leaving untouched the high salaries of European, Turkish and Circassian officials. Minor irritations and conflicts multiplied until troops led by Ahmed Arabi established nearly complete control over Egypt by a coup on September 9, 1881. The puppet Khedive was compelled to dismiss his Ministers and convoke the Chamber of Notables.[12] The army seemed determined to destroy European interference in Egypt, and the French bondholders protested loudly to Jules Ferry's Cabinet.

Egypt During Ferry's First Premiership

During his first Premiership, Jules Ferry was quite content to let Egyptian affairs take their course. He was very well satisfied with the Dual Control system and wanted to cope with all Egyptian difficulties with the full support and cooperation of Great Britain. When an outburst in February 1881 in Cairo threatened the position of Tewfik, Barthélemy Saint-Hilaire arranged through Lord Lyons in Paris to have identical instructions sent the French and English representatives in Egypt. The note set forth the desirability and necessity of full and complete cooperation between the French and English consular representa-

---

[8] On this commission see: C. Rivers Wilson, *Chapters from My Official Life* (London, 1916), Chapters XI–XIV.

[9] Wilson was Minister of Finance and De Blignières, Minister of Public Works.

[10] The Khedive learned of his deposition upon receiving the Sultan's telegram addressed to the "Ex-Khedive Ismail Pasha." *DDF*, II, Nos. 407, 432–439; *Livre Jaune Egypt, 1880*, Nos. 320–325; *GP.*, II, 660.

[11] Langer, *op. cit.*, pp. 263–265.

[12] Freycinet, *op. cit.*, pp. 197–198; *DDF*, IV, Nos. 119, 120, 122.

tives. In view of the improved administrative and financial situation in Egypt, effected with the aid of the two nations, it was "a question henceforth of guaranteeing the survival of a financial regime which functions to the general satisfaction." The agents were instructed to support the administration of the Khedive jointly and fully and to discourage any attempts to overthrow Tewfik or bring about a violent change in the system of government.[13]

The French Consul General at Cairo who twice received a deputation from the rebellious army officers early in February and apparently gave them some measure of cooperation, was immediately recalled and dismissed when Tewfik protested.[14]

During the Spring and Summer of 1881 Ferry was busy with his Tunisian campaign and had no interest in taking any action in Egypt. Fortunately for him, the mutterings that portended the more serious nationalist revolt could be overlooked as local incidents. From the European point of view, the financial and administrative reorganization was proceeding smoothly.

However, with Arabi's revolt in September, Egyptian problems suddenly demanded attention, for regular payment of the French bondholders and the Dual Control were jeopardized. Since French resources were already absorbed in suppressing the last of the recalcitrant tribes in Tunisia, and as Ferry's parliamentary position was weak at the time, he had little interest in undertaking any action in Egypt. His real desire was to preserve peace and the interest payments, and maintain Egypt's attenuated ties with the Sultan, while keeping actual authority, under the Dual Control system, in France and England.[15] However, after the uprising, the previous arrangement could only be restored by some definite intervention.

The keynote of Ferry's policy in meeting the crisis again was cooperation with England. He carefully made clear his intention to London,[16] and, when action became absolutely necessary, moved only in conjunction with the British. He opposed every attempt to make the Egyptian question one of international concern, for he did not want any other powers to share in the direction of Egyptian policy.

However, the French were confronted with England's willingness to accept the Sultan's proposal to send Turkish troops to quell the nationalists.[17] Barthélemy Saint-Hilaire foresaw disaster here; he feared

[13] *DDF*, III, 393; Barthélemy Saint-Hilaire, *Fragments pour l'histoire de la diplomatie française* (Paris, 1882), pp. 172–174.

[14] *DDF*, III, Nos. 357, 372, 374, 385, 399.

[15] Rambaud, *Ferry*, p. 259; *L. J. E.*, *1881*, No. 53; *DDF*, IV, No. 123.

[16] *DDF*, IV, No. 123.

[17] Great Britain. Foreign Office. *Accounts and Papers. Egypt, No. 3* (1882), pp. 7–8; *L. J. E.*, *1881*, No. 31; *DDF*, IV, No. 218.

that the Egyptian question might as a result be laid open to all the European powers, and that France and England would thus lose their exclusive control. Moreover, such intervention might lead the Egyptians to believe that the Porte was the only legal authority for their country. In any event, Turkish intervention would create a wholly new situation. Since he felt the present status of Egypt to be the best possible, if only order were restored, he was most anxious not to take any chances with altering the *status quo*.[18] As the Foreign Minister of a nation with a large Moslem population in Algeria and Tunisia, Saint-Hilaire feared that if the Turks were at all encouraged the whole Moslem world might be upset.[19] This was a weighty consideration, for France had only recently summarily rejected the Sultan's claims to suzerainty over Tunisia. Ferry had no intention of bolstering the Sultan's hold in Africa. He had not long since been alarmed when the Tripolitanian garrisons were slightly reinforced,[20] and he had no intention of deliberately stationing more Turkish troops along the Mediterranean littoral. His caution may have been excessive, but he doubtless remembered that when the Treaty of Bardo was signed with Tunisia, Egyptian army officers had clamored for an increase in their army and fortifications.[21] Ferry, then involved in crushing rebellious Tunisian tribes, could not consent to measures that might encourage them to further resistance. In any case, French policy was to discourage Anglo-Turkish cooperation. England accepted Ferry's refusal [22] for fear of driving the French into cooperation with Bismarck.[23]

Saint-Hilaire's favorite solution, which he repeatedly proposed, was to establish French and British generals in the Egyptian army to reorganize and supervise it in the same way that controllers of France and England had revamped Egyptian finance.[24] However, London was very cool to his suggestion.[25]

A real crisis arose when the Sultan, on his own initiative and despite warnings from France and England,[26] early in October sent two commissioners to Egypt to assert his authority. Harmonious joint action and full cooperation between France and England met this situation. Saint-Hilaire readily agreed to Granville's suggestion that each send a warship to Alexandria to see that the Turks made no change in Egypt's status.[27] The commissioners were at once recalled, having accomplished

---

18 Saint-Hilaire, *op. cit.*, p. 339.
20 *DDF*, IV, Nos. 90, 102.
22 *Egypt, No. 3*, pp. 14, 21.
24 *Egypt, No. 3*, pp. 8, 13, 35; *DDF*, IV, No. 123.
25 Saint-Hilaire, *op. cit.*, pp. 338–339, 341.

19 *Ibid.*
21 *Ibid.*, Nos. 28, 34.
23 Newton, *op. cit.*, II, 259.

26 *DDF*, IV, No. 140.

27 *Egypt, No. 3*, pp. 38–41; *L. J. E., 1881*, Nos. 39–42; *DDF*, IV, Nos. 161, 164. The Powers felt unable to forbid the Sultan to send the commissioners since they had so recently called in the Sultan to depose Ismail. Saint-Hilaire, *op. cit.*, p. 349.

nothing during their thirteen-day stay,[28] and the warships departed after only a twenty-four hour call, the Porte having been effectively checkmated. The French and English Consuls General had received identical instructions and had acted in unison throughout this incident.[29]

The conduct of negotiations during the Egyptian crisis was in the hands of Barthélemy Saint-Hilaire who had acquired a considerable interest in Egypt during a visit there with De Lesseps some years before. However, as usual during his Ministry, Ferry kept a guiding hand on the course of action. The Foreign Minister was undoubtedly expressing Ferry's sentiments as well as his own when, at the conclusion of this episode, he wrote the French Consul General in Cairo that Egypt was rightly of considerable interest to France and must be maintained under the Dual Control. He cited France's cultural and economic ties with Egypt which made intervention there an old national tradition. The chief aim of French policy was to ensure the payment of Egypt's creditors—among them, of course, the French bondholders. Therefore, the country must be made as prosperous and stable as possible. This could best be accomplished, he said, under the tutelage of France and England each of whom had equal interests there and between whom there should be no rivalry. He wished a long life for the Dual Control system.[30] Throughout the whole period neither the French nor the British displayed any understanding of Egyptian nationalism. Egypt was considered chiefly in its relations to the Europeans there, their investments and the effect it had on international alignments.

French Withdrawal from Egypt

Advocate of vigorous action in Egypt, Gambetta persuaded Lord Granville to join him in a note to the Khedive on January 8, 1882, asserting that the two governments believed the maintenance of Tewfik on the throne to be essential for Egypt.[31] However, it soon developed that the Gladstone Cabinet, contrary to Gambetta's desire, had no intention of taking action. Therefore, the Gambetta note served chiefly to anger and unite the nationalists.[32] Bismarck rallied his Three Emperors' League to protest any Anglo-French action.[33] In any event,

---

[28] *Egypt, No. 3*, pp. 56–58; 67–68.   [29] *DDF*, IV, No. 160.

[30] Saint-Hilaire, *op. cit.*, pp. 365 ff.; *L. J. E., 1881*, Nos. 52, 58; Freycinet, *op. cit.*, pp. 200–202.

[31] *DDF*, IV, Nos. 203, 224, 226.

[32] Cromer, *op. cit.*, I, 228–229; Lowell J. Ragatz, *The Question of Egypt in Anglo-French Relations, 1875–1904* (Edinburgh, 1922), pp. 94–95.

[33] *DDF*, IV, Nos. 227, 229, 249.

Gambetta resigned and Freycinet was not disposed to risk action against the Powers.[34] His plan was to establish a European concert on Egypt, which he termed "internationalizing" the question. Since neither France nor England would act alone or together, in the event of any new outbreak, the major Powers should meet to decide on a course of action. With this policy, Jules Ferry, as a cabinet member, agreed.[35] As Minister of Public Education, Ferry took little part in the conduct of foreign affairs, devoting himself to the problems of his new educational system. On such an important matter, however, it was necessary for him to be in substantial agreement with the Cabinet.

The calm in Egypt was disturbed by the Khedive's appeal to Europe to support him against the nationalists.[36] Freycinet, still anxious to work with the Powers, but also to restore order in Cairo, proposed sending French and English squadrons to Alexandria; the Powers, except Turkey, agreed.[37] No landing force was provided, the French refusing to accede to the use of Turkish troops. The French and English Consuls interfered enough in Egypt to cause discomfort to Arabi, now become Minister of War, but not enough to dislodge him. They succeeded only in greatly weakening Tewfik.[38] While the Powers conferred in Constantinople,[39] anti-foreign riots broke out in Alexandria. Arabi became virtual ruler and, in early June, began construction of fortifications at Alexandria which allegedly threatened the squadrons at anchor. The English government, on July 3, ordered a bombardment of the earthworks and batteries, in which Freycinet refused to cooperate. He claimed that bombardment was an act of war which needed the consent of the French Chambers and was a violation of the engagements of the then-conferring Powers not to take separate action. He also observed that it was unwise since there were no troops to land.[40] Jules Ferry apparently agreed with his views.[41]

A brief bombardment destroyed the forts on July 11, and subsequent fires damaged considerable European property. Meanwhile the English prepared to send troops into Egypt. Granville and Freycinet sought a

---

[34] Freycinet, *op. cit.*, pp. 230–236. [35] *Ibid.*, p. 237.
[36] Cromer, *op. cit.*, I, 265. [37] *DDF*, IV, Nos. 254, 256, 259, 269, 274, 327.
[38] *Ibid.*, Nos. 337, 341, 346, 347, 351.
[39] An ambassadorial conference beginning late in June debated the question of allowing Turkish troops to intervene, a proposal that Freycinet intensely disliked. By the time it was agreed to ask the Sultan to send troops for three months to reestablish the status quo, Alexandria had been bombarded. *DDF*, IV, Nos. 355, 357, 359, 367, 392, 404, 429, 471; Newton, *op. cit.*, II, 284–285; *L. J. E., 1882*, II, Nos. 102–164.
[40] Freycinet, *op. cit.*, p. 284; *DDF*, IV, Nos. 463, 467, 483, 484.
[41] Freycinet, *op. cit.*, pp. 297–299.

mandate from the Constantinople conference to protect the Canal in the name of Europe, only to be refused on the insistence of Germany. While further proposals were under discussion by the conference, Freycinet was defeated in the Chamber of Deputies on July 29 on a bill to provide funds for protecting the Canal. By this vote France virtually gave predominance in Egypt to England.

Intervention Before Parliament

Unlike Jules Ferry on many similar occasions, Freycinet observed his constitutional obligation to ask Parliament for funds before acting in a foreign theater. A weak Ministry, typical of the combinations patched together by this most opportunistic of all French politicians, his satisfied neither the supporters of intervention nor withdrawal in Egypt. When Freycinet asked the Chamber on July 6 for six million francs for the naval squadron at Alexandria, he stated his intention of supervising the Turks, keeping the Suez free and acting only in concert with the other Powers. He intended to preserve both the condominium with England and the European concert. The Radicals accused him of waging war, but the majority agreed with Gambetta when he demanded protection of French interests in Egypt and preservation of England's friendship. The credits were voted overwhelmingly, 424–64.[42]

In late July, Freycinet asked the Chamber for nine million francs for a few thousand troops to protect the Canal together with English troops. This was not, he said, intervention in Egyptian affairs, but a necessary police measure for the security of commerce. But there was general disapproval of Freycinet's stand. The Radicals who wanted no expeditions outside France could point to the fact that the Powers at Constantinople had just refused France and England a blank cheque for policing the Canal. The Premier asserted that the Powers had no objection to the proposed undertaking, but he could produce no written proof. Clemenceau was therefore able to play on the fears of the timorous that this step would lead to others and that French military strength might be weakened by operations in Egypt when the rest of Europe was, he said, a tense and waiting armed camp, each country making certain that it was free for all contingencies. He rallied the Radicals and some of the more moderate Republicans to the slogan of preserving France's "liberty of action." Although they did not speak out, Ferry and Gambetta, however, thought the proposed sum unworthy of France.[43] Ferry voted for the appropriation but Gambetta swung his block of votes

[42] *J. O. C.*, 7/19/82.   [43] Rambaud, *op. cit.*, pp. 262–263.

into a coalition with the extreme wings and thus the credits were refused 75–417.[44]

At the moment, the full consequences of this vote were not clear;
actually France thereby indicated she would not participate in military
operations in Egypt, thus yielding her share in dominance to England.
Ironically, the country which had once been most forward in pressing
the demands of her investors and, at least once before, most ready to
intervene, lost her opportunity to secure more complete control over
Egypt by a turn of domestic politics and an attack of nerves.

No intention existed of impeding England's action in Egypt. Lyons
was told that the French government wanted to see England guard the
Canal and crush the revolt.[45] Neither was it expected, however, that
the English should establish themselves in Egypt indefinitely. In fact,
when Wolseley landed and defeated the Egyptian forces on September
13, England found she held Egypt almost in spite of herself, having plan-
lessly floundered and blundered in.[46] It was the declared and honest
intention of the British government to move her troops out when the
Khedive's position was firmly established, but revolts and reorganization of the administration held her inextricably in Egypt for years.[47]
Granville set forth his government's position in a note to the Powers
on January 3, 1883: Great Britain had no intention of subjugating
Egypt but would recall her troops as soon as the Khedive's authority
was reestablished; in the near future a convention on the Canal should
be agreed upon by all the Powers providing the right of unhindered
passage under all circumstances, even for belligerents, but barring
hostilities in or near the Canal. Economies in the Egyptian administration and new codes for the mixed tribunals were promised.[48]

However, the continuing occupation annoyed the French who soon
felt themselves duped. High on the list of complaints was the abolition
of the Dual Control, which in fact had ceased to exist on December 30,
1882, over the repeated protests of Paris.[49] The French further weakened
their position when the Duclerc Ministry declined the Presidency of
the Debt Commission for France. Britain was left a free hand in Egypt,
but French resentment grew nevertheless.

As England proceeded to pacify and reorganize Egypt, the former

---

[44] *J. O. C.*, 7/30/82. Freycinet asserted that on the following day he had word
that Germany was ready to propose collective protection on terms he wanted, and
Russia, Turkey and Italy were agreed. This might have saved him, could he have
told the Chamber. Freycinet, *op. cit.*, p. 313.

[45] Newton, *op. cit.*, II, 293.

[46] Langer, *op. cit.*, p. 276; Freycinet, *op. cit.*, pp. 284–285.

[47] Langer, *op. cit.*, p. 282.   [48] *DDF*, V, No. 592.   [49] *Ibid.*, No. 573.

Anglo-French working agreement and friendship withered.[50] This change, originally due to the distrust aroused over the Egyptian question, was a most important development in the latter quarter of the nineteenth century, for it marked the beginning of twenty years of unfriendly relations between France and England. The aggressive expansionist policy of Jules Ferry, evidenced in Egypt and many other parts of Africa and Asia, contributed importantly to the Anglo-French estrangement.

Egyptian Affairs in the Second Ferry Ministry

For seven months preceding the formation, late in February, 1883, of Jules Ferry's second Ministry, the weak Governments of Duclerc and Faillières, heeding the demands of the Radicals, had consistently refused to participate in Egyptian affairs. Over a year elapsed thereafter before Ferry was able to initiate a concrete policy in this field. Not only did he lack the opportunity, but as soon as he took over the reins of government, he also had under way absorbing expeditions in Madagascar and Indo-China. It was not until the last year of his Ministry that he undertook to regain for France a share in the control of Egypt.

The change in Egypt's status in 1882 and 1883 altered both Ferry's problem and his approach to it. During his first Premiership, he had wanted merely to maintain the Dual Control and to avoid the necessity of action. During the second, three problems confronted him: to assure the continuation of interest payments to bondholders; to regain France's lapsed share in the political control of Egypt; and to combat England's efforts to enlarge her power there. Therefore, he now found himself compelled to reverse the policy of his first Premiership to attempt "internationalizing" the question of Egyptian control. Unlike Freycinet's "internationalization," a device whereby France and England avoided action, Ferry's program was designed to force England to share her control of Egypt with all of Europe. Ferry fully expected that France, as the continental power with the largest Egyptian interests, would play the leading role in such a scheme. To make Egypt an international problem was about the only method whereby France could again secure some measure of political authority. To this end he successfully enlisted Bismarck's support at a moment when the Chancellor was annoyed at

[50] Bismarck sat on the sidelines and watched this rupture which he had not engineered but with which he was not entirely displeased, even though his usual policy was to seek a balance between France and England. He remarked that Germany could afford to watch the French and British locomotives collide because England would then be more dependent on German aid and France would be isolated. *DDF,* IV, No. 573; Hohenlohe, *op. cit.,* II, 328.

the British for their unfriendly attitude toward German expansion in Africa and the Pacific. The many elaborate plans laid by Ferry had few lasting results, but that they had even temporary success was largely due to the embarrassment of Great Britain and the ambition of Germany, both of which Ferry exploited to his advantage.

Internationalizing Financial Control

The Egyptian government was still in financial straits due to the cost of the Sudan expeditions against the Mahdi,[51] the high administrative expenses, the debt burden, and the award of large damages for destruction in the Alexandria bombardment. The troubles of Egypt were not only her own, however. The campaigns against the Mahdi sacrificed not only Egyptian troops and treasure, but also English officers and honor. The indemnities awarded European claimants for damages in the Alexandria bombardment fell upon the Egyptian treasury, but it was the English who had to devise ways and means of raising the monies to pay for the destruction they had wrought, as well as for Egypt's other expenses, and persuading Europe of the necessity and wisdom of the measures. Solutions for these problems were undertaken with respect for law and international obligations. In this invasion there was no cutting of Gordian knots. Therefore, Granville invited the Powers on April 18, 1884 to confer on modifying the Law of Liquidation.[52]

Perceiving an opportunity again to make Egypt a European question, Ferry opened discussions with the other Powers before replying. He informed Italy that since the Dual Control was dead, he would try to make Egypt a European question, thus avoiding the great danger for Mediterranean powers of an English protectorate over Egypt with the Suez an English canal.[53] When consulted, Bismarck assured Courcel he would not object to French refusal to separate Egyptian financial from political problems in the discussions, even if such a refusal should cause the conference to be forestalled.[54]

When Ferry replied to London, he tentatively accepted the conference idea depending on a preliminary exchange of views and an agreement upon an agenda.[55] He renounced aggressive intentions, stated that France would not attempt to reestablish Dual Control or move troops in when England left, but would like to have some idea of how long the English intended to tarry.

[51] The Mahdi was a religious fanatic who rebelled against the Cairo government and dominated the Sudan for several years.

[52] This law specified the revenues to be used for meeting interest and amortization on Egypt's debt. *DDF*, V, No. 235; *Egypt, No. 17* (1884), p. 1.

[53] *DDF*, V, No. 239.   [54] *Ibid.*, No. 246.

[55] *Ibid.*, No. 254; Newton, *op. cit.*, II, 330–331.

In the preliminary conversations Ferry proposed immediate enlargement of the Debt Commission to make it an international financial commission with power to regulate the budget and supervise expenditures.[56] The negotiations proceeded rather stormily, Granville refusing to yield to Ferry's suggestion that the president of the Debt Commission be other than English or that a majority of the Commission decide all questions.[57] Waddington, now French Ambassador, finally dropped insistence on these points lest the conference be aborted and the most important problem—namely that of providing for English evacuation —not be settled.[58]

Their negotiations eventuated in an exchange of notes on June 17 in which the English Government stated its intention to withdraw its troops early in 1888 "provided that the Powers are then of the opinion that this evacuation can take place without endangering peace and order in Egypt." It further agreed to enlarge the authority of the Debt Commission so that it should be consulted annually on the Egyptian budget. England promised to submit to the Powers, before 1888, a plan for the neutralization of Egypt similar to the guarantees on Belgium and a proposal relative to the liberty and neutrality of the Suez Canal. All these agreements were to be contingent on a satisfactory new financial agreement. France, for her part, renewed her promises not to invade Egypt.[59] Ferry was especially pleased at his success in setting a definite date for its evacuation.

The supporters of the Dual Control system interpellated the Ministry on June 23 when the preliminary agreement with England was announced. The Radicals criticized the vagueness of the evacuation date and terms, and of the measures to be taken to neutralize the Canal. Ferry set forth his basic formula: Egypt was "essentially an international and European problem," not simply one for France and England.[60] Defending himself again on June 26, Ferry flayed the Radicals who would have adopted a negative policy toward Egypt. That was a land, he said, where France must maintain an interest because of the old and great French traditions of aid to Egypt in both cultural and economic fields. Such great national traditions should not be abandoned. More immediately, Egypt was important because of the sizeable stake of French investors which he intended to protect. Dual Control was a "chimera" which he had replaced by much more dependable assurances from England. Confidence in the Ministry's Egyptian policy was voted unanimously by 460 votes.[61]

[56] *DDF*, V, No. 259.
[58] *Ibid.*, Nos. 291, 294.
[60] *J. O. C.*, 6/24/84.

[57] *Ibid.*, Nos. 286, 289, 291.
[59] *Ibid.*, No. 311.
[61] *Ibid.*, 6/27/84.

The London conference on Egypt, convening June 28, was to deal only with financial problems since England had already set a date for withdrawal. The British proposal for reducing the debt's interest rate by one-half of one percent, and consolidating certain loans were essential for that government, but the French refused to agree to this, contending that Egypt could pay.[62] Upon this rock the conference foundered, for Granville had predicated the English concessions on other points upon a settlement of the financial problems. Accordingly, he refused to entertain the proposition to increase the power and functions of the Debt Commission.[63] Ferry had expected to overcome this not wholly unexpected refusal by the united pressure of Germany and her allies whose support had been promised him.[64] However, he reckoned without the hostility of Count Münster, the German Ambassador, whose great friendship for the British led him to ignore Bismarck's instructions to support France.[65] Thus, Granville was able to refuse to make any change in the powers of the Debt Commission.[66] The French delegates were forced to oppose England single-handed, since Münster refused even to speak in their support, although he expressed sympathy for the French view of the financial problems.[67] He asserted that he was neutral and that the two powers most concerned in Egypt must make their own arrangements.[68] His Austrian and Russian colleagues also held back.[69] Ferry's hope had been to add Russian, German and perhaps Turkish members to the Debt Commission, thinking that these delegates would usually be a counterweight to the English.[70] Here again Münster failed to support France against the English refusal. When Russia asked for a Commission seat, the German Ambassador, contrary to Bismarck's instructions, mildly said that he would insist on a place for his country only in case Russia secured hers.[71] Consequently, no additions to the Commission were made. When the British Foreign Secretary effectively ended the conference asserting ". . . that we have not been able to find . . . a satisfactory basis for arranging the financial regime of Egypt," Münster again refused to support the French move to set a reconvening date. He expressed only vague regrets that the conference had failed.[72] Ferry was greatly angered and disappointed by the fruitless outcome of the conference which ended on August 2.

[62] *Egypt, No. 30* (1884), pp. 6–7, 12, 15.
[63] *Ibid.*, pp. 22, 37.
[64] *DDF*, V, No. 268.
[65] *Ibid.*, Nos. 345, 347, 349.
[66] *Egypt, No. 30*, p. 37.
[67] *DDF*, V, Nos. 339, 340.
[68] *Egypt, No. 30*, p. 16.
[69] *Ibid.*, pp. 16–17; *DDF*, V, No. 347.
[70] *DDF*, V, Nos. 312, 313, 328. There were already Austrian and Italian delegates as well as French and British.
[71] *Egypt, No. 30*, pp. 25–26; *DDF*, V, No. 405.
[72] *Egypt, No. 30*, pp. 37–38; *DDF*, V, Nos. 347, 349.

To his mind the entire responsibility for the failure rested on Germany who had not fulfilled her pledges.

From this time forward, Ferry cautiously but steadily worked to secure by a European *démarche* what France alone had been unable to accomplish: the immediate internationalization by England of the financial control of Egypt which in time he thought would affect the political sphere. Later England might be compelled likewise to establish international control of the Suez Canal, thus considerably strengthening France's communications with her growing Far Eastern holdings. Only in the first part of his tri-partite plan was he successful.

Two major factors enabled Ferry to attain some of the objectives which he had failed to secure in the London conference. The first was the fact that Egypt's finances steadily deteriorated, and some solution simply had to be found by the British. The second was Bismarck's great anger at the English who were apparently trying to curb his new appetite for a colonial empire. A series of crises in Anglo-German relations arose over Southwest Africa, West Africa, the Fiji Islands, and New Guinea at the same time that Ferry was anxious to curtail England's power in Egypt. After his London experience, Ferry would not move without the certain support of the other Powers. Bismarck knew he was furthering his own designs when he encouraged France to thwart England and to reaffirm her erstwhile right of sharing in the control of Egypt. In measure as the English government failed to satisfy Bismarck, or actively opposed his designs, so he supported and urged Ferry on. All this was perfectly evident to Ferry who had no intention of being used as a cat's-paw, but who intended to use German support when it was useful and certain. He constantly strove to commit Germany to support his plans and urged her allies, Austria and Russia, to do likewise. He was always careful, however, not to break completely with England.

During their negotiations concerning West Africa, Ferry unsuccessfully endeavored to persuade Bismarck to join him in an agreement on Egypt as well. Actually, as he made clear, Ferry would much rather have made a settlement of the Egyptian question than any other.[73] But the Chancellor only urged the French to strike out on their own, and Ferry would not again risk facing England on this question without full and assured support.[74] When Courcel visited Bismarck late in August, after having been in Paris for conferences with Ferry, he found the Chancellor still unwilling to do anything to satisfy France, merely urging her to call another conference which representatives of Germany,

[73] *DDF*, V, Nos. 366, 369, 372; *GP.*, III, 680–682, 686–689.
[74] *DDF*, V, No. 377.

Austria, and Russia would attend.[75] He was surprised and annoyed at Courcel's indifference to this suggestion.[76] Ferry did not fail to point the moral: France's reserve was due to Münster's failure to support her at London as Bismarck and Hohenlohe had promised he would.[77] Bismarck then and many times thereafter disavowed Münster, but both Courcel and Ferry suspected that the Ambassador's conduct was not wholly undirected by Berlin.[78]

The first occasion on which Ferry could test Bismarck's professed new interest in Egyptian questions and his many recent expressions of friendliness toward French interests on that score came when the Egyptian government, on September 17, seized revenues intended for debt service and used them for administrative expenses. Such a step had been recommended in the most recent investigation of Egyptian finances by Lord Northbrook, and Granville had expressed his approval.[79] However, the Law of Liquidation and the decree establishing the *Caisse de la Dette* had been violated, as Ferry was quick to point out. He asked Bismarck to join him in protesting this action before the mixed tribunals in Egypt. The Chancellor who was then in a towering rage at the British over Angra Pequena and had recently spoken of an anti-British naval league,[80] immediately agreed and urged Austria, Russia and Turkey to support Ferry's move. Again he stated in advance his consent to any proposal for a new conference on Egypt to be held in Paris.[81] He was ready to accept Hatzfeldt's suggestion to undertake some action if necessary to ensure the freedom of the courts on this question.[82] However, the identical notes of protest from the Powers [83] had their effect and the funds were restored to the Debt Commission. Egypt, and indirectly England, had been backed off the board by this cooperative action.

Altogether these were happy days in Franco-German relations, as the West African conference [84] was called and as Bismarck gave encouragement to France in the Far East.[85] Courcel was delighted by the major evolution in German policy which had taken place when Bismarck changed to the side of France in the Egyptian question. He counted on the German search for colonies to develop further Anglo-German friction whose corollary was Franco-German collaboration.[86] Herbert Bismarck was then in London endeavoring to make the English agree

---

[75] During these talks they reached substantial agreement on the question of West Africa. *Supra*, pp. 98–100.

[76] *DDF*, V, No. 385. [77] *Ibid.*, No. 391.

[78] *Ibid.*, Nos. 347, 349, 356, 391, 399, 405. [79] *Egypt, No. 36* (1884), pp. 6–12.

[80] *Supra*, p. 101. [81] *DDF*, V, Nos. 403, 408; *GP.*, III, 430.

[82] *GP.*, III, 429–430. [83] *DDF*, V, Nos. 409, 410.

[84] *Supra*, p. 101. [85] *Infra*, p. 164. [86] *DDF*, V, No. 410.

to the recent German annexations in Africa, and he did not hesitate to use the new success in Egypt as a weapon. He told Dilke that Franco-German relations were of the "friendliest," that they would be cultivated, and that Germany simply could not support such a policy as that of England in Egypt.[87] To Waddington he stated the German intentions in the strongest of terms saying that, "the actual state of relations between Germany and England is becoming intolerable and that if it is not changed at once we have decided to refuse all Egyptian arrangements and even to exact evacuation."[88]

Bismarck's son went on to Paris for his interview with Ferry on Egyptian problems, since the West African questions were already settled.[89] Each was pleased with the manner of the other and after agreeing on the unreasonable attitude of England, Herbert expressed the opinion that an understanding on Egypt would be possible.[90] Ferry found that the elder Bismarck's views on Egypt were still "vague" but evolving to his taste.[91] The Premier told Herbert that the only way to check England in Egypt was by a strong union of the Powers. He expressed great regret that France had not stood firm in July, 1882.[92]

Herbert suggested again that France, with Germany's backing, call a conference on Egypt. But Ferry replied that to do so would be useless unless full evacuation could be secured and that this was now impossible. The French Premier believed that the German strategy was to push France ahead but he was determined that his country should await the assured support of the rest of Europe.[93] He was delighted to hear that Bismarck Sr. was anxious to uphold Gladstone, for the latter was one of the few English statesmen who still wanted to quit Egypt.[94]

The rosy glow in Franco-German relations dimmed briefly in mid-November when Bismarck found Ferry intransigent on several Congo problems and was angered by the steady stream of vituperation poured on him by the French nationalist press.[95] Moreover, he had found that his disagreement with Great Britain over the West African questions was not as great as he had supposed.[96] However, new British proposals which would practically have given Egypt to England, as Waddington acidly remarked,[97] threw the continental powers back together.

The British plans for reorganizing Egyptian finances, based on Northbrook's report, contemplated a loan of nine million pounds to be guaranteed by England, the taxation of foreigners, most notably by taxing bond interest, a slight reduction of interest rates on certain bonds, and a reduction of the land tax. Northbrook himself said the program meant

[87] *GP.*, IV, 755. [88] Daudet, *op. cit.*, pp. 129–130. [89] *Supra*, p. 101.
[90] *GP.*, III, 694. [91] *DDF*, V, No. 421. [92] *GP.*, III, 694.
[93] *DDF*, V, No. 421. [94] *GP.*, III, 694. [95] *DDF*, V, No. 450.
[96] Crowe, *op. cit.*, p. 76. [97] *DDF*, V, No. 465.

substituting English for international control of Egyptian finance. His assumption that the Powers would not object [98] was naive and he certainly misjudged Jules Ferry. The latter now found himself compelled both to fight England's attempt to extend her hold on Egypt and to try to recover ground previously lost by France.

The new proposals were given to Waddington in the hope, said Granville, of securing French acceptance before their communication to the rest of Europe. According to the English Minister, Bismarck had said he would gladly see French prior agreement; this the Chancellor heatedly denied.[99] In any event, Ferry would not consider discussion on plans with which he so thoroughly disagreed, and they were sent to the Powers. For nearly four months thereafter, Ferry devoted a large part of his energy to working out counter-proposals and negotiating acceptance of part of them. At the same time he endeavored to link a financial settlement to England's promise to evacuate Egypt in the near future and establish an internationalized regime for the Suez Canal.

In a long interview with Bismarck on November 27, Courcel learned that the Chancellor had refused to discuss the English proposals before they were presented to France, but had rather suggested that some plan for international control of Egypt be offered instead.[100] He returned to his usual suggestion of a Paris conference which he would gladly attend. Courcel suspected privately that Bismarck would give only scant support to such a conference should it convene and take credit for it if it succeeded.[101] To Bismarck, however, he emphasized that, although France had large interests there, Egypt was important to all of Europe. Because of its strategic location this would become more so as European interests in the Far East developed. In the course of this interview, Bismarck expressed warmest feelings toward France, frankly saying that he had for years sought to make France forget the war of 1870 and stating "We already have too many French territories . . ." His suggestion that France might forgive Sedan as she had Waterloo rankled in Courcel's mind.[102] However, assuring Bismarck that Ferry's Government appreciated Germany's friendship and recent assistance, he belittled the importance of the nationalist press.

Courcel was following Ferry's advice in maintaining a reserved attitude on the Egyptian question, waiting for Bismarck to show more concrete expressions of friendship.[103] He suspected that the latter's game was to force France to show her hand to him and also to embroil France with England. But he was greatly encouraged that the Chancellor showed such interest in Egypt. Considering the small stake German

[98] Cromer, *op. cit.*, II, 370.   [99] *DDF*, V, Nos. 462, 463, 469.   [100] *Ibid.*, No. 469.
[101] *Ibid.*, No. 475.   [102] *Ibid.*, No. 471.   [103] *Ibid.*, No. 475.

investors had there, the reason was clearly to be found in power politics but, whatever the motive, Ferry and Courcel hoped to use his interest to their own advantage, while avoiding being caught in any outright commitments against England. Courcel's haunting fear was that England would yield in colonial matters and that Germany would immediately give in on the Egyptian question.[104]

The French reply to Granville's proposals was considerably delayed while Ferry worked out his own counter-proposals, reinforced with the knowledge that Russia, Germany and Austria all considered the English plan unsatisfactory.[105] To add to England's worries, Germany and Russia asked the Khedive for seats on the Debt Commission.[106] Granville, vainly trying to enlist Bismarck's aid, pressed France to answer. After several failures to elicit a reply, Lyons correctly surmised that the Powers were collaborating and observed to Granville, "The best card in your hand, and it is not a high trump, is the reluctance of the French to be thrown irretrievably into the clutches of Bismarck by a distinct quarrel with us." [107] Before the French counter-proposals were dispatched to England, they were indeed sent to Bismarck who accepted Ferry's whole program and even advised him to take his full measure of time to let England's manifold troubles make her more tractable.[108]

The memorandum of Ferry, presented to Granville January 17, asked for an international inquiry into the state of Egyptian finances, an international guarantee of the new loan to Egypt and establishment of an international accord concerning the status of the Suez Canal based on the note of January 3, 1883. Ferry still professed that it was not clear that Egypt was unable to pay her full obligations. The new survey to end all surveys should be conducted by the Debt Commissioners (including new German and Russian commissioners) and the Cairo diplomatic agents of the major Powers. The important question of providing for free access to the Canal, said Ferry, should be taken up by a conference at once without waiting for the report of the new investigation.[109] England should consent to settle the Canal question in return for the concessions made her by the Powers.[110] His clear intention was to link the question of international control of the Canal with the financial reorganization of Egypt, which England felt she must have, by means of a treaty which England did not want.

Ferry's desire to minimize the French origin of the proposals [111] was gratified by the German answer to London which made the same points, merely emphasizing the German interests at stake.[112] Soon afterwards,

---

[104] *Ibid.*, Nos. 518, 529.   [105] *Ibid.*, No. 501.   [106] *Ibid.*, No. 495.
[107] Newton, *op. cit.*, II, 338–339.   [108] *DDF*, V, No. 507; *GP.*, III, 696.
[109] *DDF*, V, No. 515.   [110] *Ibid.*, No. 523.   [111] *Ibid.*, No. 518.
[112] *Ibid.*, Nos. 520, 532.

Austria, Russia and Italy likewise supported him, much to his delight.[113] However, Ferry hung back when Bismarck suggested that they make a joint approach and exert pressure, if need be, on England on the question of paying the long-overdue Alexandria indemnities.[114] Ferry feared that England would immediately link such a problem to the whole financial settlement and delay her answer,[115] Bismarck, together with Russia, was meanwhile pressing the Khedive to answer his requests for seats on the Debt Commission, a proposition the French Consul at Cairo was told to support before Tewfik.[116]

Franco-German relations were now riding high with the Congo conference drawing to a conclusion, Bismarck having ceased encouraging France's rivals in this sphere, and it was at this point that he expressed his desire to have a personal meeting with Ferry.[117]

Faced with such a coalition, at the same time she was harassed by Germany in Africa and the Pacific, and Russia in Afghanistan, England accepted in principle all the points in Ferry's memorandum save for the Commission of Inquiry which England wished to postpone for two years. If at the end of that time, it were still necessary to tax the coupons by five percent, then she would consent to an investigation. The most important concession was the collective guarantee by the Powers of the nine million pound loan. Waddington expressed Ferry's thought:

. . . it implies the eventual surveillance of Europe over Egypt's finances. It is the beginning of the international system applied to Egypt. After the negotiations for the freedom of the Canal will come the question of neutralizing Egypt and, by necessary consequence, the evacuation of the country by the English.[118]

Ferry was pleased with the British answer since the key points of the collective guarantee of the loan and freedom of the Canal were admitted. The postponement of the inquiry he thought not important since the principle was granted.[119] After consultation with the other major Powers, all of whom agreed with him,[120] Ferry proposed that the loan should be the subject of a guarantee convention to be signed at London by the representatives of the guaranteeing Powers. The proceeds of this loan were to be used to pay the Alexandria indemnities and the remainder should go to the Egyptian government. The temporary five percent tax on the interest of the privileged and unified debt should be established for two years by a Khedival decree which should also

113 *Ibid.*, Nos. 524, 525, 536.   114 *Ibid.*, Nos. 526, 530.   115 *Ibid.*, No. 530.
116 *Ibid.*, No. 527.   117 *Supra*, p. 101.   118 *DDF*, V, No. 533.
119 *Ibid.*, Nos. 537, 538. Only the French agents in Cairo were unhappy because it appeared that Egypt was being abandoned to England. *Ibid.*, No. 543.
120 *Ibid.*, Nos. 554, 573, 576; Newton, *op. cit.*, II, 342.

establish the new taxes. For the Suez question, Ferry recommended that an international committee should sit at Cairo from March 2 to examine the technical questions and draw up an arrangement for the Canal. Each major Power as well as Turkey and Egypt should have two delegates. Their recommendations should be adopted by a later conference.[121]

Although the proposals went to England early in February, just after the news of the Khartoum disaster and the loss of General Gordon had shaken the Gladstone Cabinet, Granville objected to the last proposition, arguing for direct negotiation.[122] The rest were accepted.[123] The English Government turned to the idea of an international commission to cope with the Canal problem, so, with the agreement of Germany and her allies, Ferry substituted Paris for Cairo.[124]

At the last moment Bismarck appeared to weaken, for he sent Hohenlohe to suggest to Ferry that France should not press England too hard but should sign the financial agreements before the Suez question was settled.[125] Ferry quickly retorted:

> It was never my intention to conclude with England an arrangement for the Egyptian finances without obtaining at the same time the settling of the other questions posed in the memorandum.

That was why he linked the questions in the original statement. Though no definite commitment had appeared practicable, he had settled for a fixed date for the meeting of an international commission on Suez.[126] Now that England had agreed to a meeting in Paris,[127] Ferry hoped an agreement on the Canal could be made before the parliaments of the various countries had ratified the loan convention. He pointed out that this convention would be tied to the Khedival decree and that these two measures vital for England would stand and fall together. If necessary, the ratifications of the convention would be delayed until the Suez question was settled. Ferry observed that among the two houses of France, the four houses of Austria-Hungary, the two houses of Italy and the chamber of Germany, there should easily be found ample opportunity to delay ratification. "Our Parliaments will cover us better than a damaging clause against the strictures of British diplomacy." [128] Doubtless, the staunch French Republican enjoyed calling to the Chancellor's attention the advantages of the parliamentary system of which the latter had often complained. At any rate, Bismarck did not persist in his objections to hastening the Suez settlement.

121 *DDF*, V, No. 550.   122 *Ibid.*, Nos. 579, 596.   123 *Ibid.*, Nos. 579, 583, 586.
124 *Ibid.*, Nos. 594, 596.   125 *Ibid.*, No. 599.   126 *Ibid.*, No. 601.
127 *Ibid.*, No. 602.   128 *Ibid.*, Nos. 602, 606.

Without further difficulty the convention on the internationally guaranteed Egyptian loan was signed in London on March 18.[129] Simultaneously the Khedival decrees were authorized and the Debt Commission enlarged.

The conference on the establishment of a regime on the Suez Canal to provide for navigation on the basis of the British circular of January 3, 1883, met in Paris on March 30. Ferry's hope was to put through the meeting his plan for making the Canal an international zone with an international police force.[130] Thus the Suez would no longer be primarily a British-dominated area. However, only a single meeting of the Commission took place [131] the very morning before Ferry was defeated in the Chamber of Deputies as a result of the Langson reverse in Tonkin. The following sessions were fruitless. Later French statesmen were unable to call another conference on the question.

Both France and Germany had fared well in their passage of diplomacy with England during late 1884 and early 1885. Germany's interests in Egypt—prompt payment of the claimants for the Alexandria bombardment damage, uninterrupted interest payments and a seat on the Debt Commission were met. But Egypt had been only a weapon to force England to be more agreeable toward German colonial expansion.[132] By the Spring of 1885 Germany found a satisfactory solution to her ambitions in Africa and the Pacific, England yielding on every score. Gladstone backed down completely when he told the House of Commons on March 12 that he was pleased Germany was becoming a colonial power and that England wished her Godspeed. This was in marked contrast to an earlier exchange of bitter words with Bismarck over alleged German promises of support in Egypt. Gladstone's speech was the prelude to a truce between England and Germany. Bismarck began to taper off his support of Ferry. Doubtless he was disappointed by Ferry's determination that the entente should be limited and specific, and his studied coolness to proposals for a general alliance against England. Before long the only Franco-German entente between 1870 and 1914 was to peter out. It had been useful to both parties. Without it, Ferry certainly could not have conducted his many colonial campaigns with such impunity on the continent, and especially, it had enabled him to make some progress in Egyptian questions.

Jules Ferry had easily undertaken an active policy in regard to Egypt when the occasion arose. He had a solid bourgeois respect for French

---

[129] *Egypt, No.* 7 (1885), pp. 1–3.
[130] Rambaud, *op. cit.*, pp. 272–273; *DDF*, V, No. 609.
[131] *L J. Commission internationale pour le libre usage du Canal de Suez,* 1885, No. 1.
[132] *GP.*, IV, 758.

investments and investors there, although he himself had no financial connection with Egypt. He could never hope to make Egypt a French colony, but he could hope during his second term to enlarge France's controlling share. Not only was he moved by the respect for old French traditions which he upheld in overseas areas whenever he had the opportunity, but Egypt's new importance was her contiguity to the Suez through which trade passed to the increased French possessions in the East. Then, too, Ferry believed that any enlargement of French power was a good in itself.

On the ledger of accomplishments, Ferry had much to enter. During his second Premiership, with Bismarck's aid, he had prevented the British from making Egypt their exclusive preserve. He kept intact the tradition of European financial control of that country and, moreover, he actually increased it. He was later disappointed in seeing the beginnings he had made toward achieving international political control of the Suez wasted by his successors who, unlike him, did not have Bismarck's blessing. He believed, himself, that if he had only somewhat more time he could have carried his ideas out successfully. At any rate, he had rather skillfully used the irritation of Bismarck and the embarrassment of England to stop England and to increase France's chances of regaining a position in Egypt.

French Somaliland

The movement of Egyptian troops to the vicinity of Obock first brought Jules Ferry into action on the question of Somaliland. France's claims to part of this region on the Southeastern hump of Africa [133] were strengthened and enlarged by Ferry partly to counter the advance of the English and partly to establish a more secure naval station on the road to Indo-China and the Southwest Pacific.

The small port of Obock on the Gulf of Aden had been ceded to France by its Sultan in 1862.[134] However, no settlement was made and three trading posts, established in 1881 as possible termini for caravan routes, failed.[135] Gambetta sent a warship in 1882 to aid a French merchant from Réunion who was being molested,[136] but still there was no continuous occupation.

Ferry demanded the withdrawal of the Egyptian troops on June 22,

---

[133] The Khedive Ismail had laid claim to most of the desert waste that is Somaliland by establishing posts along the coast in 1874 and 1875. He paid tribute to the Sultan for this area but in reality it was ruled by several independent Moslem chieftans.

[134] This was secured when a warship called to exact punishment for the death of a French subject.

[135] Hanotaux *et* Martineau, *op. cit.*, IV, 582.   [136] Hanotaux, *Mon Temps*, II, 196.

1883 [137] and shortly thereafter the flag of Egypt was torn down by a French force.[138] The British had inspired this movement of the Egyptians to various Red Sea and Gulf of Aden seacoast towns in order to protect the shore and the Canal route from the Sudanese tribesmen.[139] It was asserted in Commons that France had only some vague claims on Obock but when Waddington protested that it actually was a French holding, Granville readily yielded.[140] Shortly thereafter the French claims were extended.

By 1884 there was another reason for Ferry to strengthen the hold on Obock, for French ships were refused permission to coal at English ports during the Franco-Chinese hostilities.[141] To establish a coaling station and small colony at Obock, Paul Lagarde was sent in July, 1884 with twenty-seven soldiers.[142] Upon Ferry's instructions, Lagarde proceeded to secure for France the shoreline around the Gulf of Tajura, on one side of which stands Obock and on the other Jibouti. The Sultanate of Tajura was placed under protectorate on September 21 and the Egyptian troops there withdrawn,[143] although no French occupation was made. Through the remainder of the year, Sagallo, Ras Ali and Angar were set under French control.[144] In January 1885 protectorates were extended over Raheita and Gobad and finally Jibouti, later to become the capital of the colony.[145] These areas formed the major part of the colony of French Somaliland.

The Italian occupation of the Red Sea littoral around Massawa was protested by Ferry in February, 1885 as a violation of Turkish integrity. France, he said, had claims to Adulis Bay and Dessé Island.[146] However, since Italy had the approval of her allies, Germany and Austria, and of England,[147] Ferry's protests were unavailing. Obock remained as the single French-occupied port in Somaliland serving only as a naval station on the route to Indo-China accessible both to the Cape and the Suez routes.

[137] *DDF*, V, No. 451.   [138] Rambaud, *France Coloniale*, p. 420.

[139] *Egypt, No. 15* (1885), p. 10. To this end England had urged the Ottoman Empire to take possession of that coast although it had failed to do so. Later Italian occupation of part of Somaliland was looked upon favorably for the same reason. *Ibid.*, p. 81. Britain was meanwhile occupying Zeyla farther down the coast.

[140] *Ibid.*, p. 4.   [141] *Infra*, p. 178.

[142] Hanotaux *et* Martineau, *op. cit.*, IV, 582.

[143] *DDF*, V, No. 479; *Egypt, No. 14 (1885)*, pp. 11, 56.

[144] *Egypt, No. 14*, p. 56; *No. 15*, pp. 52, 58.

[145] *Egypt, No. 14*, p. 75; Hanotaux *et* Martineau, *op. cit.*, IV, 583.

[146] *DDF*, V, Nos. 547, 549, 574, 593.

[147] *Ibid.*, 593; *Egypt, No. 15*, p. 81; Daudet, *op. cit.*, p. 20; Newton, *op. cit.*, II, 341; Cromer, *op. cit.*, II, 57.

Chapter Seven

EMPIRE AND WAR IN INDO-CHINA

The most famous colonial affair of Jules Ferry's second Ministry was the extension of a French protectorate over Annam and its province of Tonkin in Indo-China. Together with Tunisia, this acquisition is Ferry's greatest claim to fame as an empire-builder, for Tonkin and Annam were striking additions to the existing French possessions in Cochin-China and Cambodia. Rich prizes of imperialist rivalries in the Far East, they were not easily won, especially since Tonkin involved France in a war with China.

French interests in and claims to the parts of Indo-China adjacent to the French colonies of Cochin-China and Cambodia long antedated Jules Ferry. As in other colonial theaters, so here there were a few established economic ties, some missionary activity, and, more important, an aggressive spirit on the part of colonial administrators. Again the familiar pattern of Ferry's imperialist activities recurs: when he came to office there was an old French claim to the area and a military expedition all ready to move against the native rulers. Ferry lost no time in ordering the expedition to proceed. During two years thereafter—that is, throughout his second Premiership, he was engaged in military operations in the Far East. This particular colonial venture dominated his overseas policies. It was the most costly of all his projects. In the end it proved successful for France but provided the military reverse which brought about Ferry's personal defeat and sent him to political limbo.

French Indo-Chinese holdings were revived only under Napoleon III, for the older French establishments in Annam and Cambodia had withered away early in the nineteenth century. The Second Empire's hope that Cochin-China and Cambodia [1] would give access up the Mekong River to reputedly wealthy Southwestern China [2] proved illusory. In the next decade interest shifted North to Annam's province

---

[1] After a military demonstration against Annam, that kingdom ceded to France in 1862, the provinces of Saigon, Mitho, and Bianhoa in Cochin-China. Three more provinces West of these were seized in 1867, but no settlement was made with the Annamites. The province of Cambodia was annexed in 1863.

[2] Roberts, *op. cit.*, II, 422.

of Tonkin whose Red River provided a commercial route to the Chinese province of Yunnan.

The Annamites were an energetic, well-organized people of Chinese culture who had long held most of Indo-China, having conquered Tonkin in 1802.[3] The heavily populated Red River delta offered potential markets, but the river and the province were swarming with Chinese bandit gangs. The Annamite mandarins, moreover, were very hostile to Europeans, and endeavored to keep Tonkin and the Red River closed to them.[4] Their kingdom's vassalage to China was observed only when convenient.[5]

French officials in Cochin-China had been spoiling for a chance to extend their nation's rule over neighboring Annam.[6] They found their instrument in the person of a French merchant, Jean Dupuis, who, in 1871, had found the Red River to be navigable to Yunnan.[7] Having established a trade in salt and arms in exchange for metals, he vainly sought aid in Paris to clear the river of the pirates. On a subsequent trip up the river in 1873, Dupuis was held a virtual prisoner at Hanoi by the Annamites who demanded his recall. The Governor of Cochin-China used the occasion to dispatch an expedition ostensibly to enforce the Annamite demand, but actually to establish a protectorate.[8] Sent in violation of orders from France,[9] the expedition of eighty-three men was led by one Francis Garnier, a colonial official and explorer who dreamed of a great Eastern French Empire.[10]

After Garnier's arrival at Hanoi,[11] the Annamite court at Hué was told that the Red River and the ports of Tonkin must be opened to Europeans.[12] On November 18, 1873, Garnier carried out his real orders and, instead of ordering Dupuis to leave, proclaimed the Red River open to French, Spanish and Chinese trade from the sea to Yunnan's border.[13] When the Annamite troops refused to leave the citadel, it

[3] *Ibid.*

[4] Jean Dupuis, *L'ouverture du Fleuve Rouge au commerce* (Paris, 1879), p. 3.

[5] *Ibid.*, p. 424.

[6] Albert de Pouvourville, *Francis Garnier* (Paris, 1931), p. 189.

[7] Dupuis, *op. cit.*, p. 2.

[8] Dupré, the Governor of Cochin-China, instructed Garnier to stay at Hanoi and "prevent the recurrence of such incidents." Pouvourville, *op. cit.*, pp. 195–202.

[9] *Ibid.*, p. 193.

[10] A native of Lorraine, Garnier had been an official in Cochin-China for years, had been second in command of an expedition that explored the Mekong and, as early as 1863, had begun to urge France to open Indo-China to French commerce. He fancied himself the heir and successor to Dupleix. *Ibid.*, pp. 4, 179.

[11] Where he had to face the hostility not only of the Annamite mandarins but also of the Spanish Dominicans. *Ibid.*, p. 205.

[12] *Ibid.*, p. 204.

[13] Three Tonkin ports were also opened and customs duties set. *Ibid.*, p. 207.

was stormed and easily taken.[14] Garnier then undertook to free the region from the piratical Black Flags.[15] He had cleared nearly the whole delta when he was slain in an ambush. After this reverse, the French withdrew on orders from the Duc de Broglie, then Foreign Minister, much to the annoyance of the Governor of Cochin-China who thought the subsequent treaty to be a shameful surrender.

The Treaty of Saigon of 1874

An accord, known as the Treaty of Saigon, was signed with Annam on March 15, 1874. Although the specific term was not used, it established a poorly defined protectorate over that country. Annam was declared to be independent, but the suzerainty of China was not explicitly ended. The ports of Hanoi, Haiphong and Quinh-On were declared open to commerce; a garrison of one hundred French troops was to be established in each; and French consuls were given exclusive jurisdiction over foreign residents. France made no territorial claims on Tonkin, but the navigation of ships of Western nations up the Red River to China was permitted.[16] Various gifts were presented to the King, Tu-Duc. In the National Assembly at Versailles only an oral vote was taken for quick ratification on August 3, 1874, after Admiral Jaurés, Minister of the Navy and Colonies, spoke of the special opportunities the treaty brought for French commerce.[17] China was duly notified of the arrangement,[18] but entered no protest. The loosely drawn agreement could be variously interpreted, and led to many later misunderstandings.

French expansion in Indo-China stagnated from 1874 to 1880. Several objections were mildly presented to China against the presence of her troops in Tonkin, and there were other protests to Annam about the poor treatment of French nationals and the persecution of Christians. Annam was also repeatedly requested to rid the Red River of pirates, but these protests received no satisfaction.[19]

The early Foreign Ministers of the Republic like the Duc de Decaze

14 *Ibid.*, p. 211.

15 These were bands of Chinese bandits and mercenaries who had filtered down into Tonkin after the Taiping rebellion in China and were now ravaging the countryside.

16 Text in: *Livre Jaune Tonkin* (Paris, 1883), No. 1.

17 *J. O. C.*, 8/4/74. Only Georges Perin, who always predicted dire consequences from colonial expansion, protested against the complications to which this partial protectorate might lead. A commercial agreement between France and Annam was signed in the same month and passed by the Chamber without discussion on July 6, 1875.

18 *L. J. T.*, No. 24.

19 The French Consuls had little authority, and were constantly hampered by the mandarins. E. Hippeau, *Histoire diplomatique de la Troisième République* (Paris, 1889), pp. 451 ff.

were anxious to avoid complications in this area.[20] Waddington [21] and Freycinet showed slight interest in the Far East despite many urgent protests from Admiral Jauréguiberry, several times Minister of the Navy and Colonies, and Le Myre de Vilers, Governor of Cochin-China.[22]

The imperialists had small prospect of success until Annam renewed her recently neglected vassalage to China as a counterpoise to French designs.[23] Alarmed, De Vilers and the French Minister in Pekin urged that a firm stand be taken to reassert French rights at once lest France lose her position.[24] Freycinet was persuaded to prepare an expeditionary force and received German acquiescence.[25] An appropriation of 2,700,000 francs was passed by the Chamber on July 18, for measures to enforce the 1874 treaty.[26] By July 26, Freycinet had plans to send three thousand troops to the Red River, but he was forced to resign before he could act, just as he had been overthrown at the moment he was preparing to occupy Tunisia.[27] Such was the situation when Jules Ferry became Premier for the first time in September 1881.[28]

Ferry and Annam in 1881

Jules Ferry was no more interested in taking action against Annam than against Tunisia [29] when he first assumed the Premiership. His attention was wholly absorbed by domestic problems. His Minister of Foreign Affairs, Barthélemy Saint-Hilaire, at first intended to continue with the Tonkin project,[30] but in late October or early November the Cabinet decided against it.[31]

During that Fall and Winter the Ferry Government contented itself with informing China again that only France had suzerainty over Annam in accordance with the terms of the 1874 treaty,[32] and that she

[20] Giving instructions to a new Governor of Cochin-China in September 1877, Decazes said of Tonkin: ". . . we have renounced openly establishing a protectorate . . . originally in the personal views of the negotiator. . . . [We are] not in a position to undertake aggrandizement. . . . We have had . . . by interpretation to reduce the meaning of certain clauses of the treaty." He urged that French rights over Annam should still be asserted, however. *L. J. T.*, No. 40.

[21] On the urging of his Minister of the Navy and Colonies, Waddington instructed the Governor of Cochin-China to negotiate a treaty of protectorate over Tonkin on January 10, 1879, but nothing came of it. *L. J. T.*, No. 40. German explorers had been urging Bismarck to take Annam, but when Waddington asserted France's intention of upholding the 1874 treaty rights, the Chancellor promised not to attempt such a step unless France should relinquish her rights. *DDF*, IV, No. 561.

[22] *L. J. T.*, No. 53; Grandidier, *op. cit.*, p. 32; *DDF*, III, No. 14.

[23] Tu-Duc sent tribute to Pekin, and China revived her claim in a notice inserted in the Pekin *Gazette*. *L. J. T.*, No. 62.

[24] *DDF*, III, No. 138. [25] *Ibid.*, No. 197. [26] *J. O. C.*, 8/19/81.
[27] *Supra*, p. 42. [28] *Supra*, p. 20. [29] *Supra*, p. 42.
[30] *L. J. T.*, No. 91. [31] *Ibid.*, No. 72.
[32] *DDF*, III, Nos. 344, 345; *L. J. T.*, No. 165.

intended to preserve it. Governor de Vilers continued his exhortations to take over Tonkin, for Chinese action there was steadily increasing, he reported, and the Chinese were even interfering with the court at Hué.[33] Admiral Cloué, the Minister of the Navy and Colonies, was so disturbed by these reports that by April 15 he asked Barthélemy Saint-Hilaire to support him in a demand for funds to assert French rights in Annam.[34] Saint-Hilaire agreed to support the request, declaring that his office favored a "strict execution of the treaties of 1874." [35] This decision was reached less than ten days after the Ferry Government had determined to uphold French claims in Tunisia.

The plans for Indo-China, like those for Tunisia, soon grew more extensive. By late May, Admiral Cloué decided that the best solution would be a "true protectorate" over Tonkin and Annam, thus ending the jurisdiction of European consuls which had greatly vexed the French.[36] His attitude was undoubtedly encouraged by the success and apparent ease of placing Tunisia under a protectorate on May 12.

The Ferry Government brought a bill for an appropriation of 2,400,000 francs for an expedition to clear the Red River of pirates and explore the upper regions of Tonkin before the Chamber on July 21. At this time the Ministry was in a weak parliamentary position,[37] but the debate was brief and quiet. Ferry himself did not take part in it. The measure was urged upon the Chamber as necessary to support French prestige and national honor. The *rapporteur* of the bill denied that there was any intention of establishing a French protectorate over Tonkin. There was surprisingly little said about the commercial possibilities of the region. The measure was attacked by Perin of the Extreme Left and Delafosse, the Bonapartist: both were men who always opposed the Ferry Government. The bill passed, 309–82.[38] This was a larger majority than the Government had obtained after an interpellation on its Tunisian policies on June 30 (248–219) or on July 25 following an interpellation on the shifting of the election date (214–201). The fact that the vote came just at the time when considerable criticism was being levelled against the Tunisian expedition confirms again that there was no body of parliamentary opinion consistently opposed to all colonial expeditions as such.

The only difficulty with a foreign power came from China which immediately entered a protest against the contemplated French action, refusing to recognize the validity of the treaty of 1874, as it conflicted

---

[33] *DDF*, III, No. 461.   [34] *Ibid.*   [35] *Ibid.*, No. 470.
[36] *DDF*, IV, No. 113.   [37] *Supra*, p. 60.
[38] *J. O. C.*, 7/22/81. Perin was perhaps the most consistent anti-imperialist in the Chamber, protesting against every new expedition France sent out during these years, while professing to love the colonies France already held.

with Chinese claims of suzerainty.[39] The Chinese claimed, and the French denied, that they had protested against that accord when informed of it in 1875. At least there is no record of such a protest among the available documents, and the Chinese were never able to cite chapter and verse to substantiate their accusation.

However, the caution of Admiral Cloué grew apace, undoubtedly because the French had fifty thousand troops engaged in the Tunisian campaign in September and October. There were no forces to be spared for the Far East. Governor de Vilers was informed late in September that a full scale military expedition could not be undertaken; only limited measures against the pirates and a demonstration against Annam were possible. These were to take place after the garrisons at Hanoi and Haiphong in Tonkin were secretly reinforced with troops from Cochin-China. De Vilers was also told that no trouble was expected from China.[40] With all these restrictions, little was done in Indo-China for the time being.

The Gambetta Ministry took no action in that theater, although Gambetta told the Chinese ambassador that Chinese claims were of purely historic interest.[41] The Governor of Cochin-China was ordered to avoid hostilities and his protests of the need for immediate action went unheeded.[42] When Freycinet returned to the Quai d'Orsay he quite typically pursued a cautious policy, acquiesing only to limited policing measures.[43]

French Action Against Annam

In accordance with instructions to sweep the pirates from the Red River, Commander Henri Rivière was sent with four hundred men from Saigon to Tonkin where he quickly exceeded his formal instructions and captured Hanoi itself. He reported that the "threatening attitude" of the Mandarins had necessitated the action of April 26, 1882 and it was approved by Vilers.[44] After this definite involvement, France had to push on or lose face. As in so many other theaters, action was forced by the military men on the scene faster than the Ministry in Paris desired.

China immediately protested Hanoi's capture and continued vigorous protests throughout the Spring. Freycinet at first refused an explanation, maintaining that France was enforcing her treaty rights, which were no concern of China's.[45] In Annam, Tu-Duc became more unfriendly point-

[39] *DDF*, IV, No. 143. [40] *DDF*, IV, No. 152.
[41] A. Debidour, *Histoire diplomatique de l'Europe* (Paris, 1918), I, 70.
[42] *DDF*, IV, No. 220; *L. J. T.*, No. 105. [43] *DDF*, IV, No. 277.
[44] *Ibid.*, No. 304. [45] *Ibid.*, Nos. 360, 534.

ing out that the French action was a violation of the 1874 treaty since he was not consulted. The French attributed his attitude to Chinese support.

As in 1880, Admiral Jauréguiberry, again Minister of the Navy and Colonies in the succeeding Duclerc Cabinet, urged a swift move to take all of Tonkin. He proposed to seize it not just for economic advantage, but as a point of honor to protect the flouted French flag.[46] The Cabinet voted to act on October 21, Duclerc stating that the situation was due to the capture of Hanoi, contrary to the original plans.[47] Duclerc consented on November 14 to use the troops to establish a "full protectorate" over Tonkin and Annam.[48] His justification, the necessity for France to move a small expedition into Tonkin to save the fruits of many years' work and forestall other nations,[49] bears a striking similarity to that he gave for the Madagascan operations decided on six weeks later. A force of three thousand men was organized: three hundred to move on Hué, the rest to go to Tonkin. Jauréguiberry asked the Chamber for ten million francs for the expedition.

Although the French Government had expected the Chinese to acquiese,[50] the Empire had been moving troops into Tonkin on the invitation of Tu-Duc, and clashes with the French troops were imminent. China maintained that her troops were there only to suppress brigands, but the French were uneasy,[51] until suddenly the Chinese announced on December 5 that they would withdraw their troops [52] as the result of an agreement made with the French Minister in Pekin.

Negotiations in the Chinese capital by Bourée, the French Minister, had been underway since November 5, unknown to Paris. On the 27th, they resulted in an agreement providing for the withdrawal of Chinese troops from Annam, and in return France was to renounce "any idea of conquest . . . [or any] enterprise against the territorial sovereignty of the King of Annam." The Red River was to be open to commerce but the territory between the Red River and the China border was to be evenly divided, China to assume the policing of the Northern half and France the Southern.[53] This arrangement was a retreat from the French demands, but Duclerc accepted it provisorily as soon as he heard of it,[54] and, to Jauréguiberry's disgust, ordered the troops halted.[55] Duclerc's eagerness was like that he displayed when an opportunity for a peaceful solution was presented in the Madagascar affair. Nothing further was done before the fall of the Ministry on January 30, 1883. The succeed-

46 *Ibid.*, No. 542.   47 *L. J. T.*, No. 133.   48 *Ibid.*, No. 137.

49 *DDF*, IV, No. 581.   50 *L. J. T.*, No. 137.   51 *Ibid.*

52 *DDF*, IV, No. 545.   53 *Ibid.*, No. 370.   54 *Ibid.*, No. 582.

55 *Ibid.*, Nos. 587, 590.

ing weak Fallières Ministry took no action in the Far East.[56] As in other theaters of operations, here was a colonial problem in suspension that needed the energetic action Jules Ferry would bring in his second Ministry.

Ferry's Inheritance

When Jules Ferry returned to the Premiership for the second time, an expeditionary force was already stationed in the Tonkin delta. If the Bourée agreement with China were not accepted, it would be necessary only to set this force in motion. For the moment, although Ferry had no long-range, specific plans for action in Indo-China or in other colonial fields, nevertheless a new element was present in his thinking. Now he was convinced from the beginning, as he had not been during his first Premiership, of the value of an imperialistic policy. It is not surprising, therefore, that without a perfectly clear idea of where his decision might lead him, he soon acted opportunistically to seize Far Eastern territory.

As with the other colonial ventures of his career, Ferry found himself heir in Indo-China to an old policy. The French had first been led into Annam and Tonkin by a combined search for markets and the imperialistic ambition of the colonial administrators in Cochin-China. The economic considerations were soon buried beneath those of national honor and prestige, for, having gained a precarious hold in Tonkin, French administrators and military men felt they had to keep going to avoid losing face. The expansionist drive then came not from merchants but from these men and diplomats in the Far East who found their best supporter to be Jules Ferry. To them territorial gain was a good in itself, a contribution to the prestige and glory of their country. Using the opportunities that came to hand, they were now well able to forward the French cause, and Ferry backed them because he, too, was a staunch patriot to whom these arguments appealed.

In discussing the reasons why Ferry pushed ahead in Indo-China, scholars have often assumed that economic determinism was very important.[57] Because, in the course of defending his policies before Parlia-

[56] The only sign of interest in the problem was that expressed by François de Mahy, the ardent expansionist from Réunion who served in the ministry as Minister of Commerce and Agriculture and *ad interim* Minister of the Navy and Colonies. He had helped launch a determined drive against Madagascar from this post. He was horrified to learn that an arrangement had been concluded with China wherein France abandoned her rights and virtually recognized the suzerainty of China over Annam. On the last day of the Ministry he wrote a memorandum expressing his angry but unavailing protest against the accord. *DDF*, IV, No. 612.

[57] Woolf, *op. cit.*, p. 25; Moon, *op. cit.*, pp. 42–45; Roberts, *op. cit.*, II, 425–428; Schuman, *op. cit.*, pp. 81 ff.

ment and the country, the Premier gave classic expression to the tenets of economic imperialism: the need for markets and investment fields for France, some have believed that Ferry had a clear and present interest in the economy of Annam and China. Actually, his pleas for imperialism on economic grounds represented rationalizations *ex post facto* rather than his primary motives for acting. As a good bourgeois politician, he had a healthy regard for the possibilities of business advantage for French commerce. Doubtless that prudent thought was constantly in the back of his mind for it was an integral part of his outlook. It also was advantageous to appear before Parliament as the champion of French trade and industry. But economic advantage in the Far East was a matter of speculation rather than immediate fulfillment.

In 1883 France had but small economic stakes in Annam and Tonkin and French trade and investment were very slow to enter even after the conquest. The economic, like the cultural, ties of Annam were chiefly with China both before and after French intervention. There could be only limited markets for European goods among the poor, agricultural population. In 1885 Tonkin imported only seven million francs' worth of goods from France [58] despite the high hopes of Ferry and his friends. There were few French traders in the region, the outstanding exception being Dupuis. That ambitious merchant did describe to Ferry the great potentialities of the Red River delta and the even greater wealth of Southwestern China [59] and may have been partly responsible for the Premier's optimistic expectations.

Ferry's hope of finding good new fields for investment was also slow to be realized. There were then no French investors in Annam and Tonkin. There were no railroads there as yet,[60] and Tonkin had no French bank until the Bank of Indo-China, operating from Cochin-China, established a branch there upon invitation of the French government.[61]

There was no personal profit for Ferry, his family or friends in the Indo-Chinese expansion, any more than in any of the other colonial expeditions in which he was interested. No charges of personal gain for Ferry were ever substantiated.[62] If he had been speculating here it is

[58] In 1885 the chief imports were wines to the extent of three million francs, and textiles to about half a million.

[59] Albert Duchêne, *La politique coloniale de la France* (Paris, 1928), p. ix. One of the greatest attractions of the Red River route was that the freight rates were so much lower than on the Yangtze. Roberts, *op. cit.*, II, 424.

[60] Railroad construction began only in 1897. Godfernaux, *op. cit.*, p. 34.

[61] Henri Baudoin, *La Banque de l'Indo-Chine* (Paris, 1903), p. 27.

[62] One radical pamphleteer charged that Ferry profited from his various colonial expeditions but he had no evidence for his accusations. See A. Chirac, *L'agiotage sous la Troisième République, 1870–1887* (Paris, 1888), II, 147, 190.

certain that his opponents would have uncovered and dwelt on it in 1885 after his resounding defeat.

A certain amount of responsibility for initiating and pursuing the expansionist policy in the Far East belongs to Ferry's subordinates, for he had a number of advisors who were ardent imperialists. Among the most influential of them with regard to the Tonkin policy was Albert Billot, Director of Political Affairs in the Ministry of Foreign Affairs during Ferry's second Premiership. Just as Baron Courcel had been influential in launching the Tunisian expedition,[63] so now Billot helped greatly in shaping a firm policy toward Annam and China over Tonkin.[64] The influence of this ardent advocate of French expansion is attested by many who were close to the control of policy,[65] Billot himself later complained that the Radical Republicans disliked him for his behind-the-scenes role in the Tonkin matter.[66] Ferry's Foreign Minister, Challemel-Lacour, had no policy-forming role in Indo-Chinese affairs, merely following with gloomy expectation of failure the decisions that the Premier made.[67]

The initial declaration of policy of the new Ferry Cabinet gave no hint of any intention to pursue new conquests in the Far East. The Premier promised the Chambers that he would pursue "a pacific policy. . . . But a pacific policy is not necessarily an inactive policy . . . in all questions where our interests or our honor are involved we shall maintain for France the rank that belongs to her." [68]

Ferry turned his attention to Indo-China soon after the pressing domestic matters had been arranged. He had no intention of minimizing French claims there; hence Bourée who had made the new arrangement with China, calling for the surrender of part of Tonkin, was recalled on March 5 with the explanation that his proposed accord overlooked France's treaty rights.[69] China was informed that France wanted to maintain friendly relations with her, but intended to secure observance of the 1874 treaty with Annam.[70] Reinforcements were dispatched to the detachment in Tonkin on March 23.

As China persisted in asserting her rights over Annam, she was warned

[63] *Supra*, pp. 49–50.
[64] As he also did in the Madagascar episode. *Supra*, p. 120.
[65] Hanotaux, *Mon Temps*, II, 250; SDA, *Dispatches, France*, vol. 95, No. 647; Vice-Admiral Fournier, "La France et la Chine au traité de Tien-Tsin," *Revue des Deux Mondes* 7me pér. (1921), t. V, 770, 790.
[66] A. Billot, *France et l'Italie* (Paris, 1905), I, 4. Unfortunately Billot's own memoir on the Tonkin question is not available in this country. Apparently it has not been consulted by previous writers on this subject.
[67] Emile Krakowski, *La naissance de la Troisième République; Paul Challemel-Lacour* (Paris, 1932), p. 298.
[68] *J. O. C.*, 2/23/83.   [69] *DDF*, V, No. 6.   [70] *Ibid.*

that France would not be frightened out of that country.[71] Paris did not credit the warnings from Bourée that China intended to fight,[72] a miscalculation that cost them dearly.

The expedition in Tonkin was voted a credit of 5,300,000 francs with very little opposition in the Chamber save from a few speakers on the extreme wings. Challemel-Lacour told the deputies that French honor was at stake and that this appropriation would enable her troops to insure the observance of the rights granted by the 1874 treaty. He misled the Chamber when he assured it that China had no interest in Tonkin and offered no objection to French action there. The bill passed with the large majority of 351–48.[73]

Hostilities in Tonkin

Out in Tonkin, Rivière defeated the Black Flags at Nam-Dinh; turned back when he found his base at Hanoi threatened, and was killed in an ambush on May 18.[74] Soon afterwards the amended Tonkin appropriation came back to the Chamber of Deputies from the Senate. The bill was passed unanimously with 494 votes [75] in a burst of patriotic enthusiasm for vengeance on those who had insulted the French flag. A force of four thousand men and a squadron under Admiral Courbet was sent to crush the Black Flags and their pirate allies, and to expel any Chinese troops found in the Tonkin delta region.

Ferry's intention of extending a protectorate over the whole region was clear, although he did not yet publicly admit his plans. A new Civil Commissioner for Cochin-China, General Harmand, was instructed on June 8 to be ready to organize the Tonkin protectorate, limiting French occupation to the delta of the Red River. It was hoped that he would be able to do this in the near future.[76]

France experienced little difficulty with other European powers in the early stages of the Tonkin affair. England was not pleased, but would not take action. Germany supported France, refusing to aid China and advising her to yield when China asked for assistance.[77] The United States sounded France on July 18 on the possibility of mediating the Tonkin dispute, but Challemel-Lacour politely declined, stating that there was no trouble between China and France.[78] The American Minister persisted, however, and on August 10 handed to the Foreign Minister the Chinese demands that France leave Tonkin. Challemel-Lacour was distinctly annoyed at this intrusion and refused even to

[71] *Ibid.*, Nos. 22, 24.   [72] *Ibid.*, No. 24.   [73] *J. O. C.*, 5/16/83.
[74] *L. J. T.*, No. 199.   [75] *J. O. C.*, 5/29/83.   [76] *DDF*, V, No. 46.
[77] *Ibid.*, No. 61.   [78] SDA, *Dispatches, France*, vol. 92, No. 372.

consider the demands which asked complete abandonment of the French claims.[79]

At this stage Parliament objected only slightly to the Tonkin expedition. On July 10 the Government had to answer an interpellation on its Far Eastern policy submitted by the deputies Granet and Delafosse. Granet charged that the expedition was ill-advised and warned of the dangers of complications with China. Rising to speak in his own defense, Challemel-Lacour promised that France would stay in the Delta region of Tonkin, a promise which was not observed and which was often later flung at Ferry to his embarrassment. Lacour further promised not to act without consulting Parliament. He blundered when he stated that France was at "war" with Annam: such a situation was, of course, quite unconstitutional, for only Parliament could declare war. At least the fiction of peace had to be maintained. The opposition made much of this admission, both then and later. Lacour denied that there was any trouble between France and China, at the very time when China was bitterly protesting the French action. Cassagnac, the noisy Bonapartist, accused Jules Ferry of personally profiting from the expedition, and when he could not produce any proof of this charge he was expelled from the Chamber in a tempestuous scene. Confidence in the Ministry, however, was voted by the large margin of 362–78 votes.[80]

Ferry's parliamentary position was very strong at this time, his measure to purge the judiciary having just been passed with a comfortable margin. His prestige was bolstered when the Republicans won in the elections to the departmental assemblies on August 12 and 19, thereby strengthening the Republican cause in the bodies that chose the Senators.

The contemplated French action in Tonkin was ostensibly directed against the Black Flags whom Tu-Duc had employed to combat the French, but in reality the French forces were also faced with regular Chinese troops, even though at this time China denied their presence.[81] Ferry told Marquis Tseng on June 21 that he intended only to establish a protectorate, not to annex either Annam or Tonkin; that he would realize the provisions of the 1874 treaty, and clear the Red River. Tseng was pointedly warned that the Chinese forces in Annam would be attacked if they opposed the French.[82] China continued at frequent intervals to protest the French action and refused to recognize the treaty of 1874,[83] but only on August 9 did Tseng admit that there were Chinese troops in Tonkin, which he averred had gone there to repress the bandits.[84] Therefore, there was now danger of war with China if the

[79] *Ibid.*, No. 397.   [80] *J. O. C.*, 9/11/83.   [81] *DDF*, V, No. 50.
[82] *Ibid.*   [83] *Ibid.*, No. 56.   [84] *Ibid.*, No. 68.

French and Chinese troops should clash. On the same day that Tseng admitted the presence of Chinese troops in Tonkin, France exercised her rights under the Treaty of Saigon to establish a blockade against the munitions traffic in the ports of Annam.[85]

Protectorate Over Annam

The whole situation was suddenly changed to the benefit of the French, when the elderly Tu-Duc was poisoned by a faction at his court. Immediately, Ferry sent French reinforcements of five thousand men to the Far East without consulting Parliament, then on vacation. General Harmand and Admiral Courbet took advantage of the confusion to impose a new treaty on his successor, Disiep-Hoa, on August 25.[86] Signed after a brief bombardment of Hué, the capital, under a threat of occupation, the Treaty of Hué compelled Annam to accept an unreserved military, diplomatic and financial protectorate giving France full rights of intervention in Annam and complete French control of Tonkin. Harmand went beyond Ferry's instructions when he also arranged for the annexation to Tonkin of the provinces of Ha-Tinh, Ngue-Ann and Thank-Hoa and the province of Binh-Thuan to Cochin-China. These annexation provisions were dropped by Ferry from the final treaty in consideration of his explicit promises not to annex any territory. The treaty was ratified only more than nine months later, June 6, 1884, for France still had to pacify Tonkin and drive out the Chinese troops.

Chinese Stalemate

Negotiations with China in Shanghai to secure agreement to the French protectorate broke down when Li-Hong-Tchang, the Chinese Viceroy in charge of foreign affairs, refused to accept the new treaty.[87] Tension mounted as the Chinese reportedly sent more troops into Tonkin in late August.[88] The French were now the victims of a subtle Chinese delaying action in which Li, Tseng, and the Tsong-Li-Yamen, the Chinese Foreign Office, each claimed that the other was the proper one to carry on negotiations and that he himself could do nothing.[89] The French position was made worse by the tactlessness of the French Minister, Tricou, of whom Ferry said that he "treated the Chinese like Arabs." Tricou was replaced on September 7, but the new Minister, Patenôtre, did not take up his duties at once.[90] On September 11 the

85 *L. J. T.*, No. 238.   86 *Ibid.*, No. 253.   87 *DDF*, V, No. 58.
88 *L. J. T.*, No. 250.   89 *DDF*, V, No. 58.   90 *Ibid.*, No. 92.

French concessions at Canton were burned by a mob, and the Europeans in that port had to take refuge on the ships.[91]

In September, on Ferry's instructions, England's good offices were sought to settle the Franco-Chinese differences. France proposed that a neutral zone between Tonkin and China be established and that in case of disturbances there the two powers should act in concert to quell them. Man Hao on the Red River should be an open port; China must agree not to intervene in the administration of Annam, but the Annamite king was to be allowed to send presents to the Emperor, if he desired, although his doing so was not to be considered an act of vassalage.[92] China rebuffed this French concession and demanded the recognition of her sovereignty over Annam. Such demands France refused to discuss.[93] When France suggested that England support her proposals at Pekin, Granville declined on September 14, and the negotiations died.[94]

Ferry was very anxious to settle this affair now that he had his protectorates, but, as he complained to his wife, China was "as ungraspable as a stream." [95] China repeatedly proposed in Paris and Pekin that France leave Tonkin,[96] a suggestion Ferry termed "grotesque." [97] The Pekin talks were finally broken off by Tricou on October 29.

During the summer parliamentary recess the press of the Left was highly critical of the Far Eastern policies.[98] It claimed that France was being involved in a war with China, and Parliament was not being kept properly informed. When the Chambers reconvened on October 23, copies of a Yellow Book containing the documents on the Tonkin affair from the previous May were distributed. The August Treaty of Hué was not included. The publication of the documents materially weakened the case against the Government, and the Radical Left now refused to attack the Ministry. Therefore the Extreme Left, with some reluctance, undertook to support Granet's interpellation [99] in the debate that took place on October 30 and 31.

The opposition now dwelt on the known hostility of China, pointing out that Ferry and Lacour untruthfully had denied its existence. It criticized the Government for insufficient preparation and for dispatching troops to Annam during the parliamentary recess without authoriza-

91 *Ibid.*, No. 97.   92 *Ibid.*, No. 101.   93 *Ibid.*

94 *Ibid.*, No. 102.   95 *Ibid.*, note.   96 *Lettres*, p. 347.

97 *DDF*, V, No. 125.

98 *Supra*, p. 28. Its annoyance was increased by Ferry's attacks on the Left following the insulting reception of the King of Spain by a Paris crowd. Ferry's alleged remark that "the danger is on the Left" was made in the middle of October.

99 *Année politique*, 1883, p. 332.

tion. Clemenceau accused Ferry of weakening the French defenses on the continent, but General Campenon, Minister of War, replied that most of the 25,000 troops in the Far East were Algerian troops. Clemenceau attacked the policy of colonial expansion as being contrary to the principles of 1789, betraying the brotherhood of man ideal.[100]

Challemel-Lacour defended himself by stating that the death of Tu-Duc had changed the situation so that action had to be taken quickly, and that it would have alarmed the country to have the Chambers reconvened so soon after adjournment. But Lacour was an ill man, scarcely able to deliver a speech. The real task of defending the Government was left to Ferry.

He now made the most explicit defense of his colonial policy to date, justifying it on the twin grounds of national traditions and honor that must be upheld, and markets that must be assured for future prosperity of French industry.

Asserting: "It is not I who first undertook an enterprise which is based on national traditions," he cited in proof the treaty of 1874, the credits asked by Freycinet in 1880, and the action begun by Duclerc in late 1882. ". . . this Tonkin affair [is] not a personal affair for one or another Minister. . . . From the beginning to the end it is a French affair and a national question."

Tonkin had been a concern since 1879 because:

All the portions of the colonial domain, its least waifs, should be sacred for us because, first it is a legacy of the past and then because it is a reserve for the future. Should the Republic have an ephemeral, short-sighted policy, only preoccupied with living from day to day? Shouldn't it, like every other government, consider the future of the generations which are entrusted to it? . . .

Cast your eyes on the map of the world and see with what vigilance, with what eagerness the great nations who are your friends or your rivals are reserving outlets for themselves. It is not a question of the future of tomorrow but of the future of fifty or one hundred years, of the very future of the country which will be the heritage of our children, the bread of our workers. See with what eagerness each of these industrial races—rightly occupied with that serious question of outlets which is a vital question for every producing nation—strain to take their share in the still unexplored world, in that Africa, in that Asia that holds so much wealth and particularly in that vast Chinese empire. It is not a question, of course, of wanting to conquer that

[100] *J. O. C.*, 11/1/83.

great Chinese empire. . . . But we must be at the gateway of that rich region. . . . And it is for that that we admire and thank the vigilance, the wisdom or deep instinct that pushed our predecessors toward the mouth of the Red River and which established for them as a goal the possession of Tonkin. . . . It would be anti-French to forbid the Republic to have a colonial policy.

Discussing the manner in which the French protectorate was established over Annam, he said that when Tu-Duc died the Ministry had to take advantage of the opportunity to start the new regime in Annam on the right foot. Reading the new Treaty of Hué, which he claimed gave France great advantages at slight cost, he maintained that it would have been ludicrous to have convoked the Chambers to ask whether the Cabinet should take advantage of a favorable opportunity.

Discussing French relations with China, Ferry continued, ". . . the negotiations that we have begun with China have not succeeded because China has no interest in outstripping accomplished facts." He described the government of China as chiefly composed of men who disliked Westerners but, "faced with accomplished facts, Asiatic good sense bows and accepts them." The Premier cited Marquis Tseng as authority for the contention that there were no regular Chinese troops in Tonkin. Ferry said that he intended to maintain diplomatic relations with China. "We are not at war with China. . . . I believe that China will not make war on us, and we do not intend to declare it on her." The only French desire was "to establish ourselves firmly in the Delta" and he was sure that the Chinese would bow before this occupation.[101]

This espousal of a philosophy of national expansion to insure France's future markets went almost unchallenged in the Chamber. Clemenceau protested Ferry's "building for future generations," maintaining it would be a greater mission to spread the democratic doctrines of the French Revolution. This is the only instance in the debates on Ferry's Indo-China policy when it was attacked on such ideological grounds.

Ferry made it clear that he intended to push forward. Troops in Tonkin were to move ahead, avoiding clashes with the Chinese as best they could, but there was to be no hesitation. Following so resolute a statement of policy, confidence in the Government's Tonkin policy was voted, 325–115.[102]

Shortly afterwards, Challemel-Lacour resigned as Foreign Minister, partly because of illness, partly because of disgust at the petty parliamentary attacks to which he was subjected.[103] He had not really carried his duties for months, leaving them to Ferry. With reluctance, Ferry

[101] *J. O. C.*, 11/1/83.   [102] *Ibid.*   [103] Krakowski, *op. cit.*, p. 299.

gave up his favorite portfolio of Education [104] and took over that of Foreign Affairs in addition to his Premiership.

Tseng was informed by Ferry that the French forces were going to move forward and that it was China's responsibility to avoid any conflict.[105] Granville protested to France when he heard of it and sounded Ferry anew on November 18 on the possibilities of arbitration.[106] Lyons was correct when he said that he thought such an offer was useless.[107] Nothing daunted, Granville, on December 10, transmitted another Chinese proposal demanding that France quit Tonkin. As he delivered this, Granville protested to Waddington that Tonkin would give France access to the interior of China. That was the great concern of England, jealous of her predominant position in the East. When both of these overtures were rejected,[108] Anglo-French relations, already strained over Madagascar, grew still cooler.[109]

Another appropriation of nine million francs for Tonkin, together with an interpellation on the Government's policy, was debated on December 9 and 10. A supplementary *Livre Jaune* published for the event showed that China had warned that she would fight, if necessary, to hold Tonkin. There was little in this debate that had not been discussed in October. Clemenceau and Ribot repeated the old accusations that the Government was waging an undeclared war, and that, in spite of warning of China's hostility, it had pressed ahead recklessly without proper provision for carrying on a conflict as great as that which would develop. Renault, the *rapporteur* of the bill, and Antonin Proust rallied to the defense to state that French honor and prestige were at stake in Tonkin; any retreat or weakening would be a blow to *la patrie*.

Ferry argued that the conquest of Annam's province of Tonkin was necessitated by the potential threat to Cochin-China from such an unfriendly and turbulent neighbor. It was the same argument he had used in the case of Tunisia, justifying a new acquisition as necessary not for markets but for the defense of French possessions. After his appeal to patriotism, the appropriation was voted 383–109.[110] An Order of the Day expressing the Chamber's conviction "that the Government would employ all the necessary energy to defend in Tonkin the rights and honor of France" was passed 308–201.[111] Although the Tonkin expedition received more votes than did the Ministry itself, the Government's majority still remained very impressive.

On December 15, Ferry introduced a bill to appropriate twenty million francs to send an expeditionary force of fifteen thousand men to

[104] *Lettres*, pp. 347–348.
[105] E. Hippeau, *Histoire diplomatique de la Troisième République*, p. 45.
[106] *L. J. T.*, No. 138.   [107] Newton, *op. cit.*, II, 320.   [108] *L. J. T.*, No. 155.
[109] *Supra*, pp. 123–124.   [110] *J. O. C.*, 12/10/83.   [111] *Ibid.*

Tonkin. Following so closely upon the previous debates, the discussion was rather brief. Lockroy, Granet and Perin from the Left asked the Government for a statement of policy on the nature of the expeditionary force, its plan of operations and the concessions that were to be made to China. Ferry refused to reply on the ground that matters of vital importance to the State might be compromised.

The most remarkable incident in this debate was a declaration of Bishop Freppel of Angers in favor of a strong policy in Tonkin. This spokesman for the conservative, clerical group opposed the Government on all except matters of colonial policy.[112] He declared that "political divergencies should disappear before national interests; and the flag being involved, as it is, by a regular vote of Parliament, no one could any longer ask whose are the hands that hold it." Following this peroration, the bill was passed 327–151.[113] The Senate passed both bills by a vote of 207–6 on December 21.[114] Throughout all Ferry's colonial expeditions the Senate always supported him. Only one or two individuals in that body like the Duc de Broglie objected; criticism came almost entirely from the lower House.

Little progress was made on settling the Tonkin affair throughout the Fall and Winter, negotiations with China remaining at a standstill until March. The French Chargé in Pekin had almost no relations with the Yamen.[115] The munitions blockade was extended to Tonkin, and the French pushed on slowly, taking Bac-Ninh on March 12. China was embarrassed in March when the Hong Kong–Shanghai bank refused to make a new loan or continue payment on a loan previously contracted until relations with France were stabilized. This appears to have been a spontaneous action on the part of the bank, interested only in being repaid.[116]

Convention of Tien-Tsin

Li-Hong-Tchang suddenly reopened negotiations in April with a Captain Fournier of the French navy, an old acquaintance,[117] who was invited to Tien-Tsin to discuss the Sino-French difficulties. Before going, he insisted that as a mark of good will Tseng be removed from his Paris post, a request easily granted on May 1, since Tseng was Li's rival at court.[118] Ferry approved Fournier's undertaking the mission at his own risk.[119]

On his way, the Captain learned that Li was piqued at the British Minister to Pekin, who had gone to Korea to negotiate a treaty directly

---

[112] Freppel also supported Ferry's Madagascar policy.   [113] *Ibid.*, 12/16/83.
[114] *J. O. S.*, 12/21/83.   [115] *DDF*, V, No. 201.
[116] *Ibid.*, No. 221.   [117] Fournier, *loc. cit.*, p. 759.
[118] *Ibid.*, p. 780; *DDF*, V, No. 255.   [119] Fournier, *loc. cit.*, p. 780.

with that vassal of China, although such a function properly belonged to Li. The viceroy was therefore agreeable to French propositions which would not humiliate China.[120] After brief negotiations, the draft was approved by Ferry on May 8.[121] Fournier received full powers on May 10, and the Convention of Tien-Tsin was signed on May 11.[122] China agreed to respect the new treaty between France and Annam, and to withdraw her troops from Tonkin; France promised to respect the southern border of China; between Annam and China there was to be freedom for trade and an advantageous commercial treaty was to be negotiated. When the differences with China had been thus composed, the Treaty of Hué was formally signed and ratified on June 6, 1884.[123]

It appeared that Ferry had obtained everything that he sought, for he had protectorates over Tonkin and the kingdom of Annam connecting Tonkin and Cambodia, and commerce could freely ascend the Red River to China. Both French commerce and prestige were well provided for and only technical details remained to be arranged.

Undeclared War with China

Fournier and Li had made arrangements for the most pressing problem, the withdrawal of the Chinese troops from Tonkin. Orders had been sent to the commanders, when a new turn in palace politics deposed Li and put an official unfriendly to France in his place. A counterorder from the Yamen halted the withdrawal, but the troops were instructed not to fight.[124] The Tien-Tsin Convention was under severe criticism in Chinese court circles as having been too precipitately and poorly drawn, yet there appears to have been no intention of deliberately violating it.[125] The Convention was a weak reed to lean upon, since it was so largely a product of Chinese domestic politics and the personal feelings of a viceroy, but apparently these limitations were not realized by Ferry.

Although the French forces in Tonkin had received no confirmation of the June 6 withdrawal date set in the Tien-Tsin talks,[126] they continued to move forward toward Langson. A French column under Colonel Dugenne met a Chinese force and a slight skirmish developed. In parleys the Chinese officers recognized the validity of the Tien-Tsin agreement but asked six days to withdraw to their border. Because of a disagreement over protocol the commanders of the two forces did not confer. The French colonel insisted on moving forward at once, fighting developed near Bac-Lé when the Chinese resisted and the French

---

[120] *Ibid.,* p. 781.   [121] *DDF,* V, No. 260.   [122] Text, *L. J. T.,* pp. 5–7.
[123] *DDF,* V, No. 293.   [124] Fournier, *loc. cit.,* p. 787.   [125] *DDF,* V, No. 607.
[126] Fournier, *loc. cit.,* p. 787.

were forced to fall back on June 23 with eighteen killed and seventy-eight wounded.[127] The incident was reported by the commander of the column and the naval officials in Tonkin as an "ambush" and an "attack" in their first wires to Paris.[128] From June 26 to July 4 this distorted description was the only one available to Ferry.

Immediately upon receipt of the telegram, Ferry protested to China the violation of the Tien-Tsin Convention, laying full blame upon her troops. He ordered Admiral Courbet to sail North with two squadrons ready to take retaliatory action.[129] Admirals Courbet and Lespès, and Patenôtre in Shanghai all urged Ferry to send a punitive expedition against China.[130] He had not the resources for doing so, but he did order Courbet to stand ready to seize Foochow, destroy its arsenals and defenses, and then move against Kelung on Formosa. Such an order was sent two days after the news of the "ambush" was received.[131] The Chinese protested that the blame was not theirs, holding that no date for withdrawal had been set and contesting the validity of the French text of the agreement to withdraw the troops. They strongly protested against the naval demonstrations being made, and suggested that all troops hold their positions until an evacuation plan could be arranged.[132]

It was only after these steps had been taken that Admiral Peyron received a full report on the incident from General Millot in Hanoi. Although Ferry himself later admitted that the French colonel had been wrong, excusing him on the grounds of "patriotic haste," [133] he nevertheless continued to speak of a "deliberate ambush."

An ultimatum, sent July 6, and presented to China on July 13, demanded the publication of a decree immediately evacuating the troops from Tonkin; an indemnity of two hundred million francs and an answer to these demands in a week, or France would seize proper indemnities.[134]

It is a little hard to understand why Ferry was so rash, for such an ultimatum, if it were refused, was certain to lead to war. When he sent Courbet northward he had a distorted picture of the Bac-Lé skirmish, but, by the time he sent the ultimatum, he must have known the true story, though there is a bare possibility that it had been withheld from him by those most anxious to move energetically.[135] It is unlikely that Ferry would countenance such insubordination. Since he had already committed himself to the first account of the attack and to avenge such treachery, it is possible his own stubbornness may have kept him going. The Bac-Lé "ambush" had become a matter of French prestige; French

[127] *L. J. T.*, No. 36.   [128] *Ibid.*, No. 21.   [129] *DDF*, V, No. 323.
[130] *Ibid.*, No. 332.   [131] *Ibid.*, No. 332, note.   [132] *L. J. T.*, No. 33.
[133] *J. O. C.*, 7/15/84.   [134] *DDF*, V, No. 333.   [135] Schuman, *op. cit.*, p. 86.

honor was at stake and it was difficult to stop short. In any case, Ferry was not the man to quail at the use of force to wrest a concession from a weak opponent. Certainly there was no hope of gain for French commerce in the prospect of a war. The indemnity might have helped defray the cost of the Tonkin expedition but it was so quickly reduced in the negotiations that followed that he could not have counted very seriously on the large figure.

His advisors on the Far East and the men in the field wanted to pursue a vigorous policy toward China. Patenôtre and Courbet in China and Peyron, the Minister of Navy and Colonies, all wanted action. Ferry realized that Courbet was "devoured by a desire for glory" and would do anything he could "to lead us to Pekin" while Patenôtre, too, "would like action on a grand scale." The Premier was determined not to be led along by these men to dangerous complications.[136]

Billot told the American Chargé that he himself had strongly recommended the policy adopted toward China.[137] Probably he really was largely responsible, for he was a personal friend of Ferry's as well as being the most important permanent official in the Foreign Office. He had urged the Premier to strike against Annam and had pushed French demands in Madagascar.[138]

All his advisors and Ferry himself misjudged China's will and capacity to resist. In Paris they were poorly informed and unwilling to believe that China would be recalcitrant. She had often before been bullied by European powers, including France, into giving whatever was demanded. Ferry believed he would gain more by action than negotiation.[139] Success in the Far East would help compensate for the dragging affairs in Egypt and Madagascar. China was to prove a difficult and intractable adversary and Ferry never could command sufficient force to impose his decisions on her. But he expected little difficulty and only a brief struggle.[140]

China accepted the ultimatum's provision for withdrawal of her troops at once, but refused to accept the remaining demands.[141] Ferry granted an extension of the expiration date to August 1, and indicated on July 19 his willingness to reduce the indemnity to one hundred million.[142] China refused to consider this, refused to accept responsibility for the incident and offered to pay only three and a half million as an indemnity for the soldiers killed. Ferry rejected the offer.[143] He told Patenôtre to bargain for fifty millions of indemnity to be paid over three years.[144] Four hours after sending this instruction, Ferry learned

[136] *Lettres*, p. 360.
[138] *Supra*, p. 120.
[140] *Lettres*, p. 360.
[143] *L. J. T.*, No. 76.

[137] SDA, *Dispatches, France*, Vol. 95, No. 647.
[139] SDA, *Dispatches, France*, Vol. 94, No. 592.
[141] *DDF*, V, No. 317.   [142] *Ibid.*, No. 343.
[144] *DDF*, V, No. 352.

of an offer made through Sir Robert Hart, the Inspector General of the Chinese Customs, which he accepted at once, to pay eight million over ten years.[145] Then he found that Hart could not get the Chinese to accept it.[146] Thereupon negotiations broke down. France already had announced on August 2 that she was going to take action.[147]

Although war was not declared, the fortress at Kelung was shelled and captured by Lespès' squadron on August 5,[148] and China was threatened with even more severe punishment. But Patenôtre maintained that this was inadequate to force China to yield; nothing short of occupation of Foochow and an expedition to Pekin would suffice.[149] He constantly reiterated his demand during the next nine months.

The Chamber of Deputies debated an additional appropriation of 38,482,000 francs for Tonkin on August 14 and 15. All the charges so often made before about Tonkin were repeated by the opposition in these debates: Tonkin was of small value to French commerce, the struggles for it had been expensive, the Ministry had involved the country in a state of war without the consent of Parliament. But the debate was less violent than others had been, for the Chamber was half-empty on the eve of vacation and Ferry himself considered the discussion very mild.[150]

Ferry's defense assumed a more patriotic tone than any of his previous apologias. He called the colonial empire then being founded "one of the greatest achievements of this time, one of those which have been most warmly upheld by the Republican majority of the country." He excused the Bac-Lé action as a case of "patriotic haste" on the part of the commander attributable to "traditional French bravery."

To his critics who accused him of being too hasty in dealing with the Chinese government, he replied that the fault, if any, lay in delaying too long before acting. He termed the Chinese government "strange and inefficient," wound up in the red tape of its own bureaucracy, hostile on principle to all Westerners. He considered it most unfair of the Chinese to have appealed to the United States and Germany to intervene under the terms of their treaties. He attributed China's resistance to a contemptible "mixture of pride and weakness." Asked if France were at war, he replied, "We are not in a state of war with China; we are in a state of negotiations," to which a deputy aptly added, ". . . with cannon balls." A vote for the requested appropriation, said Ferry, would show Pekin France's firm will to prevail and "will be more than half the victory won."[151]

145 DDF, V, No. 353.   146 Livre Jaune Chine et Tonkin (Paris, 1885), No. 12.
147 Ibid., No. 6.   148 Ibid., No. 22.   149 Ibid., No. 29.
150 Lettres, p. 352.   151 J. O. C., 8/15/84.

In these debates the opposition and majority vied with one another in their expressions of patriotism. Ferry was taunted with overlooking the best interests of the country when he violated the Constitution by waging an unauthorized war. Each opposition speaker was careful to say that he spoke as a true patriot. Whenever a deputy suggested that there might be some justice in the claims of China, he was accused of believing the word of a mandarin rather than of a French officer. The doctrine of national infallibility was invoked particularly against Frederick Passy who proposed to put the whole matter to arbitration.[152] Perin and others insisted that the expenditure of French military resources in Tonkin had jeopardized France's continental position and left her friendless in Europe.

Such sentiments were not widely shared among the deputies as their vote, passing the appropriation 334–140, indicated. The same evening the Ministry received a vote of confidence only by the narrow margin of 173–50, but which was not a fair test of strength, for it was taken on the eve of adjournment for the Summer holidays and few deputies still remained in Paris.[153] The Senate passed the bill the following day, 193–1.[154]

Encouraged by the vote, Ferry decided to seize part of Formosa despite Patenôtre's insistence that this was not enough. To his wife he wrote that he had no intention of trying to strike at Pekin, now or later.[155] A final ultimatum demanding that China agree within forty-eight hours to pay an indemnity of eighty millions was refused on August 22.[156] The Chinese Minister left Paris and the French Minister left Pekin although both legations were kept open. China sent a protest to the Powers.[157] Foochow was shelled, a number of Chinese ships there were sunk; Formosa was blockaded, its port occupied and coal mines seized. There was still no declaration of war, although Courbet urged that one be made in order to prevent neutrals, especially the British, from sending through supplies.[158]

China was unmoved and Patenôtre and Courbet insisted that no satisfaction would be obtained from Pekin until a large squadron was sent North to blockade the Gulf of Pechili, Port Arthur, and to threaten Pekin.[159] Ferry would not consider this for fear of offending the other Powers interested in the Far East. Therefore a stalemate lasted through the Fall and Winter much like that in Madagascar. Ferry did not command enough strength to strike an effective blow against the vast Chinese Empire.

[152] *Ibid.*, 8/16/84.   [153] *J. O. C.*, 8/16/84.   [154] *J. O. S.*, 8/17/84.
[155] *Lettres*, p. 353.   [156] *DDF*, V, No. 374.   [157] *L. J. C. et T.*, No. 55.
[158] *Ibid.*, No. 73.   [159] *Ibid.*, No. 101.

The operations in Tonkin dragged along with neither distinction nor glory. A French garrison, besieged by the Chinese at Tuyan-Quan, was relieved only in November. The small French forces were bottled up in the cities along the river and on the Delta.

France had less difficulty with other Powers in the Far East than she had in some other colonial ventures, although she could hardly be called free. Bismarck was very cooperative, for this was the period of the Franco-German entente over African affairs and their understanding extended to Indo-China in which Germany had small interest.[160] Bismarck had refused from the beginning to lend the Chinese any aid. On August 28, he assured Courcel that the German Fleet had orders to avoid the French zone of operations and that German army officers on active duty would not be allowed to resign for the purpose of entering the Chinese service on the tempting terms offered by the Chinese.[161] In return, Ferry gave the Chancellor assurances that the French would be careful not to disturb the treaty ports of China or the foreign concessions.[162] When the Chinese Minister asked Hatzfeldt for German mediation, Bismarck gave instructions that China should be referred to Paris. To Courcel he said, "Do in the Far East what suits you," adding that he had no objection if the French should try to take even more from China.[163] But to Bismarck's suggestion that he mediate the question, Ferry returned a refusal, saying that any German action would embarrass France.[164] When the Chancellor was asked by the Chinese to convoy some corvettes, built for China in Germany, he refused and considered the resulting Chinese inability to move a fine joke.[165] Bismarck did arrange a secret meeting between Courcel and the Chinese Minister at Hatzfeldt's house on September 19, but it produced no results since even a French plan to occupy Formosa for ninety years in lieu of an indemnity was rejected.[166]

Bismarck subsequently suggested that the French take more active measures against Formosa in order to bring the affair to a conclusion. He told Courcel he was resisting the demands of the Hamburg merchants that he intervene because he was on the side of "civilization" in this struggle against "semi-barbarism." Nevertheless he made it clear that he had to preserve friendly relations with China for the sake of German commercial interests.[167] Upon Ferry's request, Bismarck had a formal statement published in the *Norddeutsche Allgemeine Zeitung* that German officers were not being allowed to enlist in the Chinese forces.[168] Ferry had been embarrassed by statements in the French op-

---

[160] Hohenlohe, *op. cit.*, II, 348.   [161] *DDF*, V, No. 380.

[162] *Ibid.*, No. 381.   [163] *Ibid.*, No. 396.   [164] *Ibid.*, No. 397.   [165] *Ibid.*, No. 399.

[166] *Ibid.*, No. 401.   [167] *Ibid.*, No. 436.   [168] *Ibid.*, No. 512.

position press that such enlistments were permitted. In February, 1885, Bismarck prevented German bankers from making loans to China.[169]

Relations with England over the China war were not as smooth because of England's large interests in the Far East and because of the many other points of friction between her and France. After the failure of the London Conference on Egyptian finance in July, 1884, Anglo-French relations were very cool and remained chilly because of conflicts over Egypt, the Congo and Madagascar. English merchants in Shanghai were asking their government to intervene because the French were disrupting trade: [170] the English and French press were filled with recriminations.[171]

Granville sounded Waddington on the possibilities of English mediation on October 6, suggesting that France had sufficiently avenged her honor by the success at Foochow. Waddington immediately replied that mediation was not desirable, that the United States had already offered its good offices and that they had been refused.[172] But Ferry's attitude was not so arbitrary, and he took up the proffer after some small successes in Tonkin, suggesting that the English might mediate the question of Formosa's occupation but that the French must receive an indemnity of at least forty millions.[173]

The English Minister for Foreign Affairs promised to talk with the Chinese, but at the same time he expressed the opinion that England might soon find herself forced to proclaim her neutrality because of the Formosa blockade.[174] This suggestion worried Ferry who pointed out on November 3 that France was not at war with China, but was merely "recalling [China] to the observation of its international duties." England had exercised such rights in the past, and France had recognized their legitimacy.[175] Granville let the matter rest for a few months.

When some Chinese proposals were submitted to England, Granville himself had to admit that they were "unacceptable" being like the terms of "victors," for they proposed the return of Annam and Tonkin to China and that France evacuate Formosa without an indemnity.[176] In December, Waddington informed Granville that the French must soon act decisively and that his last chance to intervene was approaching. New Chinese proposals were virtually the same as before and were rejected by Ferry on January 7.[177]

England invoked the Foreign Enlistment Act in January, 1885, to prevent French ships from provisioning in English ports. Ferry was very much annoyed and expressed his "surprise" at the English change

[169] Daudet, *Courcel*, p. 133.   [170] *L. J. C. et T.*, No. 97.
[171] Newton, *op. cit.*, II, 334.   [172] *DDF*, V, No. 420.   [173] *Ibid.*, No. 434.
[174] *Ibid.*, No. 434.   [175] *Ibid.*, No. 442.   [176] *Ibid.*, No. 462.   [177] *Ibid.*, No. 510.

of attitude, but he had to admit its legality. He warned that now France would have to seek belligerent rights but that this move should not be considered as "directed against the English government." [178] Accordingly the Powers were notified that France laid claim to the rights of a belligerent.[179] Ferry asserted that the French ships would have no difficulty supplying themselves, but it was after this lesson that the French proceeded to develop a naval base at Obock and that they held the bay at Diégo-Suarez in Madagascar with more determination.

Further to harass China, a rice blockade was established on February 26 to prevent ships carrying this staple to the North.[180] This was not to apply to Shanghai's shipments, however, lest the business of Europeans be injured. All these measures did not seriously affect the sprawling Chinese Empire. In St. Petersburg Giers aptly described the situation when he remarked to the French Ambassador that the operation at Formosa was like "the bite of a flea on an elephant's back." Only a blow at Pekin could induce China to yield.[181]

During the Summer and Fall of 1884 the United States made several attempts to bring about a settlement of the Sino-French conflict. China had requested the United States to act on its behalf under the terms of their 1858 treaty. Accordingly, the United States offered on July 23 to have the President arbitrate the indemnity question. Ferry politely refused and spoke confidently of success.[182] On August 1, the American Minister Morton suggested arbitration of the matter by the United States or others. This the French Premier firmly refused, for he would admit no questioning of the facts.[183] China pressed the United States to renew her arbitration offer but Secretary of State Freylinghuysen replied that two refusals made further advances impossible. At the same time, China asked Young, the American Minister to Pekin, former correspondent of the New York *Herald,* and friend of China, to attempt to make a settlement with the French in Shanghai. Billot now showed only mild interest.[184]

After the bombardment of Foochow, Billot hinted to Morton that the good offices of the United States might now be acceptable, but the Americans insisted on being asked formally.[185] Ferry claimed on September 12 that he could not do this, for it would be interpreted by the Chinese as a sign of French weakness.[186] Young shortly afterwards offered terms to Patenôtre in Shanghai but these, too, provided for American arbitration on the indemnity and so were unacceptable.[187] Further

[178] *Ibid.,* No. 541.
[180] *Ibid.,* No. 587.
[182] SDA, *France, Dispatches,* Vol. 94, No. 592.
[184] *Ibid.,* No. 605.
[186] *Ibid.*

[179] *Ibid.,* No. 556.
[181] *L. J. C. et T.,* No. 163.
[183] *Ibid.,* No. 601.
[185] *Ibid.,* No. 619.
[187] *Ibid.,* No. 633.

talks in Paris from October 16 to 27, between Morton and Ferry, again were fruitless because the United States insisted on a formal request to arbitrate and Ferry refused to make it.[188] He made it clear that he feared that an award might go against France, and this was not only unthinkable for him personally but impossible politically. In his resolve not to allow French statements to be questioned, he was bolstered by Billot.[189] However, Ferry did want the United States to press on Pekin the French demands including the occupation of Formosa until the indemnity was paid. These terms the United States refused to present,[190] as had England and Germany. A final attempt was made when Young sent a proposition nearly identical with his earlier one through Washington to Paris, on November 20.[191] Again Ferry termed the proposal impossible and the negotiations died.

The Tonkin affair occasioned considerable debate in France during 1884 and 1885 largely because it coincided with several colonial affairs, with the entente with Germany which alarmed the nationalist press; and, above all, with Ferry's program of moderate reform at home. The enactment of additional laic laws, the limited revision of the Constitution, and the law on municipal government each angered some groups in the Chamber. The real role of Tonkin in French domestic politics was to give an already determined opposition a point vulnerable to attack by patriotic arguments, a course made possible because the campaign in the Far East was going poorly. Ferry was embarrassed because he was obviously waging war, but could not admit the fact.

Shortly after hostilities began in August, the Extreme Left, in a letter to the President, demanded the convocation of Parliament in order legally to declare war.[192] The demand was not seriously considered, but it foreshadowed the violent attack that faction was preparing to launch when Parliament reconvened. The opposition found its opportunity when Ferry had to ask for more large appropriations in November: 16,147,368 francs for 1884 and 43,422,000 francs for 1885. A four-day debate from November 24 to 28 examined all the details and ramifications of the Far Eastern policy.

The accusations against Ferry were not new. Lockroy, Granet and Clemenceau for the Left all attacked Ferry for his deceptions, his waging of an unauthorized war and his heavy demands on China. Lockroy criticized the Ministry for not accepting the three and a half million franc indemnity that China once had offered. Delafosse, from the Bonapartist benches, painted a dreary picture of army disorganization, an exhausted treasury, and a France weakened in its European military

---

[188] *Ibid.*, No. 648.   [189] *Ibid.*, No. 641.   [190] *Ibid.*, No. 651.   [191] *Ibid.*, No. 668.
[192] *Année Politique*, 1885, p. 222.

and diplomatic relationships. He admitted that he would oppose any Republican cabinet but therefore claimed disinterestedness, for this one seemed to him to be the worst possible.[193]

Ferry made another defense of his policies, especially able considering the handicap under which he labored, as events in the field offered him scant support. He again reminded the Chamber that France had been pursuing a firm policy against Annam and China long before he came to the Presidency of the Council. Each of the actions taken in the Far East had been approved by Parliament either immediately before or after the event. The latest approval, in August, had authorized him to proceed against Foochow and the island of Formosa. Formosa was, he said, a good "gage," for the blockade was inflicting serious damage on Chinese revenues. He read the dispatches on the latest overtures of the Chinese Government presented through Great Britain which demanded that France leave both Annam and Tonkin. To enable the Government to thwart these unreasonable terms, Ferry asked approval of the "credits for energetic and persistent action."

Despite the heated attacks on his proposals by Clemenceau, both measures were passed with a good margin. The money for 1884 was approved by a 354–157 count; that for 1885 passed 342–170. When it came to an Order of the Day that demanded "the full and complete execution of the treaty of Tien-Tsin" and expressed confidence in the Government's "energy in assuring respect for the rights of France," the Ministry secured only 295 votes against 196.[194]

These votes indicated that a majority of two hundred deputies was willing to support the Tonkin expansion even when it was reasonably certain that to do so meant war with China. Ferry obtained a better vote on the appropriations for Tonkin than he did on many concurrent domestic questions.[195] When the Premier announced that he intended to adopt a firmer policy in dealing with the enemies of France, he secured appropriations from a patriotic parliament. But the declining power of the Ministry, particularly in domestic affairs, was seen in the slim vote of confidence it received.[196] Doubtless part of the falling away was due to dissatisfaction with the management of foreign affairs, but it was no very significant portion. There was very little real anti-colonial feeling in a Chamber of Deputies which was willing to back such an energetic foreign policy.

The two Tonkin appropriations were debated in the Senate on December 11. The Duc de Broglie, who was an unrelenting critic of the

[193] *J. O. C.*, 11/25/84.   [194] *J. O. C.*, 11/29/84.   [195] See Appendix.

[196] It was on December 2 that the Ministry was defeated on a question of Senatorial reform. At this time Waldeck-Rousseau had resigned, but Ferry persuaded the Cabinet to continue and was upheld on a vote of confidence December 9th. *Supra*, p. 29.

Ministry and of the policy of colonial expansion, spoke at great length reviewing the charges repeatedly levelled against the Far Eastern policy of Ferry. He attacked the overconfidence of the Cabinet in its statements to the Chambers, the failure of the Ferry Government to accept the Bourée treaty, its failure to send a professional diplomat with Captain Fournier better to draw the Convention of Tien-Tsin, Ferry's hasty action after the Bac-Lé affair, his refusal to accept the proffered three and a half million indemnity, and the reopening of hostilities with China. He claimed that colonial expansion was unwise for France because she was a weakened nation and her first duty was to establish herself in an impregnable position on the continent. German support he criticized as designed to turn French attention from her lost provinces.

Ferry, in reply, exhaustively justified his diplomatic policy chiefly on the grounds of upholding French prestige in the Far East. He declared that he demanded and still insisted on an indemnity from the Chinese ". . . to teach them that a signature is sacred and that when it is violated, one has to pay."

The Premier turned on the Duc de Broglie to say sharply:

> It is that treaty of 1874 [which Broglie had negotiated] that ill-conceived, poorly constructed, distressing and limping protectorate that has been the cause of all our difficulties. . . . Stop repeating that we are conducting an arbitrary, capricious colonial policy. We are conducting, in this affair, the colonial policy to which the precedent created by yourself condemned us.

Turning back to the Senate, he continued,

> . . . is not the colonial policy one of the great facts, one of the universal facts of our time? Isn't it apparent to you that for all the great nations of modern Europe, once their industrial power is formed, there is posed the immense and formidable problem which is the very basis of the industrial life, the condition of existence: the question of the market? Don't you see all the great industrial nations come in turn to the colonial policy . . . ? This policy is, for all of them, a necessity like the market itself.

The Senate thereupon voted the 1884 credits by 191–1, and, after a brief tirade by Broglie, the 1885 credits by 189–1.[197] Thus, as always, the Senate supported colonial expansion by overwhelming majorities.

In the Senatorial elections of January 1885, the colonial operations were criticized but were not an important issue in the campaign. Al-

197 *J. O. S.,* 12/12/84.

though the Republicans won sixty-seven out of eighty-seven contests, gaining twenty seats from the monarchists, twenty-eight deputies who belonged to Ferry's coalition were elected to the upper Chamber, thus reducing his majority.

The only discussion of Far Eastern affairs in January followed an interpellation on General Campenon's resignation as Minister of War and his replacement by General Lewal. Actually the resignation was occasioned by Campenon's desire to limit the military campaign to the Red River Delta, as Ferry frankly admitted in the debate.[198] The Premier defined the purpose of the expedition in the Far East as "the uncontested possession of Tonkin and the full and complete execution of the treaty of Tien-Tsin." Since the Ferry policy was approved by the Chamber in November, Campenon had felt obliged to resign. General Lewal assured the House that the mobilization organization had not been injured by the dispatch of troops to Tonkin and China. An Order of the Day, pure and simple, was requested for the Government,[199] and it was passed by the narrow margin of 280–225. The vote represented quite a loss for the Cabinet but constituted approximately the majority it was to hold on all questions during the Spring of 1885.

French Imperialist Literature

Although France's colonial program was by no means undertaken in response to popular demand, there was considerable discussion of Ferry's imperial policy about which a word should be said. Until expansion dramatically became a public issue with the seizure of Tunisia in 1881, discussion of colonies had been confined to a few academicians who had but a small audience. Paul Leroy-Beaulieu was perhaps the best-known of these and his *De la colonisation chez les peuples modernes* [200] had the widest circulation. A professor of Political Economy at the *Collège de France,* he upheld colonies as the most profitable place for the investment of a nation's surplus capital. They were also extremely valuable as markets, as an outlet for surplus population and were generally beneficial to the mother country by stimulating economic activity. Leroy-Beaulieu was enthusiastic about the acquisition of Tunisia in his 1882 edition, calling it "the one great thing France has done in ten years." [201] As editor in chief of *L'Economiste Française* he turned out a stream of articles on the value of overseas expansion.

Paul Gaffarel, a professor of History and Geography, followed a line of argument similar to Beaulieu's in his *Les colonies françaises* of 1880.

[198] *J. O. C.*, 1/15/85.   [199] *Ibid.*
[200] P. Leroy-Beaulieu, *De la colonisation chez les peuples modernes* (Paris, 1874).
[201] *Ibid.*, ed. 1882, p. 391.

He was especially interested in Africa but also urged that Cochin-China should be fully exploited.[202] Several other colonial propagandists were active at the same time but it does not appear that they influenced Ferry nor that they had much public following while Ferry was in office.[203]

Once France embarked on expansion nearly all the moderate Republican press gave its support to the cause. The *Temps* and the *Journal des Débats* lent their support with arguments justifying colonies as markets and fields for investment. As occasion demanded, they urged the necessity of preserving the French colonial heritage, of avenging insults, and of carrying on the French "civilizing mission." [204]

During Ferry's second Premiership discussions on the value of colonial expansion dealt primarily with the problem of Tonkin and the collaboration with Germany at the Congo Conference. The moderate Republicans defended Ferry's policy in the press as on the platform. As the Radicals accused Ferry in the Chamber, so in the press they lashed out with even more vitriolic fury.

Perhaps the ablest critic of the colonial program was the Republican economist, Yves Guyot. He, too, was a radical Republican, a journalist, strong free trader and vigorous critic of Socialism. In his *Lettres sur la politique coloniale*,[205] he poured ridicule on Ferry's program: the colonies were for the most part uninhabitable by white men; were poor markets because of the poverty of the natives; they were unnecessary if only free trade were practiced; they led to wars, and brought the natives not civilization, but death. However true many of these facts may have been, his work was without effect on French policy.

Both the Monarchist and Radical papers reproached Ferry for his working alliance with Germany. Rochefort in his *Intransigeant*, Cle-

202 P. Gaffarel, *Les colonies françaises* (Paris, 1880), p. 315.

203 Among these were: Gabriel Charmes, anti-republican, younger brother of François and Xavier Charmes, editors of the *Journal des Débats*, who wrote in support of the development of Tunisia and the Mediterranean area, although he thought the Republic unfit to build an empire; Edward Guillon who wrote a school text on: *Les colonies françaises* (Paris, 1881), extolling the glory that would accrue to France from a new colonial empire; Arthur Bordier, author of *La colonisation scientifique et les colonies françaises*, proposing a strengthening of the French "race" by a "fusion with races" in the colonies, to forestall the depopulation of France; and M. Raboisson, a conservative champion of colonization who urged in *Etudes sur les colonies et la colonisation au regard de la France* (Paris, 1877), that a nation could only be great if it held an empire, and held France could never grow great under a Republic that would not expand.

A number of geographical societies sprang up in the late 1870's throughout France. In 1881 the geographical societies of France counted 9500 members. Their publicity was of some slight aid in rallying support for Ferry's projects. Their subsidy of exploration, expositions and congresses served to create interest in expansion. Donald V. McKay, "Colonialism in the French Geographical Movement," *The Geographical Review*, XXXIII (1943), 214–232.

204 E. Malcolm Carroll, *French Public Opinion and Foreign Affairs, 1870–1914* (New York, 1931), p. 85.   205 Paris, 1885.

menceau in his *Justice,* and the monarchist *Gazette de France* all were fearful of the friendship of Bismarck. The *revanchards* were, of course, furious at this collaboration with the despoiler of France, and Mme. Adam in her *Nouvelle Revue* castigated Ferry, whom she had hated for a long time.[206] By and large, the attitude of the press toward colonial expansion was determined by its attitude toward the whole policy of Ferry. There were no important defections among his friends although they chided him from time to time about the conduct of specific undertakings.

Negotiations with China

Relations with China throughout the Fall of 1884 remained hopelessly stalemated with the French occupation continuing, and the Chinese insisting on complete French withdrawal. In conversations in Paris early in November, the Chinese proposed a truce, with each side keeping what it held; but Ferry insisted on recognition of the principle of an indemnity and the talks came to naught.[207] Consequently the Chinese became more adamant, sending through England in December renewed demands for complete French withdrawal.

During that month, Chinese-Japanese relations in Korea were strained as fighting broke out in Seoul, the capital. Ferry hoped that this would work to his advantage,[208] but rejected a Japanese proposal for joint action against China. China requested German aid against the Japanese, but Bismarck, after consulting France, refused any support.

The Tonkin campaign was renewed as a result of the new War Minister's energetic policies and the reinforcements. The army, under General Brière de l'Isle, of Senegal fame, took over from the navy land operations in Tonkin.[209] Early in the new year, a Chinese force was defeated and after another engagement, the citadel of Langson was taken on February 13.[210] The blockade was extended on February 26 to cut off contraband of war going to China and especially the rice supplies for Canton from Shanghai.[211]

Fruitless negotiations were carried on in Berlin between the French and Chinese military attachés from February 18 to 28. The Chinese official opened the conversations, but he had nothing new to offer and French hopes of settlement were dashed. The attaché of the Celestial Empire claimed that if he transmitted home any indemnity demand it would cost him his head.[212]

---

[206] Carroll, *op. cit.,* pp. 96-97.
[208] *DDF,* V, No. 487.
[210] *Ibid.,* No. 582.
[212] *Ibid.,* No. 603.

[207] *L. J. C. et T.,* Nos. 125-131.
[209] *Ibid.,* No. 511.
[211] *Ibid.,* No. 587.

The Inspector General of the Chinese Customs, Sir Robert Hart, offered on January 17 to open negotiations with Ferry through his secretary in Paris, James Duncan Campbell.[213] Hart was anxious to arrange a peace because the Treasury was strained by the falling customs revenues due to the blockade, and because the vital rice supply of North China was threatened.[214] Ferry replied cautiously, having once before been disappointed by a Hart overture not acceptable in Pekin. He indicated he was willing to talk, but made it clear from the beginning that France demanded full execution of the Tien-Tsin Convention and a guarantee that future treaties would be observed. Conversations with Campbell were begun by Ferry on February 6, and by the 26th the Premier felt confident of a settlement.[215] Only Billot was privy to these conversations: Patenôtre in Shanghai was not informed, probably because Ferry realized that his agent, so closely identified with an aggressive policy, would not be acceptable as a peace emissary.

China proposed, in terms sent on February 28, to recognize the Tien-Tsin agreement; that France should ask nothing more of China; hostilities should cease at once, and the Formosa blockade should be lifted. Campbell was authorized by the Tsong-li-Yamen to sign such an agreement.[216] Hart set forth the Chinese contention that since the Bac-Lé incident was an accident of war, not premeditated, China should not pay an indemnity.[217] Ferry was very loath to abandon his indemnity claim and asked what else China would offer.[218] He was told China offered nothing but peace. Ferry hesitated, still hoping for an indemnity, but he soon would have to accept the proposal as the best he could obtain.

Soon afterwards, Li-Hong-Tchang in Tien-Tsin made a new effort on March 8 to open negotiations.[219] Campbell had told Ferry that Li had no authority in this matter.[220] There was considerable bad feeling between Li and Hart and the former was not hesitant in denouncing the customs official.[221]

When Patenôtre reported to Paris the overture by Li, he was told for the first time of Ferry's talks with Campbell during the past two months. But even then he was not given a full idea of how far they had progressed, for Ferry's personal conversations were only mentioned as one of several talks including that in Berlin.[222] Patenôtre continued to urge Paris to take more vigorous action. He was distressed to hear that the Government intended to leave Kelung, a withdrawal he termed "de-

[213] *L. J. C. et T.*, No. 165.   [214] Fournier, *loc. cit.*, p. 789.
[215] *L. J. C. et T.*, No. 178.   [216] *Ibid.*, No. 176.   [217] *DDF*, V, No. 607.
[218] *L. J. C. et T.*, No. 178.   [219] *Ibid.*, No. 179.   [220] *DDF*, V, No. 607.
[221] *Ibid.*, No. 617.   [222] *Ibid.*

plorable."[223] He solaced himself with the illusory hope that the Pescadores were to be retained.[224]

On March 15, Hart wired Ferry to hasten to accept the terms of the February 27 offer, saying that the Yamen was getting restless. Ferry wanted to check on Hart's authorization and therefore asked that the Yamen secretly communicate a confirmation of Hart's powers to Ristelhueber, the French consul in Tien-Tsin. Patenôtre was informed that a message which he should quickly pass along was coming through these channels.[225]

Patenôtre, however, first learned from his subordinate, Ristelhueber, the news that Li would give him a note to be sent directly to Paris on Ferry's orders. It came as a shock to the Minister to find that he had been so completely ignored in the important negotiations, but he loyally said that he would efface himself if such actually were Ferry's commands. However, he strongly hinted that Hart was not strictly honorable in all his intentions. Apparently Hart had annoyed Patenôtre by boasting in Shanghai of his negotiations with Ferry.[226] The Yamen's note, when it came, confirmed Chinese acceptance of the conditions Ferry received on February 28 and the authorization for Campbell to sign such an agreement.[227] Ferry then told Patenôtre the full story of the negotiations for the first time.

The Chinese offered to take the first step by publishing the edict ordering execution of the Tien-Tsin Convention, but Ferry demanded that at the same time the order be given for the imperial troops to recross the frontier. This postponed the signing of the Convention—and forced what proved to be a fatal delay for Ferry.[228]

The Langson Incident

At this juncture the French troops in Tonkin met with a series of reverses. The news of the first check suffered at Dong-Dang arrived on March 25 and gave rise to a violent debate in the Chamber on March 28. Ferry was accused of gross mismanagement and flouting Parliament. He appealed for a calm attitude in the face of reverses, but the vote for the Government on an Order of the Day was only 259–209. It not only reflected anger at the turn of affairs in Tonkin, but was typical of the slim majority Ferry could command during this Spring of 1885.

On March 28 a report arrived of the wounding of General Negrier and the abandonment of Langson, after the French troops had been overwhelmed by superior numbers and had exhausted their ammunition. General Brière de l'Isle marred a good military record by sending

[223] *L. J. C. et T.*, No. 182.   [224] *Ibid.*, No. 189.   [225] *DDF*, V, No. 627.
[226] *L. J. C. et T.*, No. 191.   [227] *Ibid.*, No. 192.   [228] *Ibid.*, No. 195.

a panicky message saying that he hoped to hold on to the Red River Delta.[229] Actually the situation did not justify such great alarm, but that was known only some days later. Much later it developed in a senatorial investigation that a Colonel Herbinger, while intoxicated, had unnecessarily ordered a precipitous abandonment of Langson.[230]

Ferry realized, the moment that the message was telephoned to him in the middle of the night, that he would be defeated. He felt that the Chamber would not believe the status of the Chinese negotiations if he told them the truth; he was sure that the Chinese would use the French defeat to procrastinate.[231] But he made one last effort to induce China to come to an agreement. A telegram sent to Berlin early in the morning of March 29 suggested that Germany might advise China to come to terms at once.[232] Bismarck stood by Ferry, making overtures to the Chinese both in Berlin and Pekin to say that he hoped China would settle at once before France felt obliged to avenge this new reverse.[233] But the Chancellor's advice came too late to help Ferry.

The Radical and Monarchist press on the following day treated the Langson skirmish as a great national catastrophe, to be compared with Waterloo. Especially the journals of Rochefort and Clemenceau seized on this opportunity to flay the Ministry on the grounds that it had humiliated France. The Paris mob was aroused, and the boulevard crowds shouted against the *"tonkinois"* who was responsible for this disaster.[234] Only *Le Temps* and *La République Française* stood by the Ministry.

The Cabinet met and, on Ferry's insistence, determined to face the Chamber with a demand for an appropriation of two hundred million francs to avenge the reversal. Ferry refused to try to save himself by revealing the progress he had made in the negotiations with the Chinese, lest he compromise the outcome.[235] He may, too, have feared that the arrangement would be considered a surrender since the indemnity demand had been dropped.

The bloc of Republicans of the Center met in the editorial offices of the *Journal des Débats* and decided that it was necessary to overthrow the Premier, but "his domestic policy rather than his colonial policy determined that question," declared an eyewitness who was a seasoned politician.[236] This was the opinion of most observers, including Lord Lyons.[237] Leaders of the Republican Union and the Democratic Union, the two largest Republican groups, came to persuade Ferry to resign be-

[229] *DDF*, V, No. 637.
[231] Hanotaux, *Mon Temps*, II, 448.
[233] *GP.*, III, 699, 700.
[235] Leyret, *op. cit.*, p. 415.
[237] Newton, *op. cit.*, II, 350.

[230] *Discours*, V, 519.
[232] *DDF*, V, No. 638.
[234] Carroll, *op. cit.*, p. 502.
[236] Marcère, *op. cit.*, II, 30.

fore the Chamber met.[238] Other supporters, panic-stricken by the outcry in the opposition press and mindful of the coming elections, came to him with the same advice,[239] but he refused to yield.

He faced a turbulent Chamber on March 30, knowing defeat was certain and knowing that he held in his pocket an agreement with China that conferred the fruits of victory on France. Ferry could scarcely make himself heard in a brief statement of the position in Tonkin and a request for the additional funds as a patriotic move in the face of the enemy.

Clemenceau venomously delivered the *coup de grace* to the Ministry:

I consider that now no debate can any longer take place between the Ministry . . . and a Republican member of the Chamber . . . We no longer want to hear you, we can no longer discuss with you the great interests of the country . . . They are no longer Ministers whom I have before me, they are men accused of high treason!

The credits were refused by a vote of 306–149 and Ferry and his Cabinet stalked out of the Chamber. After his departure, the Chamber defeated a motion to bring the Ministry to trial, 287–153.[240]

As the vanquished Premier left the Chamber he was threatened by the mob gathered around the Palais Bourbon and he had to slip out by a side door.[241] As he crossed the bridge to the *Place de la Concorde* a mob of urchins, urged on by Cassagnac and Rochefort, threatened to push him into the river, and a crowd very nearly invaded the Ministry of Foreign Affairs.[242]

The ensuing ministerial crisis, which lasted a week, made it impossible to conclude the Convention with China, since the defeated Ministry was not entitled to terminate such matters and there was no one to bridge the gap, President Grévy being unwilling to order Billot to act.[243] Hart was afraid the negotiations might fail altogether and urged Paris to sign at once. On April 3 he warned that a week's delay would jeopardize the arrangement, as the war party in Pekin might gain the upper hand.[244] The Chinese did not try to take advantage of the Langson engagement, but there was every reason to fear that they might.

Billot was then directed by Ferry to sign the Convention with Campbell on April 4. It embodied the terms offered on February 27, under which France kept Annam and Tonkin and abandoned claim for an indemnity. An "explanatory note" provided for an armistice and stated that a definite treaty of peace, friendship and commerce would be drawn

[238] Leyret, *op. cit.*, p. 415.
[240] *J. O. C.*, 3/31/85.
[242] Hanotaux, *Mon Temps*, II, 405.
[244] *DDF*, V, No. 647.

[239] Hanotaux, *Mon Temps*, II, 449.
[241] Freycinet, *op. cit.*, p. 279.
[243] Schuman, *op. cit.*, p. 95.

later.[245] This method of signing was highly irregular, since Ferry was a repudiated minister, but it was necessary to prevent a resumption of hostilities.

Freycinet, the Foreign Minister in the succeeding Boisson Cabinet of April 6, had no intention of abandoning Tonkin. The Convention was respected and a definitive peace formula was worked out by April 19, with a commercial treaty with China still postponed. Finally, on June 9, a peace was signed by Patenôtre and Li-Hong-Tchang at Tien-Tsin, embodying the provisions of the April 4 Convention. China relinquished all claims to Annam and Tonkin; France was to be allowed to trade with China along the Tonkin frontier, enjoying lower tariffs on the trade over the land frontier than prevailed in the treaty ports, and France was to evacuate all Chinese territory within a month.[246] The Sino-French War over the question of an indemnity thus closed with a treaty that made no mention of it. Chinese resistance had been successful, but France had won Annam and Tonkin at a cost of over one hundred million francs and several hundred men.

Although there was no serious intention among the majority of the deputies of abandoning Indo-China, Ferry's enemies continued to harass him in their press and in Parliament. Indeed, their wrath pursued him for the rest of his life, and his death was hastened by complications from a would-be assassin's bullet, in December, 1887. In the elections to the Chamber in the Fall of 1885, Ferry was repudiated by his own constituents, but in 1889 he was sent to the Senate and became President of that Chamber. However, as a minister he was unacceptable, for he was too unpopular with large sections of public opinion for the Republicans to welcome him back. Yet France treasured the new colonies which his perseverance had won for her.

Ferry's Defense

After his defeat, Ferry several times publicly took issue with the critics of his colonial program, especially on the charges made about the Tonkin affair. He rose in the Chamber on July 28, during a debate on an appropriation for Madagascar, to make a general defense of his colonial program, and of his policy toward Madagascar and Tonkin in particular.[247] He gave the most complete and detailed justification of imperialism he had ever offered till then. All the arguments of prestige, the civilizing mission and the search for markets were developed at length, with the last-named in a predominant position.

His defense against the charges that the Tonkin expedition had been ill-planned was that all colonial empires had of necessity to be built

[245] *L. J. C. et T.,* No. 206. [246] *Ibid.,* No. 281. [247] *Supra,* p. 128.

opportunistically, step by step, because the complications involved could not be foreseen. As proof he cited the British control over India, which had been extended in the most unpremeditated way possible.[248]

The principal justification for Tonkin was that it gave "access to that enormous market of 400 million consumers [in China] . . . not poor blacks like the inhabitants of equatorial Africa, but . . . one of the most advanced and wealthy people in the world."

To the Radicals who criticized the number of his colonial expeditions, he replied:

> We have undertaken the expeditions that we needed to; we did not in the least premeditate them, and not having premeditated them, I will not let it be said that we conducted them by chance. We conducted them of necessity, and by right: we were led to them by that obligation and duty that is imposed on all civilized people to make the signature of their representatives respected by barbarous nations. There is the history of our colonial policy; it is not a policy that wavers haphazardly.[249]

He summarized his justification:

> . . . the colonial policy . . . rests on a triple base, economic, humanitarian and political. . . . I say that France which has always been glutted with capital and has exported considerable quantities of it abroad . . . has reason to consider this side of the colonial question.
>
> But, gentlemen, there is another more important side of this question which is very much more important than that I have just mentioned. The colonial question is for countries devoted by the very nature of their industry to a great export trade, like ours, the essential question of markets. . . . The foundation of a colony is the creation of a market, . . . itself of the highest importance, [and] is justified from that point of view, in these times and in the crisis through which all European industries are passing.[250]

This was the first time that Ferry had justified his colonial position on the basis of the severe effect of the prevailing long depression. He cited statistics to show that there had been an increase of seventeen million francs exported to the colonies in 1883 over 1881, most of the increase being attributable to the new colonies.[251]

He continued to lecture the deputies:

> In the economic field, I have allowed myself to place before you the considerations that justify the policy of colonial expansion from the

[248] *Discours,* V, 187.   [249] *Ibid.,* p. 189.   [250] *Ibid.,* pp. 194–196.   [251] *Ibid.,* p. 199.

point of view of that need, more and more imperiously felt by the industrial peoples of Europe and particularly of our rich country of France; the need of outlets . . . because Germany protects herself with barriers, because . . . the United States has become protectionist to the limit; because not only the great markets . . . are shrinking, becoming more and more difficult for our industrial products to reach; but because these great states are beginning to pour into our own markets products that were not seen there formerly. . . . But . . . the creation of the outlet with which we are now concerned will give us, in a certain future, free and even privileged exchange with China and, with that, markets of four hundred million inhabitants.[252]

Leaving the problem of markets, he turned on the Radicals who objected to extending French control over backward people to state frankly, ". . . there is for the superior races a right, because there is a duty for them. They have the duty to civilize the inferior races." Especially did this mean that France should work for the abolition of slavery and the slave trade as provided in the recent Congress of Berlin.[253]

Colonies had still another value for a maritime country such as France, with a world-wide commerce that must be protected and old colonies to be maintained. In a time when warships could carry only fourteen days' coal, there arose

> . . . the necessity of having on the seas some harbors for provisioning, some shelters, ports for defense and refitting. And that is why we had to have Tunisia, that is why we had to have Saigon and Cochin-China, it is for that that we must have Madagascar and why we are at Diégo-Suarez and Vohémar and that we shall never leave them.
>
> To have influence without acting, without mingling in the affairs of the world, holding one's self aloof from all the European combinations, while regarding as a trap, as an adventure, every expansion toward Africa or toward the East, to live in such a way, for a great nation, . . . is to abdicate, and in a shorter time than you can believe, it is to descend from the first rank to the third or fourth.[254]

He wrote an even more classic justification of his policy in 1890 as a preface to a collection of documents on Tonkin.[255] He reviewed the international prestige and glory that France had gained from her new colonies which brought a needed revival of the old tradition of a Greater France. She now was a great power with a world-wide empire of rich

---

[252] *Ibid.,* pp. 200–202.   [253] *Ibid.,* pp. 211–212.   [254] *Ibid.,* pp. 217–218.
[255] Léon Sentupéry, *Le Tonkin et la mère patrie* (Paris, 1890).

colonies and naval bases to protect them.[256] But most important of all was the fact that the colonies provided outlets for French products. He told his readers:

The colonial policy is the daughter of the industrial policy. For the rich states where capital abounds and rapidly accumulates, and the manufacturing regime is constantly on the increase . . . exportation is an essential factor of public prosperity and the field for the use of capital, as the demand for work is measured by the extent of the foreign market.

After reviewing the rise of tariff protectionism and the new competition from American and Russian agriculture and American, German and English manufactured goods, he continued:

The protective system is a steam engine without a safety valve if it does not have as a corrective and an auxiliary a healthy and serious colonial policy. . . . The economic crisis which has weighed so heavily on industrial Europe since 1876 or 1877, the misfortune that has followed it and from which the frequent, long and ill-advised strikes that have arisen are the most unhappy symptoms, has coincided in France, in Germany, even in England, with a notable and persistent reduction in the figure of exports. . . . European consumption is saturated; one must move out into other parts of the globe for new classes of consumers, under pain of throwing modern society into bankruptcy.[257]

Ferry certainly had not worked out such a well-formulated philosophy of imperialism when he moved into Indo-China. He had advanced a policy toward Annam and Tonkin that he had inherited from his immediate predecessors and had forcefully imposed a real French protectorate on Annam and its Tonkin province to replace a nominal claim. With little economic motivation, except from his general prudent bourgeois regard for French commerce, to open potential new markets, he had acted chiefly to strengthen the prestige and glory of France. After securing guarantees from the kingdom of Annam he had recklessly plunged into a war with China to avenge insults to French military honor and drive China from Tonkin once and for all. Only when repeatedly forced to justify his policy in Indo-China to Parliament did he develop an explanation *ex post facto* that placed increasing stress on the need for markets and fields for investment. After he had left ministerial office he was even more outspoken in preaching a Neo-Mercantilist creed.

[256] Quoted in *Discours*, V, 554, 557.   [257] *Ibid.*, pp. 557–558.

Chapter Eight

SUMMARY

Revival of the competition for empire was one of the most striking phenomena of the last quarter of the nineteenth century, for, following a period of disinterestédness in overseas possessions, the major powers raced to appropriate most of Africa, large parts of Asia and the islands in the Pacific and Indian oceans. A movement driven by intertwined nationalistic, economic and religious impulses with the first-named usually the most important, it gave France a huge overseas empire of which Jules Ferry was the chief harvester.

French expansion in the 1870's was unobtrusively begun by colonial officials without the knowledge of, or with only grudging approval from, Paris. They were predominantly naval and military men who practiced their art of war on relatively backward kingdoms and tribes for the love of *la patrie* and of adventure. Often they were encouraged and abetted by French colonists like those in Réunion, Algeria and Tunis. New oriental and tropical lands were opened up by merchant-adventurers like Dupuis in Tonkin and adventurous explorers like Brazza in Equatorial Africa. Little encouragement from the motherland was given these lonely imperialists for many years.

The leaders of France were for a decade much too busy to devote their energies to the empire. They had to repair the French economy after a war and revolution, rebuild the state with a new constitution achieved only after long struggles. The Republicans had first to secure political and then administrative and institutional control of the Third Republic. Moreover, France had no formal ally although she enjoyed the friendship of England. Bitter after defeat, she could not risk any serious involvements abroad.

Jules Ferry as a young man had no interest in colonial expansion. He was deeply concerned with domestic problems, his liberal faith was opposed to imperialism. He thought in European terms and was chiefly concerned with opposing the undemocratic Napoleonic Empire. Typical of the majority of Republicans, he was absorbed in domestic problems during the early years of the Republic and well into his first term as Premier of France. He had no plans for overseas expansion when he came into office and only after his sweeping educational reforms were nearly completed did he become interested in these questions. He was persuaded to embark on his first colonial venture by career diplomats and colleagues, alarmed at Italian ambitions in Tunisia, who proposed to preserve French prestige and guard Algeria by seizing the Regency. Ferry's predecessors had already secured the consent of England and Germany.

Once he was persuaded to act in Tunisia, Ferry launched into a many-pronged imperialistic drive, renewing French projects in Indo-China, Oceania and West Africa. Pronounced vigor in the colonial sphere characterized the balance of his years as Premier. Not only did he subsidize exploration of Africa and Asia as he had early done, but he undertook aggressive actions without properly informing Parliament of his intentions. He never had any long-range plan, but he moved opportunistically whenever a chance presented itself. If he thought he could easily add to the French domain, he moved in as he did in Annam and Madagascar. His formula was to subsidize, seize and suppress abroad and then to explain his actions at home. But he was seldom the initiator: his ability lay in perceiving a promising, even though precarious French foothold, organizing a campaign to secure it, doggedly hanging on, and exploiting all opportunities while holding a firm majority in Parliament. The only colony that was entirely his creation, from early exploration to final international ratification of French ownership, was Equatorial Africa, an outgrowth of Brazza's Congo discoveries. In each other field he was the heir of previous French occupation or ambition. His acquisitions included: Tunisia, the Congo, part of the French Sudan, Annam and Tonkin, several Pacific island archipelagos, and part of French Somaliland. He came close to securing Madagascar and the base he established there was later successfully enlarged, as indeed were most of his territorial gains. He nurtured French interests in the financial management of Egypt and instigated the establishment there of multiple European control, a beginning that was never carried through. He beat off diplomatic or military attacks on his conquests, by England, China, Belgium, Turkey and Italy. However, he probably dissipated his energies dangerously in attempting to take so many new colonies. Undoubtedly it was a source of weakness for him to have his energies spread so far over the globe.

Very important in persuading him to undertake several of his colonial expeditions were high civil servants, professional diplomats and military men. During his second term he needed little of this encouragement, and they merely bolstered his resolve. For the most part they were concerned about French prestige or diplomatic position. As Courcel joined Barthélemy Saint-Hilaire and tipped the balance in the case of Tunisia, so Billot, his successor at the Quai d'Orsay, was a chief advisor and goader in the case of Indo-China. The explorer Brazza fired Ferry's imagination for African expansion; Mahy, a deputy from Réunion, misled him into the Madagascar expedition. Ambassadors like De Noailles, Waddington and Saint-Vallier also encouraged the Premier, and Courcel's promotion did not cool his desire to extend French domination.

Thus abetted, and especially during his second Premiership, supported by a firm coalition in Parliament, Ferry could give energetic propulsion to French overseas ambitions. Probably he was not without the realization that political capital could be made from a successfully conducted campaign.

The aggressive imperial policy which Jules Ferry pursued would perhaps not have been possible and certainly would have been more hazardous had it not been for the support of Bismarck. The German Chancellor deliberately encouraged France to build an empire in order to distract her from the lost provinces. During 1884, Bismarck backed French imperial ambitions to use them as a weapon against England. Ferry was well aware of the reasons for Bismarck's support, which the Chancellor was fairly frank to admit. He refused to be pushed by the German statesman beyond the limits he set for himself, however. The Chancellor did not succeed in involving Ferry in any expedition or diplomatic move that did not suit his intentions. This Franco-German working agreement, a specific and limited entente, was the only cooperation of its sort between 1870 and 1914, and Jules Ferry certainly secured more concrete and lasting results therefrom than Germany. It was most useful to him in the West Africa, Indo-China and Madagascar questions, as well as in Egypt. Thanks to it, the European diplomatic ring was kept clear. Ferry could send his troops off without fear of threats or reprisals at home from hostile powers or coalitions. England was unable to protest, as she would often have liked to do, for fear of a continental alliance of secondary naval powers against her. Much of this situation was purely fortuitous for Jules Ferry. He could not possibly have engineered the Anglo-German coolness, for example —but he drew from it all the advantage possible. There must, however, be counted among the lasting results of Ferry's international policy the fact that an Anglo-French estrangement, which began shortly after the military intervention of England in Egypt, was made worse and persisted for nearly two decades. Moreover, loss of the race for Tunisia was a factor in influencing Italy to ally herself with Germany and Austria.

It has been often assumed that Ferry and his colleagues were primarily interested in acquiring new markets for French industry, new fields for French investors; or in protecting French commerce or finance when it was threatened by unsympathetic natives or the vicissitudes of the Great Depression. Such was not the case. Economic factors alone or predominantly were hardly ever responsible for the initiation of French colonial policy. The total French exports to the colonies which were acquired during Ferry's time constituted but an infinitesimal fraction of the nation's trade; French investments were small except in Egypt where France had long been supporting her bondholders. Egypt was a special case for there was no thought or hope of making it a French colony. Jules Ferry was first determined to continue to protect the bondholders because he thought this a proper function for government. In his second Ministry he added to that continuing concern a desire to regain a share in the political as well as financial control of Egypt. Elsewhere, there were French investments only in Tunisia, and on those the bondholders were having no difficulty in collecting their usurious returns when Ferry took over. Nor was there an immediate rush of French trade, private construction of utilities or investment in the newly acquired colonies. Conspicuously lacking from Ferry's creed was a demand for raw materials. Only later did imports of tropical and mineral products bulk large in French interest. In the early days of expansion the Great Depression had not yet hit France heavily, and French commerce was but slightly affected by the rising world tariff barriers. When Ferry's expansion was *in medias res*, depression conditions were setting in and he did not hesitate, on the floor of Parliament, to use the threat of rising European and American tariffs to justify his acquisition of new markets. In any case, Ferry, as a good bourgeois, strong nationalist, and good politician, would not naturally oppose measures presumably to improve his country's prosperity. But his early expansion bore only slight reference to potential markets. More often than not, economic factors were only the tools of diplomacy or parliamentary controversy.

There is no evidence of pressure or influence exerted on Ferry or his colleagues by organized pressure groups, important trading associations, manufacturers, or investment houses in metropolitan France. Doubtless some individuals like Dupuis encouraged him to push on but there were no scandalous deals and no personal peculation in this French imperialism. What economic pressure there was came mostly from French colonists. It is true that during the period there was greatly increased industrial activity and a wealth of new products that generally stimulated trade and industry, but such products did not flow in great streams to the lands over which Ferry extended his control. There were few instances where threats to marketing by hostile natives furnished a motive for expansion.

When Ferry embarked on his colonial schemes, there was no organized colonial propaganda movement. Only a few publicists and academic writers without following called for an empire. Colonial societies and their periodicals were rapidly appearing, but their weight was felt only in the succeeding decade. Popular interest in the French empire was only slowly aroused until imaginations were fired by tales of natural and archeological wonders in mysterious Africa and Asia. National pride was inflated by the prestige of owning such mysterious and reputedly wealthy lands. The saga of Brazza aroused great public enthusiasm and interest in the race for Equatorial Africa, but such feeling was not evidenced for the other territories into which Ferry sent troops. Indeed, had Jules Ferry possessed a warmer personality, a greater flair for publicity to popularize his acquisitions, he might have experienced less criticism. As it was, he drove determinedly and aggressively forward but without attempting to capture public interest, presenting France with conquests, but not with inspiring panoramas of imperial splendor.

The opposition to Ferry's program of colonial expansion has been generally overrated and misunderstood, owing to the fact that his loss of the Premiership apparently came twice as a result of his policy in Tunisia and Tonkin. Actually both defeats were accounted for chiefly by growing parliamentary dislike of Ferry's domestic program. Parliament, like the public, was not pleased by the cost in men and money of the expeditions to Tunisia, Madagascar and Indo-China, but it supported Ferry until it tired of his domestic policies and found a convenient excuse to turn him out of office in a seemingly disastrous military reverse in Indo-China. Parliament made a point of retaining the new possessions, even though it defeated the man responsible for their acquisition. On measures dealing with colonial expansion Ferry secured substantially as much support as on domestic matters, and his majorities in both cases declined together. The Radicals who disliked his moderate reforms, his domineering personality and firm management of governmental affairs, fought as bitterly on colonial as they did on domestic questions. The Conservatives, as a group, opposed most of his colonial expeditions. They supported only the Madagascar enterprise, although some few of their more nationalistic members supported all expansion.

That is not to say that all the opposition to imperialism was entirely hypocritical. Many extremely nationalistic *revanchards* were thoroughly convinced that all French energy should be devoted to preparing to strike back at Germany and recover Alsace and Lorraine. A few Radicals were pacifists on intellectual grounds, staunch supporters of the doctrines of the fraternity of mankind and opposed to all imperialism. But for the most part, Ferry was faced with an intransigent coalition of Right and Left.

The need to secure appropriations from Parliament forced Ferry to formulate a rationale of expansion *ex post facto*. On the forge of parliamentary debate, this took its shape of economic imperialism. His early explanations and justifications were principally devoted to arguments of prestige and national honor. But late in 1883 the economic arguments came to the fore, and in retirement Ferry cultivated them to full flower. Those who have read only his later explanations of policy have been misled to believe that they were characteristic of his whole imperialistic career. That this is not true may be most strikingly seen in contrasting the debates on Tunisia and Tonkin. The economic arguments advanced in the latter case were useful to win over a Parliament disposed to a tender regard for business interests. Especially this was the case when economic distress set in late in Ferry's second Ministry. Doubtless he was then really interested in opening markets, for a great race for colonies in Africa and Asia was developing, and he was faced with rivalry on every side.

Ferry also professed to champion a civilizing mission and duty that compelled France to bring the beauties and truths of French culture and Christianity to the backward peoples and free them from such barbaric practices as slavery. This argument was useful to the prosaic Ferry who believed in the power of education, but was hardly a mainspring of action. Directly bound with considerations of prestige was the necessity of global strategy for an imperial and maritime power. For that reason Ferry acquired naval bases useful both for the merchant marine and warships.

Whatever the means and motives, the policy of Ferry did endow France with a great empire. A few years later one of his young assistants, Gabriel Hanotaux, as Foreign Minister, as well as a succession of French generals and explorers extended the boundaries of the possessions Ferry had harvested for France. This empire, for all its shortcomings, made the Third Republic a major world power.

Appendix

VOTES ON COLONIAL AND DOMESTIC QUESTIONS IN THE CHAMBER OF DEPUTIES

MEASURE	DATE	TOTAL VOTE	FOR	AGAINST
	1875			
Tonkin: Ratification of Treaties of 1874	7/8 8/4	Ratified by acclamation " " "		
	1879			
Freycinet Ministry—535 Deputies from here:				
Primary Normal Schools	3/20	443	317	126
Article VII	7/9	497	333	164
Conseil Supérieur de l'Enseignement	7/19	481	353	128
	1880			
Secondary Education for Girls	1/20	470	347	123
Requirement of Certificate for Teachers	5/19	475	355	120
Ferry Ministry:				
Free Primary Education	11/29	476	356	120
Compulsory and Lay Primary Education	12/24	463	329	134
	1881			
Tunis: 5 mil. frs. to Repress Kroumirs	4/7	474	474	0
Tunis: Interpellation on Preparations, Vote of Confidence	4/12	546	322	124
Tunis: Treaty of Bardo	5/24	432	431	1
Pensions to Aged Soldiers and Sailors of Former Governments	6/7	462	255	207

MEASURE	DATE	TOTAL VOTE	FOR	AGAINST
Tunis: 6 mil. frs. for Expedition	6/13	429	429	0
Tunis: Vote of Confidence after Interpellation	6/30	468	249	219
Authorization of Action against Andrieux	7/18	396	89	307
Suppression of Paris Chapter of Ste. Geneviève Order	7/19	404	279	125
Tonkin: Credits to Preserve Order	7/22	391	309	82
Order of the Day after Shifting Election Date	7/25	415	214	201
547 Deputies from here:				
Tunis: Motion for Investigation	11/9	469	141	328
Ministry's Order of the Day—Fall of Ferry	11/9	488	176	312
Gambetta's Order of the Day	11/9	433	365	68
Gambetta Ministry:				
Tunis: Gambetta's Demand for Credits	12/1	444	395	49
Society Is.: Annexation	12/19	Ratified by acclamation		
	1882			
Vote of Confidence on Revision—Gambetta's Fall	1/15	486	218	268
Freycinet Ministry:				
Senegal: 7.5 mil. frs. for Kayes-Niger RR.	3/13	380	363	17
Election of Judges	6/10	483	275	208
Rejection of Above by Ministry	7/1	484	258	226
Egypt: Credits	7/18	488	424	64
Egypt: Credits—Freycinet's Fall	7/29	482	75	417

MEASURE	DATE	TOTAL VOTE	FOR	AGAINST
Duclerc Ministry:				
Congo: Brazza Treaty with Makoko	9/18	Ratified by acclamation		
	1883			
Rejection of Plan to Elect Judges	1/27	498	274	224
Fallières Ministry:				
Expulsion of Princes from Army	2/15	490	317	173
Ferry's Second Ministry:				
Conversion of 5% Bonds	4/19	489	387	102
Tonkin: Supplementary Credits	5/15	399	351	48
Tonkin: Above with May 26 Amendments	5/26	494	494	0
Order of the Day Pure and Simple, after Interpellation on Sale of Books	5/28	450	334	116
Judicial Reform	6/5	473	343	130
Senegal: 4.6 mil. frs. for Kayes-Niger RR.	7/13	374	273	101
Orleans RR. Convention	7/16	300	206	94
Tonkin: Vote of Confidence after Interpellation	7/18	440	362	78
Judicial Organization as Modified by Senate	8/1	291	259	32
Order of the Day Pure and Simple, after Interpellation on Parliamentary Incompatibilities	8/1	442	265	177
Tonkin: Order of the Day, after Interpellation	10/31	480	325	155
Amendment Reestablishing Central Mayoralty of Paris	11/10	478	201	277
Municipal Organization	11/10	496	432	64

MEASURE	DATE	TOTAL VOTE	FOR	AGAINST
Law on Parliamentary In-compatibilities	11/24	445	299	146
Tonkin: Postponing Inter-pellation	11/29	493	299	194
Tonkin: New Credits	12/10	512	383	129
Order of the Day of Con-fidence	12/10	509	308	201
Senegal: 3.3 mil. frs. for Kayes-Niger RR.	12/17	431	197	234
Tonkin: Funds for 1884	12/18	481	327	154
Advancing Date of Mu-nicipal Elections	12/22	419	343	76
Budget for 1884 Modified by Senate	12/29	350	321	29
	1884			
Lay Personnel in Schools	3/18	499	391	108
Madagascar: Confidence	3/27	463	437	26
Senegal: 3.3 mil. frs. for Kayes-Niger RR.	3/31	445	361	84
Egypt: Interpellation, Con-fidence	6/26	460	460	0
Resolution on Limited Revision	7/3	509	403	106
Divorce Law	7/19	470	355	115
Madagascar: Credits	7/21	441	360	81
Limited Revision as Modi-fied by Senate	7/31	470	285	185
Tonkin: Credits	8/15	474	334	140
Vote of Confidence	8/15	223	173	50
Interpellation on Economic Policy of Government. Vote of Confidence	10/18	417	247	170
Interpellation on Labor Policies of Railroads. Or-der of the Day Opposed by Ministry	10/25	431	158	273

MEASURE	DATE	TOTAL VOTE	FOR	AGAINST
Vote of Confidence	10/25	290	286	4
Bill on Wine Culture	11/13	467	211	256
Tonkin: Credits for 1884	11/28	511	354	157
Tonkin: Credits for 1885	11/28	512	342	170
Vote of Confidence	11/28	491	295	196
Universal Suffrage for Senatorial Election	12/2	517	267	250
Above Repealed	12/9	507	280	227
Ordinary Budget for 1885	12/20	482	406	76
	1885			
Tonkin: Interpellation, Order of the Day Pure and Simple	1/14	505	280	225
Extraordinary Budget for 1885	2/2	420	341	79
Raising of Tariff on Cereals	3/5	414	264	150
Scrutin de liste	3/24	511	312	199
Tonkin: Interpellation, Order of the Day Pure and Simple	3/28	468	259	209
Tonkin: Demand for Funds—Fall of Ferry	3/30	455	149	306
Motion to Bring Ferry to Trial	3/30	440	153	287
Tonkin: 50 mil. frs. for Expedition	3/31	493	493	0
Madagascar: 12 mil. frs. for Expedition	7/30	397	277	120
Congo: Adoption of Berlin Act	8/3	346	251	95
Somaliland: 624,950 frs. to Organize Obock	8/3	277	223	54

BIBLIOGRAPHY

Official Publications

France

Chambre des Députés (*or* Sénat) de la République Française. Journal Officiel de la République Française. Débats parlementaires. Paris, 1879–1885.

Commission de publication des documents relatifs aux origines de la guerre de 1914. Documents diplomatiques français, 1871–1914, 1re série. Vols. I–V. Paris, 1929–1934.

Ministère des Affaires Etrangères. Documents diplomatiques (Livres Jaunes)

    Conférence de Berlin, 1878. Paris, 1878.

    Affaires de Tunisie, 1870–1881. Paris, 1881.

    Affaires de Tunisie, supplément, avril–mai, 1881. Paris, 1881.

    Nouvelles-Hébrides et les Iles-sous-le-Vent. Paris, 1887.

    Affaires du Congo et de l'Afrique Occidentale. Paris, 1884.

    Affaires du Congo et de l'Afrique Occidentale. Paris, 1885.

    Afrique: Arrangements, actes et conventions, 1881–1898. Paris, 1899.

    Affaires de Madagascar, 1881–1883. Paris, 1883.

    Affaires de Madagascar, 1882–1883. Paris, 1884.

    Affaires de Madagascar, 1884–1886. Paris, 1886.

    Affaires d'Egypt, 1878–1879. Paris, 1879.

    Affaires d'Egypt, 1880. Paris, 1880.

    Affaires d'Egypt, 1881. Paris, 1881.

    Affaires d'Egypt, 1881–1882. 2 vols. Paris, 1882.

    Affaires d'Egypt, 1882–1883. Paris, 1883.

    Affaires d'Egypt, 1884–1893. Paris, 1893.

    Commission internationale pour le libre usage du canal de Suez. Paris, 1885.

    Affaires du Tonkin. Paris, 1883.

    Affaires du Tonkin, convention de Tien-Tsin du 11 mai 1884. Incident de Langson. Paris, 1885.

    Affaires de Chine et du Tonkin, 1884–1885. Paris, 1885.

Ministère de l'Instruction Publique et des Beaux-Arts. Compte définitif des dépenses de l'exercise, 1878–1884. Paris, 1879–1886.

Ministère de la Marine. Compte définitif des dépenses, 1878–1885. Paris, 1879–1886.

Direction générale des douanes. Tableau général du commerce de la France avec ses colonies et les puissances étrangères, 1881, 1885, 1889. Paris, 1882, 1886, 1890.

Germany

Auswärtiges Amt. Aktenstücke betreffend die Kongo-frage. Berlin, 1885.
Aus den Archiven des belgischen Kolonialministeriums. Berlin, 1918.
Die grosse Politik der europäischen Kabinette, 1871–1914. Vols. I–IV. Berlin, 1922.

Great Britain

Foreign Office. Accounts and Papers.
Tunis No. 4, 1881. C 2908. London, 1881.
Tunis No. 5, 1881. C 2886. London, 1881.
Africa No. 2, 1884. C 3885. London, 1884.
Egypt No. 3, 1882. C 3161. London, 1882.
Egypt No. 17, 1884. C 4000. London, 1884.
Egypt No. 30, 1884. C 4130. London, 1884.
Egypt No. 36, 1884. C 4242. London, 1884.
Egypt No. 7, 1885. C 4341. London, 1885.
Egypt No. 14, 1885. C 4417. London, 1885.
Egypt No. 15, 1885. C 4423. London, 1885.

Portugal

Ministero dos Negocios Estrangeiros. Questão do Zaire. Vol. II. Lisbon, 1885.

United States

National Archives, Washington, D. C. Department of State Archives. Consular Letters.
Tunis. Vol. 12, November 6, 1877–May 26, 1883.
Tahiti. Vol. 7, January 1, 1875–December 31, 1886.
Tamatave. Vols. 3–4, July 1, 1880–December 31, 1886.
Gabon. Vol. 1, April 2, 1856–February 24, 1888.
France, Despatches. Vols. 87–96, September 1, 1880–August 26, 1885.
France, Instructions. Vol. 21, February 21, 1884–September 24, 1889.
China, Instructions, Vol. 3, January 1, 1879–February 28, 1885.
U. S. Senate. Executive Document No. 196. 49th Congress, 1st Session. Correspondence in Relation to the Affairs of the Independent State of the Congo. Washington, 1886.

Secondary Works, Memoirs, Collections of Letters, Speeches

Acomb, Evelyn M. The French Laic Laws, 1879–1889. New York, 1941.
Adam, Juliette. Mes angoisses et nos luttes. 4me éd. Paris, 1907.
—— Nos amitiés politiques avant l'abandon de la revanche. 5me éd. Paris, 1908.
Aldao, Martin. Les idées coloniales de Jules Ferry. Paris, 1933.
Andrieux, Louis. A travers la République. Paris, 1926.
Anonymous. Les batailles électorales de la Troisième République. Paris, 1932.
Aydelotte, William O. Bismarck and British Colonial Policy. Philadelphia, 1937.
Banning, Emile. Mémoires politiques et diplomatiques. Paris, 1927.
Barisien, P. Le parlement et les traités. Paris, 1913.
Barthélemy, Joseph. Le gouvernement de la France. Paris, 1919.
—— Démocratie et politique étrangère. Paris, 1917.
Baudoin, Henri. La banque de l'Indo-Chine. Paris, 1903.
Bentham, Jeremy. Jeremy Bentham's Works. Ed. J. Bowring. Edinburgh, 1843.
Billot, Albert. La France et l'Italie. Vol. I. Paris, 1905.
Bordier, Arthur. La colonisation scientifique et les colonies françaises. Paris, 1884.
Bouinais et Paulus. L'Indo-Chine française contemporaine. 2 vols. Paris, 1885.
Bourgeois et Pagès. Les origines et les responsabilités de la Grande Guerre. Paris, 1921.
Bourgin, Georges. La Troisième République. Paris, 1939.
Broadley, A. M. Tunis, Past and Present. 2 vols. London, 1882.
Brogan, D. W. France under the Republic. New York, 1940.
Buckle, G. E. Life of Benjamin Disraeli. Vol. V. London, 1920.
Buthman, William C. The Rise of Integral Nationalism in France. New York, 1939.
Carroll, E. Malcolm. French Public Opinion and Foreign Affairs, 1870–1914. New York, 1931.
Cavailhon, Edouard. La France Ferrycide. Paris, 1888.
Cecil, Lady Gwendolen. Life of Salisbury. Vol. II. London, 1921.
Cerisier, Charles. La France et ses colonies. Paris, 1886.
—— Impressions coloniales. Paris, 1893.
Chambrun, Général Jacques A., Comte de. Brazza. Paris, 1930.
Charles-Roux, François. "Allemagne, Angleterre et Egypte en 1877–1878," *L'Afrique française*, XXXVIII, 1928, 175–180. "L'Allemagne et les questions de Tunisie, du Maroc et de l'Egypte de 1879–1884," *Ibid.*, 345–355.
Charmes, Gabriel. Politique extérieure et coloniale. Paris, 1885.
Chiala, Luigi. Storia Contemporanea, Fasc. II: Tunis. Turin, 1895.

Chirac, Auguste. L'agiotage sous la Troisième République, 1870–1887. 2 vols. Paris, 1888.

Clough, Shepard B. France: A History of National Economics, 1789–1939. New York, 1939.

Comte, Auguste. Discours sur l'ensemble du positivisme. Paris, 1848.

—— Catéchisme positiviste. Paris, 1852.

—— Cours de philosophie positive. 6 vols. Paris, 1830–1848.

Congrès national des sociétés françaises de géographie. Compte rendu, 5me session, Sept., 1882. Bordeaux, 1883.

Constant, d'Estournelles de. La politique française en Tunisie. Paris, 1891.

Courcel, Geoffrey de. L'influence de la conférence de Berlin de 1885 sur le droit colonial international. Paris, 1936.

Cromer, Earl of. Modern Egypt. 2 vols. London, 1908.

Crowe, S. E. The Berlin West Africa Conference. London, 1942.

Daniel, André. L'année politique, 1881–1885. Paris, 1882–1886.

Darcy, Jean. Cent années de rivalité coloniale. Paris, 1904.

Daudet, Ernest. La mission du Comte de Saint-Vallier. Paris, 1918.

—— La mission du Baron de Courcel. Paris, 1919.

Debidour, A. Histoire diplomatique de l'Europe. 2 vols. Paris, 1916–1918.

Deschamps, Léon. Histoire de la question coloniale. Paris, 1891.

—— Histoire sommaire de la colonisation française. Paris, 1894.

Deschanel, Paul. Gambetta. Paris, 1920.

Despagnet, Frantz. La diplomatie de la Troisième République et le droit des gens. Paris, 1904.

—— Essai sur les protectorats. Paris, 1896.

Dietz, Jean. "Les débuts de Jules Ferry." *Revue de France*, Année 12, t. V, 1932, 501–521, 608–627.

—— "Jules Ferry et les débuts de la Troisième République." *Grande Revue*, CXXXIX, 1932, 550–572.

—— "Jules Ferry: sa première présidence du Conseil." *Revue politique et parlementaire*, CLXV, 1935, 96–109.

—— "Jules Ferry et l'enseignement supérieur." *Grande Revue*, CXLVI, 1934, 125–138.

—— "Jules Ferry au Gouvernement de la Défense Nationale et pendant la Commune." *Revue de France*, Année 14, t. II, 1934, 493–519.

—— "Jules Ferry et les traditions républicaines." *Revue politique et parlementaire*, CLIX, 1934, 521–532; CLX, 1934, 100–111, 297–311, 495–512; CLXI, 1934, 122–141, 492–505.

—— "Jules Ferry: sa seconde présidence du conseil." *Ibid.*, CLXV, 1935, 288–311, 500–518.

—— "Jules Ferry, la révision de la constitution et le scrutin de liste." *Ibid.*, CLXVI, 1936, 515–532; CLXVII, 1936, 101–117.

Drumont, Edouard. Les tréteaux du succès; les héros et les pitres. Paris, 1901.

Dubois, Marcel et Terrier, Auguste. Les colonies françaises. Paris, 1902.

Duchêne, Albert. La politique coloniale de la France. Paris, 1928.

Dupront, A. "Jules Ferry s'opposant à l'Empire: quelques traits de son idéologie républicaine." *Revue historique*, CLXXVII, 1936, 352–374.

Dupuis, Jean. L'ouverture du fleuve rouge au commerce. Paris, 1879.

—— Tongkin et l'intervention française. Paris, 1898.

Esmein, A. Eléments de droit constitutionnel français et comparé. 2 vols. 8th ed. Paris, 1928.

Fabre, Sylvain. "Eugène Etienne." *Bulletin trimestriel de la Société de Géographie et d'Archéologie d'Oran*, XLI, 1921, 97–103.

Faucon, Narcisse. La Tunisie avant et depuis l'occupation française. 2 vols. Paris, 1893.

Faure, Fernand. "A la mémoire de Jules Ferry." *Revue politique et parlementaire*, CXXXI, 1927, 5–15.

Ferry, Jules. Comptes fantastiques d'Haussmann. Paris, 1868.

—— "Jules Ferry peint par lui-même." *Intermédiaire*, XLVIII, 1903, cols. 327–328.

—— "Au lendemain du Second Empire." *Revue politique et parlementaire*, CXLVIII, 1931, 136–138.

—— Lettres de Jules Ferry. Ed. E. Ferry. Paris, 1908.

—— La lutte lectorale en 1863. Paris, 1863.

—— "Marcel Roulleaux." *Philosophie positive*, I, 1867, 289–312.

Fournier, Vice Amiral. "La France et la Chine au traité de Tien-Tsin." *Revue des Deux Mondes*, 7me pér.: t. 5, 1921, 755–790.

Freycinet, Charles de. Souvenirs, 1878–1893. 8th ed. Paris, 1913.

—— La question d'Egypte. Paris, 1905.

Froment-Guieysse, G. Jules Ferry. Paris, 1937.

Gaffarel, Paul. Les colonies françaises. Paris, 1880.

—— Notre expansion coloniale en Afrique de 1870 à nos jours. Paris, 1918.

Gallichet, Henri. Dessous diplomatiques. Paris, 1894.

—— Gambetta et l'Alsace-Lorraine. Paris, 1911.

Galliéni, Joseph S. Voyage au Soudan français, 1879–1881. Paris, 1885.

Gheusi, P. La vie et la mort singulières de Gambetta. Paris, 1938.

Godfernaux, R. Chemins de fer coloniaux. Paris, 1911.

Gooch, G. P. Franco-German Relations, 1871–1914. London, 1923.

Goyau, Georges. "Patriotisme et humanitarisme." *Revue des Deux Mondes*, 5me pér.: t. 3, 1901, 136–142, 874–889; t. 5, 520–558.

Grandidier, Guillaume. Galliéni. Paris, 1931.

—— Le Myre de Vilers, Duchêsne, Galliéni. Paris, 1924.

Guillon, Edouard. Les colonies françaises. Paris, 1881.

Guyot, Yves. Lettres sur la politique coloniale. Paris, 1885.

Halévy, Daniel. "Ferry." *Journal des Débats*, XXXIV, pt. 2, 1927, 10–12.

—— Décadence de la liberté. Paris, 1931.

—— La fin des notables. Paris, 1931.

—— La république des ducs. Paris, 1937.

Halévy, Ludovic. "Mes carnets," *Revue des Deux Mondes,* 8me pér.: t. 43, 1938, 95–126, 375–403, 589–613.

—— Trois dîners avec Gambetta. Paris, 1929.

Hanotaux, Gabriel. Histoire de la France contemporaine. 4 vols. Paris, 1903–1908.

—— Mon temps. Vol. II. Paris, 1938.

—— et Martineau, Alfred. Histoire des colonies françaises et de l'expansion française dans le monde. Vols. II-VI. Paris, 1930–1933.

Hardy, Georges. Histoire de la colonisation française. 2me éd. Paris, 1931.

Hayes, Carlton J. H. A Generation of Materialism. New York, 1941.

—— Historical Evolution of Modern Nationalism. New York, 1931.

Hippeau, Edmond. Histoire diplomatique de la Troisième République. Paris, 1889.

Hobson, J. A. Imperialism. 2nd éd. London, 1932.

Hohenlohe-Schillingsfürst, Chlodwig zu. Denkwürdigkeiten. Vol. II. Stuttgart, 1907.

Hoskins, Halford. British Routes to India. New York, 1928.

Johnston, Sir Harry. History of the Colonization of Africa by Alien Races. Cambridge, 1899.

Keltie, J. Scott. The Partition of Africa. London, 1895.

Krakowski, Emile. La naissance de la Troisième République; Paul Challemel-Lacour. Paris, 1932.

Lamarzelle, G. de. "De Jules Ferry à M. Combes." *Correspondant,* CCXIII, 1903, 441–454.

La Gorce, Pierre de. Histoire du Second Empire. 7 vols. Paris, 1899.

Langer, William A. European Alliances and Alignments. New York, 1931.

—— "The European Powers and the French Occupation of Tunis." *American Historical Review,* XXXI, 1925–26, 55–78; 251–265.

Lebon, A. "Les préliminaires du traité de Bardo." *Annales des sciences politiques,* VIII, 1893, pp. 395–438.

Lee, Dwight. Great Britain and the Cyprus Convention Policy of 1878. Cambridge, 1934.

Leger, Eugène. La question d'Egypte et l'occupation anglaise. Paris, 1902.

Leroy-Beaulieu, Paul. De la colonisation chez les peuples modernes. Paris, 1874.

—— "La Tunisie et l'opposition." *Revue politique et littéraire,* 3me sér., t. 2, 1881, 197–201.

Levasseur, E. Histoire du commerce de la France. Vol. II. Paris, 1912.

Leyret, Henri. Waldeck-Rousseau et la Troisième République. Paris, 1908.

—— Le gouvernement et le parlement. Paris, 1919.

—— Le Président de la République. Paris, 1913.

Littré, Emile. Application de la philosophie positive au gouvernement. Paris, 1869.

—— Auguste Comte et la philosophie positive. Paris, 1864.

—— Conservatisme, révolution et positivisme. Paris, 1852.

—— De l'établissement de la Troisième République. Paris, 1880.

—— "La république française et l'extérieur." *Philosophie positive,* XXIV, 1880, 128–144.

Louis, Paul. Le colonialisme. Paris, 1905.

Lyautey, Pierre. L'empire coloniale française. Paris, 1931.

Mangin, Charles M., Général. Regard sur la France d'Afrique. Paris, 1924.

Marcère, Emile de. Entretiens et souvenirs politiques. Vol. II. Paris, 1894.

Mariol, Henri. La chronologie coloniale. Paris, 1921.

Maurois, André. Lyautey. Paris, 1931.

McKay, Donald V. "Colonialism in the French Geographical Movement." *Geographical Review,* XXXIII, 1943, 214–232.

Michon, G. Clemenceau. Paris, 1931.

Michon, Louis. Les traités internationaux devant les Chambres. Vol. I. Paris, 1901.

Mill, John Stuart. Principles of Political Economy. London, 1873.

Mitchell, Pearl B. Bismarckian Policy of Conciliation with France. Philadelphia, 1935.

Monteil, P.-L., Col. "Contribution d'un vétéran à l'histoire coloniale." *Revue de Paris,* Année 30, 1923, 97–131.

Moon, Parker T. Imperialism and World Politics. New York, 1926.

Newton, Lord. Lord Lyons. 2 vols. London, 1913.

Neymarck, A. "La statistique internationale des valeurs mobilières." *Bulletin de l'Institut International de Statistique,* XX, 1915, 1297–1539.

Osborn, Chase S. Madagascar. New York, 1924.

Passeron, René-Eugène. Les grandes sociétés et la colonisation dans l'Afrique du Nord. Alger, 1925.

Pessard, Hector. Mes petits papiers. Paris, 1888.

Pillias, Emile. Léonie Léon, amie de Gambetta. Paris, 1935.

—— et Halévy, Daniel. Lettres de Gambetta. Paris, 1938.

Posener, S. Adolphe Crémieux. 2 vols. Paris, 1934.

Pottecher, Maurice. Jules Ferry. Paris, 1930.

Pouvourville, Albert de. Francis Garnier. Paris, 1931.

Priestly, Herbert I. France Overseas: a Study of Modern Imperialism. New York, 1938.

Raboisson, M. Etudes sur les colonies et la colonisation au regard de la France. Paris, 1877.

Ragatz, Lowell J. The Question of Egypt in Anglo-French Relations, 1875–1904. Edinburgh, 1922.

Rambaud, Alfred. La France coloniale. 6me éd. Paris, 1893.
—— Jules Ferry. Paris, 1903.
Ranc, Arthur. Souvenirs, correspondence. Paris, 1913.
Raphael, Paul. "Trois lettres inédites de Jules Ferry." *Revue historique,* CIX, 1912, 85–86.
Reclus, Maurice. Jules Favre. Paris, 1912.
Recouly, R. La Troisième République. Paris, 1927.
Reinach, Joseph. "Le traité de Bardo." *Revue politique et littéraire,* 3me sér., t. 21, 1881, 641–646.
—— Le ministère Gambetta. Paris, 1884.
Roberts, Stephen. History of French Colonial Policy 1870–1925. 2 vols. London, 1929.
Robiquet, Paul. Discours et opinions de Jules Ferry. 7 vols. Paris, 1893–1898.
Rothstein, Theodore. Egypt's Ruin. London, 1910.
Russier, Henri. Le partage de l'Océanie. Paris, 1905.
Saint-Hilaire, Barthélemy. Fragments pour l'histoire de la diplomatie française. Paris, 1882.
Sauzède, Albert. "Le rôle coloniale de Jules Ferry." *Revue politique et parlementaire,* LXIX, 1911, 344–353.
Schuman, Frederick L. War and Diplomacy in the French Republic. New York, 1931.
Schuyler, Robert L. "The Rise of Anti-Imperialism in England." *Political Science Quarterly,* XXXVII, 1922, 440–472.
—— "The Climax of Anti-Imperialism in England." *Political Science Quarterly,* XXXVI, 1921, 537–560.
Seignobos, Charles. Le déclin de l'Empire et l'établissement de la Troisième République. Paris, 1921.
—— L'évolution de la Troisième République. Paris, 1921.
Sentupéry, Léon. Le Tonkin et la mère patrie. Paris, 1890.
Simon, G. "Jules Simon, notes et souvenirs." *Revue mondiale,* CLXIX, 1926, 339–348; CLXX, 1927, 3–16, 113–127, 211–218, 315–322.
Smith, Adam. Wealth of Nations. J. C. Bullock, ed., Harvard Classics, ed. New York, 1909.
Société académique indo-chinoise. Annales de l'extrême orient. 1878–1891.
Société de Géographie. Bulletin. Paris, 1878–1885.
Spuller, Eugène. Figures disparues. Vol. III. Paris, 1894.
Staley, Eugene. War and the Private Investor. New York, 1935.
Stanley, Henry M., Congo. 2 vols. New York, 1885.
Stannard, Harold. Gambetta and the Foundations of the Third Republic. London, 1921.
Stephans, Winifred. Madame Adam. New York, 1917.
Straus, Paul. Les fondateurs de la République. Paris, 1934.
Thomson, Robert S. Fondation de l'état indépendant du Congo. Brussels, 1933.

Townsend, Mary E. Origins of Modern German Colonialism. New York, 1921.

Tuaillon, Georges. L'Afrique Occidentale Française. Paris, 1936.

Valet, René. La conquête de l'Algérie et l'occupation de la Tunisie devant le parlement. Alger, 1924.

Vatin, Fernand. Les chemins de fer en Tunisie. Paris, 1902.

Vignon, Louis. Les colonies françaises. Paris, 1884.

Velay, Etienne. Les rivalités franco-anglaises en Egypte, 1877–1904. Toulouse, 1904.

Vogué, Eugène, Vicomte de. Journal. Paris, 1932.

—— Le rappel des ombres. Paris, 1900.

Weiss, Jean J. Combat constitutionnel. Paris, 1893.

—— "La situation parlementaire." *Revue politique et littéraire*, 3me sér., t. 17, 1881, 513–516.

White, Harry D. The French International Accounts, 1880–1913. Cambridge, 1933.

Wienefeld, Robert H. Franco-German Relations, 1878–1885. Baltimore, 1929.

Wilson, C. Rivers. Chapters from My Official Life. London, 1916.

Woolf, Leonard. Empire and Commerce in Africa. London, 1919.

Wright, Gordon. "Public Opinion and Conscription in France, 1866–70." *Journal of Modern History*, XIV, 1942, 26–45.

Zévaès, Alexandre. Histoire de la Troisième République. Paris, 1925.

Newspapers

Le Temps. 1865–1870, 1881.

INDEX

The principal topics indicated in chapter titles have not been indexed (e.g. Tunis, Madagascar, Egypt, Tonkin), nor have merely casual references to Jules Ferry and other figures been listed. Votes by the Chamber of Deputies on important colonial and domestic questions may be found conveniently in the Appendix which, therefore, has not been indexed.